*Love and Power in the
Nineteenth Century*

Love and Power in the Nineteenth Century

The Marriage of Violet Blair

VIRGINIA JEANS LAAS

THE UNIVERSITY OF ARKANSAS PRESS

Fayetteville 1998

02 01 00 99 98   5 4 3 2 1

Designed by Liz Lester

♾ The paper used in this publication meets the minimum
requirements of the American National Standard for Permanence
of Paper for Printed Library Materials Z39.48-1984.

LIBRARY OF CONGRESS CATALOGING-IN-PUBLICATION DATA

Laas, Virginia Jeans.
      Love and power in the nineteenth century : the
   marriage of Violet Blair / Virginia Jeans Laas.
           p.   cm.
      Includes bibliographical references (p.).
      ISBN 1-55728-505-5 (cloth : alk. paper). —
   ISBN 1-55728-506-3 (paper)
      1. Blair, Violet, 1848–1933—Diaries. 2. Blair, Violet,
   1848–1933—Correspondence. 3. Women—Washington
   (D.C.)—Biography. 4. Women—Washington (D.C.)—
   History—19th century—Sources. 5. Women—Washington
   (D.C.)—Social conditions. 6. Janin, Albert—Correspondence.
   I. Title.
   HQ1413.B543L33   1998
   305.4′092—dc21   97-43715
                                                         CIP

For Fred

Acknowledgments

At the completion of a manuscript, it is always a special pleasure to recognize those who helped along the way. Librarians and archivists across the country have been unstinting in the application of their knowledge and skills, making my job much easier. I am especially grateful to Anne Van Arsdale at Princeton; Phyllis Kauffman of the History of Medicine Library at the University of Wisconsin, Madison; Gail Redmann and her intern Abby Stillman of the Historical Society of Washington, D.C.; Gail Serfaty at the State Department; Mary Williams of Blair House in Washington; Mary Ternes and Matt Gilmore of the Washingtoniana Division of the Martin Luther King Library in Washington; Peter Blodgett of the Huntington Library in California; and the staffs of the Library of Congress and the library of the State Historical Society of Wisconsin. At Missouri Southern State College, reference librarian Bob Black willingly toiled to answer my queries, and Gay Pate worked miracles with Interlibrary Loan.

The research for this project has been generously supported by a fellowship from the Huntington Library and several faculty development grants from Missouri Southern State College. My former student Shawn Hull provided translations of German documents, taking time away from his own graduate studies. My colleagues at Missouri Southern have been consistently supportive. Robert Markman read the entire manuscript, giving me the benefit of his expert editorial eye and historical understanding. They all give special meaning to the term collegiality. At the University of Arkansas, Daniel E. Sutherland and Jeannie M. Whayne have given solid advice, warm encouragement, and much-needed criticism. Generous with his time and knowledge, Williard B. Gatewood Jr. has been an exemplary advisor and mentor. His high standards of scholarship have been a goad and inspiration. Elizabeth Jacoway took time from her own important work to encourage me to sharpen my focus and broaden my vision.

As in our past collaboration on *Lincoln's Lee,* and on every historical project I have undertaken, Dudley T. Cornish has been a wonderful friend and sage advisor. By his example, I have seen what it is to be a fine scholar and enthusiastic teacher. My brother, Buck Jeans, who has always believed that I am better than I really am, read the entire manuscript and took care of me on my California research trips. He has been a best friend for life. Although they are now adults and have not been physically present for much of the creation of this work, my sons Matt and Gil have always been important sources of encouragement and support. My constant thanks to them. Son Andy and his wife, Cindy, have given essential practical aid, providing me a haven in Washington on innumerable research trips. They are gracious hosts and good friends. And finally, there is my husband, Fred, who has lived with Violet for a long time and without me for extended periods. He has been patient, kind, and supportive of all my scholarly endeavors. I am grateful every day for our life together.

Virginia Jeans Laas
Missouri Southern State College

Contents

Introduction

Violet Blair was always a belle. From her sixteenth year in 1864 until her death in 1933, she thought, talked, and acted with the assurance and self-confidence of one whose wishes demanded obedience. Beautiful, intelligent, proud, vivacious, accustomed to exercising authority, and demanding equality without apology, Violet tenaciously refused to relinquish the power she had felt as the leading belle of Washington, D.C., in the late 1860s and early 1870s. During the Victorian era, when the Cult of True Womanhood required women to be silent and submissive, Violet Blair rejected domination and, finding a man who accepted her independence, wed Albert Janin in 1874.[1] Violet was no shrinking flower; she set the original terms of their marriage, and Albert, for the most part, obeyed. He, however, was not simply a hen-pecked husband. Understanding precisely how to handle his difficult wife, he managed to live his life much as he wished. Both partners retained their individual identities while maintaining their marital bond. That they loved each other deeply there is no doubt; yet they struggled to find their own balance between love and power. Their fifty-four-year marriage provides abundant evidence of the variety and complexity that could exist between two fundamentally conservative people who had worked out their own definition of marriage.

Violet's experience offers an unusual opportunity to explore the motives and strategies of an especially arrogant and assertive woman who desired marriage yet rebelled against its strictures. It provides a means to test the standard conception of what it meant to be a belle and demonstrates the lingering effect of that youthful period of power on a mature woman.

Violet grew up in an era in which the ideal woman defined herself as wife, mother, daughter, sister; in marriage, the perfect wife was submissive to and dependent on her husband. At the same time, Violet's long life encompassed a transitional period for women, between the nineteenth-century ideal of domesticity and the twentieth-century stereotype of the New Woman. Thus, Violet looked to the past in feeling that marriage was the ultimate goal of every woman and faced the future in striving to maintain self-worth. She clung to many of the older attitudes toward women and their place while at the same time foreshadowing the mind set of the modern woman. Wanting equality, yet fervidly attentive to social proprieties, she searched for a satisfying marital relationship.

In many ways, Violet was a most conservative, traditional woman. To her, divorce was unthinkable; a wife never embarrassed her husband; marriage was a life-long commitment, and promises could not be broken. Throughout her life, she demonstrated profound loyalty to family and friends, deep concern for what others thought, and stubborn devotion to proper conduct. She placed such importance on propriety that in later years she became "the old families' arbiter of taste."[2]

On the other hand, her life contained significant elements of unconventionality. A great deal of the time, she was the dominant partner in her marriage; Albert almost always acceded to her wishes; and by her choice, they did not regularly live together. Most unusually, Albert never provided financial support for Violet; for much of their married life, he was dependent on her. Economic domination, a cornerstone of patriarchal power, was not Albert's prerogative.[3]

The private side of a life from a past era is always difficult to reconstruct. In this case, an abundance of intimate documentary evidence lightened the task. Because Albert toiled at his law practice and business interests in New Orleans while Violet remained in Washington, they wrote long and revealing letters to each other. She, especially, was remarkably open and frank when writing to her husband. The result is a voluminous correspondence which provides as immediate and complete a picture as the historian will ever have of the relationship between two people.

In addition, Violet kept copious and detailed diaries for many years. Unintended for perusal by anyone else, her diary was her emotional safety valve, a place where she could express her feelings and thoughts as freely as she wished. And she was starkly honest with herself. In her introduction to *A Day at a Time,* Margo Culley comments that a diary keeper begins with "a sense of self-worth," a recognition that her "individual experience is somehow *remark*able."[4] Violet gives hyperbolic confirmation to that theory, having never, ever lacked self-confidence. Diaries allowed nineteenth-century women to define themselves in the privacy of their own thoughts and to experiment with the idea of their autonomy as thinking, feeling beings. They could create a sense of self, independent of masculine influence. Violet never doubted her own independence; in her case, writing a diary allowed her to clarify her thoughts, reinforce her sense of autonomy, and give vent to her emotions. In the end, it is the sense of immediacy and honesty that makes Violet's diaries unusually illuminating.

Throughout this work, Violet and Albert speak for themselves. Because of the abundance of both his and her letters, in addition to her revealing diaries, I have quoted from them extensively. Their own words vividly recreate their thoughts and feelings, bringing us as close as possible to the reality of their lives and strengthening our understanding of their actions and relationship.

Essential to the research for this work were four manuscript collections, the most important of which is the Janin Family Collection located in the Henry Huntington Library, San Marino, California. It includes the bulk of Violet's and Albert's papers. A significant collection of the couple's papers are contained in the Blair-Janin Papers at the Historical Society of Washington, D.C. Other important repositories of the extended Blair and Lee families are the Blair-Lee Papers in Harvey Firestone Library, Princeton University, and the Papers of the Blair Family, in the Library of Congress. Ironically, for one acknowledged to be a most beautiful woman (in youth and old age), there is little visual evidence. In the collection at the Historical Society of Washington, D.C., are several photographs of Violet as a young woman; the next extant image shows her as a woman in her sixties. Violet was evidently quite accurate when she claimed in 1923, "My picture has never been in a newspaper."[5] The last known photograph of her was taken in her eighty-fourth year, in 1931.

In the past twenty years, there has been a good deal written about the meaning of feminism. While most of this work has dealt with feminism in public life, there has also been a significant effort to examine another dimension of feminism—its meaning in the private sphere, in the relationship between husband and wife. Joyce Antler has posited feminism as a "life process." Rather than viewing feminism only as a means to change society, she suggests that historians need to broaden their definition of feminism to include the personal: we need to analyze how individual women "struggle for autonomy" and how they "mold their destinies" throughout their entire lifetimes.[6] So too, in *Parallel Lives*, Phyllis Rose explored private lives by looking at marriage as a power relationship and tracing "the shifting tides of power between a man and woman."[7] Anthony Rotundo has added to the discourse by emphasizing the importance of the distribution of power within marriage, "who held the power, what the sources of power were, and how power was exercised and maintained."[8] This study offers an answer to those questions in a particular instance, that of Violet Blair and Albert Janin. It attempts to uncover what power and control meant to a particularly strong woman who bowed to most conventions of society but refused to relinquish her own individuality, independence, or authority. Hers was a feminism played out on the private stage. Her experience is a story of shifting power and certain struggle, ending in a kind of stasis in which both partners retained their autonomy while remaining dependent on each other.

Because of the wealth of archival material from both sides of this relationship, we have a unique opportunity to deepen our understanding of marriage in the nineteenth century, to follow the flow of power from one partner to the other, to observe how love itself changed over time. Violet's brother, Jesup Blair, once said that everything about his sister seemed exaggerated. He was right. There is nothing average about Violet Blair, but in the magnification of her personality, she makes it easier for those who have come one hundred years later to understand her motivations, her fears, her beliefs, her anger, and her ideals.

Youth

*"I do not believe any girl could take an
admirer of mine away from me."*

When Violet Blair Janin called on her mother-in-law in February 1879, she was subjected to a barrage of insults. In a frenzy of red-faced anger and wild gesticulation, the elder Mrs. Janin let loose a shrill stream of abuse. The spark that set off this unseemly attack had been Violet's comment that she intended to control the number of children she bore. She did not accept, as the older Mrs. Janin did, that babies were gifts from God and that it was wicked to interfere with His plan for procreation. More fundamentally, Mrs. Janin was jealous. She had lost her position of eminence in the affections of her son Albert; his wife, Violet, had stolen his love from her.

Violet responded to this ugly outburst by calling upon her training and instincts as a refined, cultured, upper-class lady. Calm, quietly assertive, and dignified, she coolly answered Mrs. Janin's charges, then, in stately fashion, took leave of the old woman. Violet refused to lose control of her emotions; even in her diary, she maintained her composure in relating the extraordinary encounter. She attributed such self-possession to her deep confidence in herself, remarking that her "calm, cool assurance" made it impossible to ruffle her. She had, she asserted, "the pleasant conviction that socially, morally & mentally I can hold my own in any company I have ever seen." Violet's self-assurance had almost no limits, and she was perfectly comfortable in defining it: "A quiet sense of superiority that comes from high birth & blood, unusual learning, enough of this world's goods to make me independent, acknowledged beauty & a spotless reputation, a thorough knowledge of the world & all society matters, & the recollection of having been a great belle & being now very much sought after & being very fashionable, gives an equanimity that it takes a great deal to shake."[1]

However vain and egotistical Violet's self-appraisal may sound, it was nevertheless quite accurate. Born on August 14, 1848, Violet Blair was the oldest child of James and Mary Serena (Jesup) Blair. Her lineage from both parents was illustrious. Violet's mother, Mary, was the daughter of Thomas Sidney Jesup, who had distinguished himself in the War of 1812 and had been appointed quartermaster general of the army by President James Monroe in 1818. He served in that position until his death in 1860. Except for two years, 1836 to 1838, when Andrew Jackson ordered him to fight the Seminoles in the old Southwest, Jesup lived in Washington, D.C., where he was a notable figure. General Jesup's wife, Ann H. Croghan, daughter of Major William Croghan, was a sister of George Rogers Clark, Revolutionary War hero, and William Clark, explorer of the Louisiana Purchase. She died in 1846, two years before Violet's birth.[2] Violet's father, James Blair, was the middle son of the politically powerful Jacksonian Democrat, Francis Preston Blair. James's brothers were destined for fame: Montgomery became Abraham Lincoln's postmaster general, and Frank Jr. later served as a congressman from Missouri and a general in the Union army.[3]

The marriage of Mary Jesup and James Blair on January 14, 1846, united two prestigious families from the most important political and military circles in Washington. Before the year had ended, their first child, Ann Jesup, was born on December 10, 1846. She lived only three months, and Violet's birth in 1848 began the Blair family, which eventually included a son, Jesup, and another daughter, Jimmie.[4] A naval officer, James worried about his ability to provide for his family. In 1849, he took a year's leave of absence from the navy, borrowed $10,000 from his father, and set off for California to make his fortune. Mary and baby Violet lived during the winter with her father in Washington and spent the summer with her in-laws at Silver Spring.[5] The ambitious James immediately amassed a tidy fortune. Within two weeks of his arrival in California, he had earned $500 surveying for the army.[6] Piloting ships in San Francisco harbor added to his capital, but his most profitable venture was a steamboat operation on the Sacramento River. By the end of his first year in California, he owned five boats and numerous pieces of property; he estimated his worth at $60,000.[7]

Shortly after his departure from Washington, James had asked his father to build a cottage near the Blair family home at Silver Spring, promising to repay the cost "from the 1st dollar I make until it is paid for."[8] True to his word, he sent money to Mary by each steamer. For her part, Mary oversaw the planning and building of her new home, the Moorings. Although she had numerous male relatives willing to assist her, she assumed the burden of directing the project.[9] Before the Moorings was completed, James began making plans for a second house to be built on the lot his father had given him on Lafayette Square. A generous-hearted young man, he felt indebted to his father-in-law, General Jesup, for providing a home for Mary when he was at sea, and he wanted to build one large enough so that Mary's father and her sisters could all live with them. Desperately homesick, he was anxious to make his fortune, return home, and draw his wife and her family close around him.[10] After his naval leave had expired, the government had assigned James to shore duty in San Francisco, which allowed him to continue his business ventures. Making a fortune, however, did not relieve his desire to be with his family, and when he threatened to resign in order to come East, Mary would have none of it. She decided to bring his family to him in California.[11] Despite the objections of her family, Mary and Violet left for California in the company of family friends John and Jessie Fremont on October 3, 1850, arriving in San Francisco on November 21.[12]

Although they had "a beautiful view of the harbour" and Mary was delighted to be reunited with her husband, the damp climate did not agree with her or with little Violet. In addition, Mary missed the companionship of their extensive families in Washington. She filled her letters with requests for photographs, assurances that they constantly talked of family members, and pleas for letters detailing the daily routine at home. She did not want Violet to forget those who loved her.[13] The birth of their son, Jesup, on February 13, 1852, only made Mary more homesick, and her husband took her back to Washington in November of that year. James had to return to California to sell out his California interests, but it took time.[14] Disaster struck in December 1853, when James died suddenly, leaving his twenty-seven-year-old widow with two small children and pregnant with their third child, who was born only weeks after his death.[15]

After the birth of Lucy James, called Jimmie in honor of her father, Mary continued to live at the Moorings, finding solace in the midst of her husband's loving family. Her brother-in-law, Montgomery Blair, spent months in California settling James's estate and prudently investing the proceeds to provide for the fatherless family. For the remainder of the 1850s, Mary moved her family into Washington to her father's house during the winters, returning to her country home near Silver Spring for the summers. Her children were always surrounded by affectionate relatives from both sides of the family. In Washington, within a few blocks lived her favorite aunt and uncle, Minna and Montgomery Blair, and their five children. Elizabeth Blair Lee, her husband, Phillips, and their son, Blair, lived next door to them, the two homes sharing a common wall. Eliza and Preston Blair, doting grandparents, made the Lee home their Washington headquarters. In addition to Preston Blair's Silver Spring home, Montgomery's country home, Faulkland, was not far away from the Moorings, and the Lees shared summer living accommodations with the elder Blairs. Thus in all seasons, Violet was never far from grandparents, aunts, uncles, and cousins. Preston Blair gave her such attention that Violet thought she occupied a special place with her grandfather, boasting, "I am his favorite grandchild."[16] In the midst of this extended family circle, Violet grew from a rather sickly baby to an attractive young girl. Many years later, one woman recalled Violet's appearance as a little girl: "How well I remember how you looked. It was in the spring and we all were putting on our light attire and you wore a little straw hat with a wreath of daisies and your *beautiful* hair was hanging in long braids down your back and oh how lovely you were."[17]

Mary Blair, who lived to be eighty-seven years old, never remarried; instead, she centered her life on her children, husbanding her resources and taking great pride in never incurring any debt. And Violet, as her eldest child, was absolutely devoted to her mother. Without any real memory of her father, she focused her love on her "dear darling Mama." Her feelings never changed from those she expressed in her diary when she was sixteen years old: "Who else can I want? She is, I do believe, the best dearest woman in the world— She is so gentle, patient, loving & lovely—She is my model, my ideal of a perfect woman."[18] Violet was well aware of the sacrifices her mother had made for her children, not only performing traditional maternal duties, such as watching over them when they were sick, but also literally denying herself sustenance. When the Civil War began and money from California investments failed to arrive, Mary refused to borrow funds, scraping along on what little she had. She made herself ill by refusing to eat so that her children might. Violet never forgot the incident.[19]

At the commencement of the Civil War, Mary feared for the safety of her family and left the Moorings, traveling to Philadelphia and finally renting a house in Bethlehem, Pennsylvania, which she shared with her sisters, Julia Jesup and Jane Nicholson. The attractive country village proved healthy and inexpensive, and Mary took advantage of the opportunity for her children to take German lessons.[20] During the winter, Mary moved to Philadelphia, sharing living accommodations with Julia and her other sister, Lucy Sitgreaves. After spending another summer in Bethlehem, the family returned to Washington in November 1862, to live in the Jesup house at 913 F Street.[21]

Violet resumed her education at Mrs. Cleophite Burr's school in a two-story brick house at Ninth and E Street. Operating an exclusive seminary catering to the best families of Washington, Mrs. Burr, of French descent, was especially proficient in teaching her native language. Although Violet loved learning and was "one of the best scholars at Mrs. Burr's," she was bored with "the stupid tiresome routine of a schoolgirl's life, getting up early, going to school, taking a walk, coming home in time for dinner, then studying & practicing until bed time."[22] Her formal schooling ended in the winter of 1865, when her mother decided that the health of her sixteen-year-old daughter was too fragile, suspecting that there might be something wrong with her heart. Violet continued to study, however, taking private French lessons and reciting lessons in geometry and geology to her mother. Her ease with languages allowed her to teach Jesup and Jimmie English, Latin, and French.[23]

Upon her return to Washington from Pennsylvania, Violet had been overjoyed to be reunited with her extended family, especially with her best friend and cousin, Minna Blair, daughter of Montgomery and Minna (Woodbury) Blair. The friendship of Violet and Minna, begun in childhood, remained a strong bond into their old age. As she explained to her diary, "I am perfectly devoted to Min & she is to me, we are more like sisters than cousins."[24] Although Minna was nearly two years younger, Violet thought her "perfectly charming," prettier, and smarter: "My darling Minna is one of the prettiest, loveliest, sweetest, wittiest & most amiable girls in the world—I tell her everything, & I love her, Oh! so much."[25] With Minna, Violet confided her adolescent flirtations, her doubts about matrimony, her unhappiness in her marriage, her arguments with her brother and sister—all her most intimate thoughts. Minna returned Violet's devotion; in addition, she had an intelligent and saving sense of fun. During the war, when Violet was living in Philadelphia, Minna described a conversation with a young girl about Minna's ring, made of Violet's hair. When the girl asked whose hair it was, Minna "told her it was Violet's hair. O said she I did not know Violets have hair."[26] On another occasion, Minna described how an "impudent" neighbor habitually turned her cows out on the Blair pasture. Minna found a simple solution for the problem: she took a bucket to the field and milked the cows. Although her father was shocked by her action, the Blairs apparently had no more trouble from stray livestock.[27]

During the winter social season of 1864–65, just a few months past her sixteenth birthday, Violet awakened to the pleasures of society. In late December, she reluctantly attended a party at Minna's, dreading her anticipated fate: "What is the use of going & sitting in a corner all the evening doing nothing." She loved books and study, felt most comfortable in a library, and ridiculed dancing as "idle, vain & silly."[28] Within a week her attitude changed. She had portrayed Mary Queen of Scots in an evening of tableaux, and all had agreed that she had been beautiful. She was flattered but tried to maintain her dislike for society. Vacillating in typical Victorian, girlhood fashion, she admitted that she clung to those "vain & worthless" things of this world, while wishing that she could be more religious: "Oh! if there were only some one living now like St. Paul or Luther that I might ask him what I can do— . . . I must wait patiently until He sends death to deliver me—I do not fear death, I long for it."[29]

She moved with youthful awkwardness from piety to worldliness. In February 1865, she wanted to ask the religious advice of the Reverend Eliphalet Potter, who was visiting them and who had been their minister at the Episcopal Church of the Nativity in Bethlehem.[30] At the same time, she confided that she thought he had "the most beautiful" face she had ever seen. In springtime and under the influence of the Lenten season, she continued to berate herself: "I wish to be unselfish, humble, self denying & penitent, but I am proud, sensitive & impenitent— . . . Oh! how can I be happy while I am so wicked." She knew she had lost her struggle for saintliness: "This world is so beautiful & so delightful I cannot help loving it."[31]

Violet realized that she had become a beautiful young woman. Five feet two, with deep blue eyes and light brown hair that was as long as she was tall, the slender Violet possessed a classic Venus de Milo profile. Family members commented on her beauty and also on her personality traits that would remain with her for her lifetime. Her aunt Elizabeth Blair Lee perceptively described the budding belle. Acknowledging that Violet was "a real beauty," Aunt Lizzie added that her niece was "disposed to be a blue stocking—Still all that will wear off with knowledge of the world—but egotism in any shape is as hard to cure as consumption & both are hereditary—on all sides of her house."[32]

By midsummer 1865, Violet had discovered her ability to attract men, but she felt tortured in trying to maintain her earlier religiosity: "Oh! how much I have changed since I came home last autumn—Then I was a gentle religious girl; . . . This world is gaining such hold in my heart."[33] She flirted to her heart's content. At a party at her aunt Janie Nicholson's in Georgetown, she had found a young Englishman, a Mr. Smythe, very attractive and enjoyed his attentions. Each Sunday, twenty-four-year-old army officer Frank Robinson walked her from St. John's Church to her home, just across Lafayette Square.[34] He called on her regularly, and one evening when they were alone, he took her hand and kissed it. She was shocked and angry, denying that she had encouraged him, even though her girlfriends had teased her that Frank was in love with her. She was incredulous when he proposed: "Be his, indeed! he must be crazy to ask it."[35] Her lack of experience was evident, too, in her relationship with the Reverend Eliphalet Potter, twelve years her senior. She had known him as her clergyman in Bethlehem, and she respected him a great deal, as a child admires an adult: "I like him so much, he is so handsome & so very good—I like so much to hear him talk for he is so intelligent & so highly educated."[36] She seemed to be unaware that his periodic visits to her family had anything to do with any special feeling for her. When her girlfriend Mag Zeilin, daughter of Marine Corps commandant Jacob Zeilin, informed her of rumors that Violet was engaged to Potter, her response was "How absurd!"[37]

Gradually, she overcame her fears of being a wallflower. At a party given by her cousin Minna, she danced for the first time. Her midshipman cousin, Andrew Blair, attractive and full of fun, cajoled her into the frolic.[38] Violet, feeling perfectly comfortable with a cousin just her age, "had a jolly time." Afterwards, she worried if dancing was a sin and consulted the Reverend John V. Lewis, rector of her Church, St. John's, on Lafayette Square. When he assured her that dancing was perfectly acceptable, she determined, "I will dance whenever I get a chance to."[39] Andrew eased Violet into mixed company, and she was soon enjoying the company of army officer Carlile Boyd and several middies from Annapolis: James Dixon, son of Connecticut senator James Dixon; Willy Emory, whose mother was a Bache and whose father was the Civil War veteran William Hemsley Emory; and Harry Lyon, her "uncle" James Alden's nephew. Her beaux were, quite obviously, all well connected socially and politically. She delighted in the opera, parties at Kate Ramsay's, jaunts to the Capitol, and gatherings at Minna Blair's.[40] Full of laughter and fun, Violet thoroughly enjoyed herself: "I do love jolly people."[41]

Warming to the pleasures of society, Violet and her friends Minna, Kate Ramsay, daughter of George D. Ramsay, commanding the Washington Arsenal, and Anna Dennison, daughter of Postmaster General William Dennison, formed a club. They named it "Belles Vites Diables," and took as their motto "Go it while you're young." Their first meeting in Minna's bedroom got off to a fast start with a decanter of wine, cigarettes, and song. Violet was not ready for such rascality and limited herself to joining in the singing. When Anna left for school, the girls chose Jeannie Augur as their new member and determined to include an equal number of gentlemen. Jamie Dixon became the first male member of the BVDs. Their primary activity during the summer of 1866 was meeting each evening in Lafayette Park, walking, talking, and flirting with other young people. Violet had "*such a jolly jolly* time!"[42] Additional entertainment was provided every Saturday night by music on the president's grounds, and Minna, Kate, and Violet spent two days at Annapolis visiting cousin Andrew, Kate's brother Frank, and other eligible midshipmen. Moonlight walks with gentlemen became common occurrences which Violet found very pleasurable. When she and Minna spent a few days in the country at the Moorings, gentlemen came out to call on them. During one moonlight walk, Carlile Boyd kissed her hand. This time, it did not make her angry as it had when Frank Robinson had done so a year earlier. But when he tried to put his arm around her, she jumped away: "I will allow no man to be impertinent to me." In early June, Violet spent a memorable evening at a party given by her aunt Janie Nicholson. "I danced all night & undressed by bright daylight." She had been very popular, dancing constantly all evening with innumerable men. Her aunt had told her that she "looked as beautiful as a little white rosebud."[43]

Her summer fun had hardly been more than girlish enjoyment, but in August, she turned eighteen and felt the weight of that birthday. "I must try to think of myself as a woman now—it is so hard— . . . it is so funny to think that I am a grown up young lady, it don't seem to be possible, I am just as happy & merry as if I were only ten or twelve."[44] That fall of 1866 brought her first serious encounter with a man. She and her mother traveled in the north, staying for some time in Bethlehem. The tall, thin, and rather awkward Potter courted her, taking her for carriage rides and horseback outings. When he said sweet things to her, she treated them as lightly as she did the comments of other men. On one of their riding expeditions, Potter proposed to her. When she began to cry, she recalled, "He said he would kill himself if I did not promise to marry him & talked so dreadfully that I told him I would if Mama said yes." Although she later thought herself "such a fool" to believe him, she was sensitive and inexperienced and did not tell even her mother of the circumstances of her promise. She tried to imagine that she could do great good in the world as the wife of a minister.[45]

Fortunately, her mother was more sensible and allowed no promises to be made until Violet had experienced at least one season in society. Despite Potter's promise to keep their understanding secret, he immediately told several of his relatives. Shocked by his breaking his word, Violet began to see numerous faults in the man: he made "coarse speeches" to her; he bragged about the number of women who had been in love with him; he had a weak character; he presented a false impression of himself to his congregation; he was not nearly as holy as he wanted people to think him. Nevertheless, Violet felt she was bound by her promise; it was her duty to love him.[46]

Meanwhile, when Violet returned to Washington, she found that her friend Kate Ramsay had broken off with Willie Emory, and Willie immediately began courting Violet. Although she felt somewhat guilty, considering her promise to Potter, she was a willing party to prolonged flirtation with Willie Emory. Walks, talks, parties, games of croquet, and the theater—Willie Emory was never far from Violet's side. Once again, a moonlight walk was significant: "Oh what a charming time I had that night. I took his arm & looked up into his face & listened to him—From that night I knew he loved me truly." It was not long until Willie proposed to her. Although Violet may not have mastered the intricacies of flirtation, she showed a natural ability to control her emotions. Despite thinking Willie "an honest noble character" and enjoying his attentions, she knew she was in no danger of falling in love with him: "I might have loved him myself if I had not made up my mind not to allow myself to do so."[47]

When Potter heard rumors that Willie Emory was in love with Violet, he indignantly wrote to her and, she reported, *"dared to presume to scold me!"* Without waiting for her answer, he came to Washington to plead with her. At first, Violet was "freezingly polite," but when he cried and threatened that his doctor had warned him that emotional upsets could kill him, Violet relented and forgave him. She then told him about her relationship with Willie ("I was too honorable not to tell on myself"), that she did not love Willie but that she cared for him more than she did Potter. The rejected suitor did not give up easily. He "became cross, overbearing, jealous, deceitful, always selfish & sometimes insulting." When Violet tried to turn him away, he would cry, and she would relent. She realized that he was intentionally playing on her softheartedness, and it made her angry: "Oh it was so wicked & unmanly of him! I hate him for it!" Potter, referred to by Minna as "the Rev Cream Cheese," continued to force his attentions on Violet, trying to hold her in his arms and finally forcing a kiss from her.[48] At the same time, she continued to see Willie Emory, and the hours spent with him were a blissful contrast to her tribulations with Potter.

The wedding of Alida Carroll, a member of that old and prominent Maryland family and daughter of William T. Carroll, clerk of the United States Supreme Court, on December 18, 1866, marked Violet's debut into society. Violet was, as usual, a belle, surrounded by various men all evening. Her enthusiasm was destroyed when she later saw a printed piece sent to her by a friend in New York. It was pleasing to read that Violet had been "the prettiest girl at the Carroll wedding," but she was infuriated when she read, "This charming creature is to be the wife of a clergyman." She blamed Potter.

"If anything was wanting to complete my hatred of Mr. Potter that was enough to do so." Her distaste for "Old Pott" only increased when he said "disgusting things" to her when they were alone. Her flirtation with Willie, on the other hand, was altogether agreeable. He danced with her at all the parties, took her ice skating, and devoted himself to her. When he left for active sea duty, he had elicited her promise not to marry for three years. She did not promise to marry him, but she felt "almost" in love with him. "It is impossible that I should love any man—I *will not* do so—My heart is *unconquered* & *unconquerable*."[49]

Potter eventually gave up his relentless pursuit and returned her letters and photograph as she had requested. She was no longer in any way promised to him, and she felt great relief that that traumatic episode was over. Unquestionably, it deeply affected Violet's attitude toward relationships with men. The emotional turmoil she had experienced because of the Reverend Potter reinforced her youthful determination never to marry and never to lose control of her feelings. Later, she termed the incident "that dreadful thing," vowing that such a situation could never happen again: "I am determined to live & die a maiden."[50] Violet threw herself into society, becoming a very popular belle of the season. A report of her mother's party given in Violet's honor appeared in a Baltimore paper and proclaimed that Violet was "decidedly one of the most poetic and lovely looking young ladies that was brought forward in society." Her list of admirers grew to prodigious lengths; among her favorites were Frank Ramsay, Enrique Valles (second secretary of the Spanish legation), the lawyer Seaton Munroe, and Willie Emory's brother Dr. Louis Emory.[51]

During Violet's belle years, social life in Washington consisted of "endless calls, receptions, dinners and balls."[52] According to Madeleine Vinton Dahlgren, the Emily Post of her day, the most socially important denizens of the capital were "the resident society," which formed "the very *elite*" of the city.[53] Randolph Keim characterized this upper class as "select and distinguished," and Violet Blair qualified in every way for membership in this upper stratum.[54] Ironically, this division of society is often dated from the time of Andrew Jackson's administration, the very period in which Violet's family on her father's side had come to Washington. The passage of time, however, saw many families like the Blairs, who originally came to Washington for political reasons, become what Barry Bulkley has called "the untitled gentry."[55]

Relieved of any obligation to Eliphalet Potter, Violet immersed herself in the Washington social whirl. Referred to by her male admirers as "Sunbeam" and "La belle blonde," she reveled in the attentions of her suitors, and the egotism recognized by her aunt Lizzie became most apparent.[56] Willie Emory continued to pursue her, and although she knew that she cared for him only in a friendly manner, she admitted, "It flattered my vanity to conquer him."[57] In that spring of 1867, she became convinced of her powers over men: "I do not believe any girl could take an admirer of mine away from me."[58] She spun her web of flirtation around Jamie Dixon, the Spaniard Valles, and even seventeen-year-old Willie May. Her sense of power leaped most boundaries. Even though Valles was a foreigner and she had no real interest in him, she confided her goal to her diary: "I wish to make another conquest—I am always delighted to conquer anyone, man, woman, or child from two month old to seventy years, but especially the other sex between sixteen & forty."[59] Her days and nights were filled with flirtation: walks in the park, Saturday evenings listening to the music on the presidential grounds, parties at the marine barracks, entertainments ranging from intimate gatherings to large, formal dances in the homes of the Washington elite. While other girls danced and flirted, gathering seemly numbers of beaux, none could compare with Violet. She reigned in that exclusive society.[60]

The peculiar nature of Washington's political and economic life shaped residents' attitudes toward society. Obvious and apparent was the feeling of superiority of long-time inhabitants toward the politicians whose lives in Washington were most often short lived. Compounding the distinctiveness of Washington society was the lack of industry and commerce common to other large cities. The fortunes of the wealthy of Washington did not compare to those of the elite of other major cities such as New York or Philadelphia. As a result, greater emphasis in society was placed on gentility and manners.[61] Violet's self-appraisal, made in 1879 after her marriage, when the full significance of her success as a belle had permeated her outlook, gives some indication of the influence of the structure of Washington society on one of its own. Her family background, beauty, social success, and intelligence combined to provide her with "a quiet sense of superiority."[62]

Conquest may have been exhilarating to Violet, but the ease of it all quickly bored her. By mid-May 1867 she was tired of her beaux: "I want someone else as a devoted admirer."[63] It was a good time for a change of scene, and she looked forward to the European tour her mother was planning. The trip was a standard part of a young woman's education. As Frank Carpenter commented in the 1880s, "The Washington nabobs are a strange conglomeration. Some have the bluest of blue blood in their veins, education acquired in the best of schools, and manners polished by long sojourns in Europe."[64] Mary Blair wanted her lovely daughter to have the benefit of honing her skills as a lady by exposure to the sophistication of European society. Before she left Washington, however, Violet met a new man at a party held in the home of General Richard Delafield, who had recently retired as commander of the Corps of Engineers. On May 13, New Orleans lawyer Albert Janin, related by marriage to the Delafield's, had caught her attention. The following week he had been a member of a large group of picnickers who had made an outing to Mount Vernon. Violet found him "quite witty" and confessed that they "had quite a little flirtation," not giving much thought to the father of the country.[65] On the eve of her departure for Europe, she had found a new, and therefore exciting, male interest.

Chapter 2

A Belle of Washington

*"I love no man & yet I wish them all to
love me."* ❧

On June 1, 1867, Mary Blair sailed from New York on the *Europe* with her children: eighteen-year-old Violet, Jesup (fifteen), and Jimmie (thirteen). Two weeks later, Mary's sister Julia Jesup met them at Havre. After a week in Paris, they set out on a typical circular tour of Europe: Brussels, Aix la Chapelle, Cologne, Coblenz, Frankfurt, Heidelberg, Munich, and Zurich. Returning to Paris on October 17, they remained there for nearly a month before departing for Nice. Violet's early descriptions of their sightseeing are rather pedestrian, mentioning cathedrals, art galleries, operas, and the beauty of the countryside. She was impressed to see the actual landscapes, particularly the Rhine Valley, which were the settings for so much of her reading.[1] Although she valued her experiences, writing on her nineteenth birthday, "I have seen more in the last three weeks than in all the rest of my life before," she nevertheless did "not feel one bit older or wiser." Violet was not ready to accept maturity and could not think of herself as "a grown up young lady yet."[2]

During their summer-long wanderings through western Europe, Violet discovered that her aunt Julia resented the admiring gazes men directed toward her niece. A striking woman herself, Julia had always been the center of attention. Unconventional, she had decided to live in Europe to pursue a singing career and had never wanted for male admiration. To Violet, she had been a beautiful and exotic idol. She described her aunt as "tall, dark, sad & handsome," and although "a magnificent looking woman . . . exceedingly bad tempered & cross." Whenever men seemed to focus on Violet, Julia became angry and retaliated with cutting and spiteful remarks. While they had both been called beautiful, Aunt Julia claimed Violet was "only a 'pretty little baby-faced blond.'"[3] Without doubt, Aunt Julia felt competition from her niece, only eight years younger than she. Her jealousy did nothing to temper Violet's ego.

Well aware of the interested looks she had received from strangers on the continent, Violet took special pleasure in the attentions she received from those who knew her in Paris. A young relative just Violet's age, Sitgreaves Adams, called on the Blair family and was "smitten." Enrique Valles, who was attached to the Spanish legation in Washington and had been her suitor there, called on Violet before he had even reported to his embassy in Paris. Years later a friend laughingly reminded Violet how Valles used to follow her around crooning, "I lof you, I lof you, I lof you Miss Vilete."[4] Another frequent visitor was her second cousin Lewis Clark, an excellent dancer and "the personification of a southern gentleman."[5]

Fortunately, Aunt Julia did not continue with the family to Nice. Had she, her jealousy would have had no limit, for Nice became the scene of Violet's greatest triumphs as a belle; it lived forever in her memory. Referring to the city as "this Paradise," Violet began her first 1868 diary entry in ecstasy: "Oh! I have had so much pleasure in these six weeks in dear Nizza—I have never know[n] the joy it is to live until now."[6] She was a sensation at her first social occasion, a matinee *dansante* at the Cercle Massena, where she "wore a green silk costume & a tulle bonnet with pink flowers." All wished to meet the "belle Americaine," the newspaper praised her beauty, and she became renowned as "the young lady in the green costume." At every party, Violet trailed a shoal of men in her wake. She confided to her diary, "From the day I began to know the gentlemen here . . . I have been a great belle & have not missed a partner for any dance . . . sometimes I have been obliged to give only part of a dance to each person—sometimes if there had been fifty more dances I could have had partners for them, for I was obliged to refuse so many." Americans (army colonel James Kinney and navy lieutenant George W. DeLong); Englishmen (a Mr. Percival and a Mr. Butler, the latter a son of an English lord); the Russian Constantin Catacazy, who became minister to the United States; the Frenchman Prince de Valori; and the Italian Marquis de Constatin all vied for the favor of her company. She was "the belle of the ball (c'est vrai!)" and relished it all. Violet reigned supreme, considering her days in Nice as her "glory."[7]

Her routine in Nice revolved around her social life. Arising late, she spent the remainder of the morning in writing letters to friends at home and studying Italian, and in the afternoon she received visitors. On the days when there was no afternoon dance, she walked on the Promenade des Anglais with her beaux. After dinner, there was time for reading—if she did not receive or go visiting or if there was not a ball.[8]

In mid-January Admiral David G. Farragut's USS *Franklin* came to port, and Violet exulted in her popularity at the ball given in the admiral's honor. "If I am not happy another moment of my life, I will think I have no right to complain for the glorious happiness of that one night is worth a life time of pain or sorrow." It was, in her words, "my triumph, my victory." She relished her role as "*the* belle of all the hundreds and hundreds of people there. . . . Oh! how they flattered me that blessed night! Oh! I was so happy!" Wearing a "white tarletan dress just like the snow drift & tiny green vines with a few red berries running in the ruches of the two skirts & around the neck & on [her] hair," Violet was a ravishing beauty and received many more bouquets from gentlemen than any other woman. After the dancing was over, she enjoyed a champagne supper with officers of the *Franklin* and did not leave the festivities until five in the morning.[9]

Although Violet already possessed an abundance of ego, her glorious days in Nice only reinforced her self-image. She recognized the effect on herself of such adulation, but it did not temper her outlook: "I am getting to be very conceited, but it is enough to make any girl so—I hear people I do not know say as I pass, 'That is Miss Blair, the prettiest girl in Nice' or 'La belle Americaine'—Oh! it is delicious!"[10] She began to refer to her admirers as "my pets" and boasted that "it is a rare privilege to dance with me twice in a evening." She found it "delightful to see how anxious people were to get just a waltz" with her.[11] When it was time to leave Nice, she was desolate: "I shall be like Eve cast out of paradise—I have never known such happiness before as I have known here. . . . Am I not the belle of Nice, the queen? Some people say the Beauty. . . . Here I am without a rival."[12] Her mastery of the males in Nice was indelibly etched in her memory; she knew she could never be the same again: "I will never be satisfied away from it—Never! Never! Never!"[13]

In American literature, the belle as a social type has generally been depicted as the unmarried daughter of an aristocratic family who was a frivolous coquette. While she was often portrayed as modest and meek, she was also acknowledged to be the center of attention, experiencing the only period in her life in which she controlled events.[14] She was, as Anne Scott has noted, "endowed with magic powers to attract men and bend them to her will." Novelists presented the belle's power to manipulate men and evoke passion; yet she was always in command of her own emotions.[15] Variously described as modest or temptress, naive or sophisticated, "madonna-like" or "bitch-goddess," the belle held sway in society.[16] Christie Farnham has provided the most complete analysis of the historical roots of the concept of the belle. Anchoring the ideal in antebellum southern society, she demonstrates that it "remained a compelling ideal" to young women because it served "as a model of empowerment."[17] Despite the contradictions within the social type, there is no doubt that Violet Blair was a genuine, real-life belle. She was not meek and mild, but she may have appeared ethereal to many men. Narcissistic and vain, she basked in her powers and knew full well what she would give up by marrying. Her conquests in Nice had been brilliant, heightening her already overextended sense of superiority.

Leaving Nice in February 1868, the family journeyed to Genoa, then visited Mount Vesuvius (awed by its eruption) and Naples before arriving in Rome in early March. There, they found an apartment with a balcony from which they could watch the parades and festivities accompanying the carnival prior to Lent. It was the custom for men to throw bouquets of flowers to lovely ladies on the balconies. Violet, of course, caught more than her share. On the first day, she received forty to fifty bouquets; on the final carnival day, admiring strangers tossed her between two and three hundred.[18]

That Violet's attitude toward men was becoming ever more cynical and cold is obvious in her diary: "I love no man & yet I wish them all to love me, it flatters my vanity to have it so."[19] That she had become even more imperious is evident in her relationship with her cousin Lewis Clark. During their Paris stay, Lewis had been with them nearly every day. He was "very tall & graceful" and "charming in society," but Violet thought that she was his superior intellectually. Nevertheless, she enjoyed his constant company and was grateful to have a devoted escort. While she loved him *"as a cousin,"* Lewis evidently had begun to fall under her spell.[20]

Having separated from the Blair family when they left Paris, Lewis joined them again in Naples and followed them to Rome. Also in the Eternal City, Percival, the Englishman, was intent upon courting Violet. When Lewis objected to her spending so much time with Percival, she was not pleased. Perhaps Lewis was too independent for her. In Paris, when she was just beginning to revel in her powers of attraction, Lewis had told her that he did not think beauty was particularly important.[21] Now, when he began to question her judgment, she commented that although she was "devoted" to him, she did not appreciate his advice: "He is disposed to find fault with me, which I permit no one but Uncle Jim & Min to do."[22] Accustomed to telling men what to do, she was especially upset when Lewis advised her mother not to allow Violet to give her photograph to Percival. Lewis's suggestion that the man would only use the picture as something to brag about at his club prompted Mary Blair to beg and cry in her attempt to persuade Violet to do as Lewis requested. Violet's retort was, "I would rather have been cut to pieces than yield to a man." Lewis had the last word, however; he bribed the servant to turn Percival away when he called. Violet therefore had no chance to give him a photograph. Outraged that she had been outwitted, she vowed revenge. It was not just that Lewis had succeeded in having his way. Violet was even more furious because she thought Percival meant to propose to her, and claimed Lewis "prevented me from having another offer."[23]

Thinking he had won the day, Lewis left the Blair family to travel in Switzerland, joining them again in Paris. The Blairs, meanwhile, left Rome to tour Florence, Venice, and Milan, before settling in the French capital. Once again, Lewis intervened in Violet's affairs. At her mother's urging, Violet showed him a letter from Eliphalet Potter, who had written to confess that he could not get over his love for Violet. She had composed "a decided but friendly letter," which both Lewis and Mary thought too friendly. Lewis then dictated a few "hard cold lines" which her mother insisted that she send to Potter. Unable to admit that she had submitted to the will of a man, she could only write, "It was so hard to hold out against Mama's wishes." When Lewis continued to try to dominate her, having "the impertinence" to tell her that she should not write to other men, she would have no part of it: "I *will* do it."[24] After a short time in London, the Blairs, along with Lewis, embarked on the *Russia* for their homeward passage.[25] Violet did not forget her vow of revenge; she made Lewis pay dearly. Playing upon his affections, she drew him on, pretending greater interest than she felt. "As we were leaning over the side of the steamer under the stars, I looked into his face with eyes full of tenderness & he thought he had only to speak to be accepted." Of course she refused him. It was a cruel ploy, but Violet felt victorious, proclaiming, "Woe to the man who dares to interfere with me again."[26]

Throughout her young life, Violet had lacked a strong male authority figure in her life. She had little memory of her father, and perhaps she felt her father had abandoned her. After his death, all the men close to the family had concentrated on consoling and comforting this fatherless brood. Grandfathers Blair and Jesup were both warm, loving, and uncritically devoted to Violet. Tolerant and forbearing, they had catered to her whims, intent on soothing and placating her. Uncle Montgomery, although concerned about the financial welfare of her family, had little sensitivity to anyone's emotional needs and was incapable of playing any role in her socialization. Her brother, Jesup, was, for years, too young to exert any influence. And by the time he came to the age at which he might have provided a strong male model, he was dominated by her. She had been his teacher at home, and when he went away to school, it was she who wrote essays for him so that he could maintain good grades. Violet liked her brother because he did "almost anything" she told him."[27] James Alden, best friend of the dead James Blair, nobly shouldered his responsibility of shielding the family from the harsh blows of the cruel world. He was a gentle, stable presence to Violet. While he was able to talk plainly to Violet, he was still not a dominating figure; Violet "allowed" him to criticize her. There was, in sum, no man to whom Violet felt subordinate. None had ever forced her to do anything; she had never felt compelled to acquiesce to any man. No man had ever been her superior. In her experience with all the men for whom she cared, she had found that they ultimately bowed to her wishes.

Violet's childhood years coincided with the period in which ideas of family and child rearing had changed from the older authoritarian model to a more tolerant and affectionate mode. In the mid-nineteenth century, as Carl Degler has demonstrated, "the attention, energy, and resources of parents . . . were increasingly centered upon the rearing of their offspring," and mothers had come to play a much more central role within the family.[28] The idea of "companionate marriage" had gained ascendancy, allowing women greater authority within marriage and significant control over child rearing. Part of the result of this change was a greater emphasis on the individuality of each child and the need to discipline and nurture a child's development through love and affection.[29]

In the Blair family, with no father present, the mother was the only central figure, and Mary Blair became the all-important figure in Violet's life. She was the fount of love, education, moral standards, self-sacrifice, and authority. The pre-eminent figure in Violet's life, for her entire life, was her mother, who quietly represented goodness, propriety, and perfect motherhood. Equally significant, it was her mother who represented female independence, who consistently refused to be controlled, directed, or governed by her male relatives.[30] She also had the signal example of her grandmother, Eliza Blair, who was known in and out of the family as "the Lioness." The wife of the *Globe* editor Francis Preston Blair, Eliza was extremely intelligent, outspoken, and self-confident and was an acknowledged advisor to her husband. Although she remained respectably within the bounds of a woman's sphere, there was no doubt that Eliza Blair was the equal of any man, including her husband.[31] Violet could hardly have missed the significance of her grandmother as a role model. Thus, the examples of both her mother and her grandmother reinforced her natural tendencies to autonomy and self-esteem, and Violet's own life experiences moved her from confidence to arrogance.

In the late spring of 1868, not long after their return to Washington, the Blairs moved into their new home on Lafayette Square, just around the corner from her Uncle Montgomery's. Although sad at leaving the Jesup home on F Street with all its memories, Violet was delighted to be living so close to her dearest friend, Minna.[32] Immediately, the men began to flock; especially attentive were her old beaux, Harry Lyon, Jamie Dixon, and Frank Robinson. Three times a week, Albert Janin called on her. Finding him "very amusing," Violet treated him as she did all the others and thought, "He cares no more for me than I do for him." She was obviously contemplating another conquest when she quickly added, "but he may if he keeps on coming."[33]

When summer came, the Blairs moved out to Silver Spring, staying with Violet's grandparents. Violet led a quiet life of reading, studying, and writing letters. Seeing the magnificent art works of Europe had made her even more appreciative of the beauty of nature, and she was content to take her books to her favorite spots in the woods and gardens lovingly constructed by her grandfather Blair.[34] Her reading had always been prodigious. While in Europe, she had read five volumes of Macaulay's *Essays,* biographies of Vittorio Alfieri, Carlo Goldoni, and Marguerite de Valois, Queen of Navarre. En route to America, she purchased Plato's *Republic,* Lever's *Fortunes of Glencore,* and Dr. Geothe's *Courtship.* Among the many works she read during the summer of 1868 were Walpole's *Letters,* DeStael's *De la Litterature,* Muhlbach's *Joseph the Second,* in addition to Chaucer, Tennyson, Schiller, Petrarch, Byron, and Scott. Studying Italian by herself, she worked at Dante in the original and also read Carlyle's *Essays,* Rives's *Life of Madison,* several Shakespeare plays, St. Beauve's *Celebrated Women,* and Tillotson's sermons. By the end of the year she had added Hawthorne's *Scarlet Letter,* Sir Philip Sidney's *Arcadia,* and Ben Johnson's poetry. All this, in addition to magazines, newspapers, and "trashy" novels.[35]

The social season was over, but Violet gave a great deal of thought to male admirers. She knew she did not want to marry Harry Lyon, although her uncle James Alden would have been gratified to see her wed his nephew. Aware that Jamie Dixon was on the verge of proposing to her, she was unmoved. Despite her admiration for Will Emory's bravery, she did not love him. "The truth is," she told her diary, "I have never known a man worthy of my love." During that summer of 1868, she renewed her vow: "I will never love & never marry—No man shall ever be my master—I will never promise to obey."[36]

When the family moved back to the city in mid-November, Violet repeated her desire to remain single. She recalled her glorious days in Nice, where she had been "the proudest, vainest, happiest girl on Earth."[37] Simultaneous with her declaration, "Society is my beloved forever," she was becoming intrigued by Albert Janin. She admitted to her diary, "I like him very much, for he sings well & has more brains than the rest of the beaux I meet in society—I like him very much indeed." Albert was clever in his courting. Where other men seemed "silly ignorant creatures . . . only fit to dance with," Albert appealed to Violet's intellect: "He & I talk more about books than anything else & I know he thinks me remarkably intelligent & well read."[38] With a well-developed sense of romance, Albert wooed her with songs in German, Italian, Spanish, French, and English. When he sang "Juanita," he substituted in place of "Nita, Juanita" the words "Letta, Violetta." It was all very amusing and tantalizing to Violet, but it was not to last. Janin had to leave Washington for his home in New Orleans. Perhaps his absence was part of the attraction; he could not stay long enough for her to become bored. Ironically, it was in this very period that Julia Copper, a friend from Violet's war-time days in Bethlehem, warned her against her coquettish ways: "Beware, my darling little flirt that when you think your heart most secure some elegant, fascinating fellow does not hook it & keep it a little longer than you bargain for."[39]

The 1869 season was, according to one newspaper report, brilliant: "the very *creme de la creme* of their select circles" enjoyed "balls, parties, soirees (musical and *dansante*), receptions, dinner parties, private theatricals and tableaux."[40] Violet, the reigning belle, continued to draw men to her, and she spent a heady season keeping her admirers in line. She loved it, but she hated it: "I love admiration so intensely . . . though I must confess that I suffer when I make them suffer."[41]

On December 23, 1869, Violet was one of ten bridesmaids in Carrie Carroll's wedding. Paired with Jamie Dixon, she wore a white tarleton dress, trimmed in pink satin. She and Jamie were acknowledged to be "the handsomest couple there." It was that night that Jamie proposed to her, and she refused him.[42] In the succeeding weeks, she attended parties nearly every night and flirted with a variety of men. Old Washington society saw fit to include in their entertainments attractive diplomats from the foreign embassies, handsome, clever military men, always in abundance in the capital, and, of course, young, attractive men of their own families, even if they worked for the government.[43] She danced with John Lothrop, a clerk in the second auditor's office. Count Gaston D'Aerschot, charge d'affaires for Belgium, told her that she was known as the Beauty of Washington, a fact of which she was well aware. The Greek minister to Washington, Alexander Rizo Rangabe, thought she had a perfect Grecian nose. Frank Robinson was spoony, and Jamie Dixon assuaged his disappointment over Violet's refusal of him by getting drunk.[44]

Toward the end of January 1869, she collected a new beau, Paul Dahlgren, who, along with d'Aerschot, became her most constant devotee. The "charming" Dahlgren, son of navy admiral John A. Dahlgren, constantly called on her, sometimes two or three times in a day. And at all the fashionable parties—the Riggs's, the Wallach's, the Carroll's—Violet spent most of her time flirting with him. "Tall with a beautiful figure, a good profile, soft eyes, fair hair & a fine expression," he was a very attractive man.[45] "They say," she noted in her diary, "he & I are having a grand flirtation & they are not far wrong."[46] At the reception after her cousin Betty Blair's marriage to General Cyrus B. Comstock, Paul declared his love for Violet. He pursued her in earnest, sending her flowers every day. She was tempted to fall in love with him, for he seemed to be "nearer my ideal than any man I have ever seen."[47] She had recently described her ideal man: "strong, tall, brave, generous, intelligent, cultivated, refined & above all high born."[48] Paul qualified on most counts, but she knew his reputation for flirtation and was wary.

When Paul finally convinced Violet that he loved her, she was confused and distressed. When she had thought him "cold & heartless," she had had no qualms about flirting with him. Discovering that he was deeply religious and "one of the noblest men on earth," she was aggrieved that she had caused Paul such unhappiness and considered whether she should marry him.[49] Although she knew she was not ready to marry, she wondered if, because he was "so good & noble," he might be able to "make me good."[50] Until Paul left the city on active military duty, Violet played with the idea of marrying him—perhaps in ten years or in five or six.[51]

With Paul gone, Violet wasted no time in resuming her old flirtatious ways. Janin had returned to Washington, and Pierce Young, a former Confederate general, began to court her. Tall, dark, and handsome, Young was "ready for a flirtation," and evidently so was Violet. She luxuriated in comparisons among her three admirers and quickly dismissed her short-lived desire for being good. Her vanity craved their attention, and her ego grew: "I like to have men in love with me, I feel so superior to them."[52]

At the same time, there is no doubt that Violet felt guilty. With regularity, she felt the pricks of her conscience. To compensate, she joined the Sisterhood of St. John, dedicated to caring for orphans.[53] She wanted to be deeply religious, to emulate St. Catherine, envisioning herself "a virgin daughter of the church." She had found a religiously acceptable excuse for not marrying: "I must have no earthly love, I must be the Lord's, a consecrated virgin bound by no earthly tie."[54] Violet could not, however, escape her own infatuation with her powers of attraction. She twisted her supposed desire to be "pure from all earthly passion" into a means for saving Janin's soul and an excuse for continuing to encourage him. Her beauty and worldliness could be justified, she thought, "if for the sake of my fair face he begins to read the Bible."[55] Her newly found piety provided a means for escaping blame for the pain she was causing her suitors. Not only had Paul Dahlgren proposed, but both Janin and Young had also offered marriage. In addition, Will Emory, a formerly rejected suitor, had written to her, and Violet did have a genuine sense of guilt.[56] Her conceit discomforted her: "Vile & wretched as I am! How can I belong to Him with all this deceit & earthliness in my heart! I love admiration so intensely—I am so vain that I am not satisfied unless men fall in love with me & I draw them on with tender looks, though I must confess that I suffer when I make them suffer."[57]

Despite any misgivings, Violet continued to collect her men. During the summer of 1869 she added to her list. She wondered if navy lieutenant Louis Kingsley might propose and become her "tenth victim." With the bashful James O'Kane (a lieutenant commander in the navy) she flirted shamelessly and "had such fun looking into his eyes & all that sort of thing."[58] Violet had cold-bloodedly decided to count coup, wishing to acquire a dozen proposals before she was twenty-one. She found it exciting that she might be able to elicit a proposal from O'Kane and even told him, "I only wanted three more victims to make my number complete."[59] Shocked by her disclosure, O'Kane nevertheless was, she proclaimed, "No. 10 of my victims"; and George DeLong, whom she had met in Nice, was number eleven.[60] She knew it was wrong: "I am reading 'Women of Christianity'—I am a fine specimen of one, trying to win men's hearts that I may refuse them."[61] She also did not know what to do with her men once she had captured them: "What shall I do? I am so worried about all these men who are in love with me—I cannot marry them all & I don't want to marry any of them—I wish I knew how to cure them."[62]

In attempting to decide how to handle these various men, Violet was shrewd in her assessments of them: DeLong's "love is too violent, if he dared he would try to be impertinent—Janin's love is much more spiritual—Dahlgren's is tender, exceedingly proper & not a bit red hot, but DeLong's is strong, hot & earthly as everything else in his character."[63] Pierce Young "has not heart enough to love me much," Violet decided, acknowledging that although he was "brave & handsome," he was also "stupid, conceited & uneducated."[64] Her analytical mind appreciated Dahlgren's character, but her heart told her, "Janin loves me best." He was the one with the "most brains" of all her lovers," but there were serious drawbacks: "Janin is Southern & has a French name, both of which are against him."[65]

Whether in the city or country, Violet's retinue followed her. After the social season ended, they continued to call on her daily, playing croquet, walking in the park or the countryside, talking, flirting, and vying for the belle's attention. Every evening, she had at least four or five men dancing attendance. Many years later, Mag Zeilin recalled her happy days spent in the country with the Blair family and remembered, "How Jim and I used to swear at your numerous men, who were so in the way—always around and interfering with each other."[66]

During the season, being a belle meant a grueling schedule. After receiving gentlemen at home on Monday, Violet wrote, "Tuesday we went to Mrs. Lothrop's ball, Wednesday to Miss Kinney's, last night to Miss Coleman's, & tonight we were going to Mrs. Fish's, but I am perfectly broken down & not able to go anywhere else—I have been very much of a belle at each place but particularly last night, I danced until my feet ached."[67] In addition to the large receptions and gala balls, from Christmas to Ash Wednesday the elite of Washington assembled night after night in each other's homes. Unlike either Boston or Philadelphia, Washington could count perhaps only eighty families who qualified as "well-established second-generation families."[68] Especially in the last three decades of the nineteenth century, the old families formed the nucleus of elite society, and with their emphasis on manners, cultivated conversation, and a curious combination of southern hospitality and worldly sophistication, these denizens held themselves aloof from association with official government society.[69] Admission into this society was not altogether closed. A clever, intellectually stimulating, or socially adept newcomer could find acceptance; good manners counted for more than money or position.[70] A relatively small number constituted this restricted society, and the same individuals who had attended an afternoon tea later met at a dinner party.[71] An article in the *Century Magazine* described that social scene: "There are perhaps two score of houses where people are at home one or two evenings in every month. As the society is still so small that there is but one set in it, one meets everybody, *i.e.,* some four or five hundred persons at these different houses." These gatherings were "composed of distinguished men and brilliant women; and it [was] the constant reunion of such people at dinners and small evening parties which [made] up the most agreeable part of Washington society."[72] Violet Blair was at the center of Washington society and never doubted her position or authority.

Among the most select events of the season were the dances given by the Bachelor's German Club. Organized in 1868, the club consisted of around fifty prominent Washingtonians; its purpose was to separate the old elite society of the city from the nouveau riche and official government groups. They represented what came to be called the Cave Dwellers of Washington—those of the oldest and most distinguished families of the city. As their class lost prestige and position during the Gilded Age, the Bachelor's German Club was one of numerous attempts to shore up their authority. The "very exclusive and select club of gentlemen" sponsored a series of dances during the season which were considered "quite 'the thing.'" Emphasizing simplicity of decor and food, refinement, gentility, selectiveness, ancestry, and etiquette, their germans were among the most excluding dances of the season. Violet, of course, was a regular participant in the festivities of the Bachelor's Club, loving most of all its elitism.[73]

During 1870, Violet continued to play the belle, pitting one lover against another, flirting with them all, and enticing as many men as possible. Kinglsey, Dahlgren, Young, Janin, the Spaniard Sanchez, naval ensign Hamilton Tallman, and even former Confederate Fitzhugh Lee sought her attention.[74] James O'Kane pressed his case from Montevideo, writing, "Though you are free, I am to you bound."[75] Louis Kingsley wrote of his devotion: "Darling, I miss you terribly, much more than I imagined I could."[76] When Willie Emory returned to Washington, he vigorously renewed his pursuit of Violet even though she had already rejected him.[77] It is probably on this visit to Washington that he wrote her, "Tell me I entreat you, if you can give me a favorable reply. If not, spare me the pain that another farewell would cause me, because I feel that I could not stand it."[78] Despite another refusal, Emory did not give up his quest.

Throughout her 1870 diary entries, Violet expressed discontent with her life, complaining, "Oh! I am weary of the life I lead & the men I know." Tired of the "worldliness" of her existence, she felt "good for nothing."[79] Her intense interest in the woman's rights movement colored her judgments: "I hate these stupid silly men, who, not knowing the tenth part of what I know, dare to think themselves superior to me by reason of being men."[80] Doubting that she could ever be happily married, Violet melodramatically declared, "I will never be a bride, I will live & die a vestal for Christ's sake."[81] In calmer moments, she came closer to the truth: "I do not believe it is possible for me to love any man."[82] She admitted, "I need only books & lovers to flatter me, I want admiration not love." Recognizing the fundamental basis for her opposition to marriage, she declared, "I will be no man's slave."[83]

Despite her aversion to marriage in 1870, Violet was becoming more and more interested in Albert Janin. As the year progressed, interspersed among her comments of discontent are periodic appraisals of the New Orleans lawyer. Janin encouraged her interest in woman's rights, bringing her books and pamphlets on the subject.[84] Although he was ugly and was not a churchman, she thought him "the most intelligent & agreeable man" she knew. "He loves me devotedly & is, I think, unselfish."[85] Uncomplaining and undemanding, Janin was "so gentle, tender & respectful" that Violet found herself considering marriage to him even though she did not love him.[86] Admiring his intelligence and his total devotion to her, Violet began to favor Albert over her other lovers. But she had not been won. Confessing, "I think sometimes his visits are almost necessary to me," she quickly reassured herself, "but when he goes away I don't miss him after a little while."[87]

Chapter 3

Courtship

"I am a thistle, & woe to the ass who tries to pluck me."

Superficially, Violet's social season of 1871 was much like those that had gone before. Dancing and flirting until the early morning hours, she was pursued by numerous men, and she remained a most popular belle. Emory persisted in his pleas for marriage, DeLong "begged [her] to marry him," and Dahlgren had not given up hope.[1] While she continued to toy with their affections and to consider their strengths and weaknesses in her diary, her rejected suitors began to turn their attentions elsewhere. Potter had long since married; word came that DeLong had wed; Emory and Dixon both became engaged to others; Young was no longer in attendance. In March Violet wrote, "I wonder who will be the next of my lovers that I get rid of."[2] She was not the least downhearted at the turn of events and had little trouble justifying her behavior: "I learned to amuse myself with men's passions & to think I honored them by allowing them to love me."[3] Although there were always others to replace these admirers, Violet began to consider the possibility of marriage more seriously.

Still maintaining that "matrimony is not my vocation," she nevertheless was frightened: "I may be weak enough to marry Janin, because he is so very persistent, but I do hope not." He seemed to Violet to need "looking after."[4] In her analysis, Janin "suits me better than any man I know." Although she claimed that she did not love him, she did "like him very much."[5] It was not uncommon for women in the late nineteenth century to deny their capacity for love. Ellen Rothman has pointed out that earlier in the century, women "lacked confidence in their worthiness to *be* loved," but that in later decades, "women were more likely to question their ability *to* love."[6] Through the years, Violet had consistently maintained that she was "as cold as an icicle": "All love is frozen in my heart," and "I cannot love a man." On several occasions she had questioned, "Why cannot I love like other people?"[7]

Thinking herself unsuited to marriage, she knew that if she took that fateful step, it could be only on her own terms: "It must be a man who understands I cannot love & who can stand all my whims & be contented with my friendship—I only know one man who can stand all my caprices, but I believe he can for his love is so great."[8] That man was Albert Janin. By mid-April, part of her vacillation was over: "If I marry, it will be Janin." In him, she found the necessary qualities: "He has most brains, a gentle temper & high principles—Perhaps if I were not too conceited to care for any man, I might care for him, he is so good to me—I consult him about nearly everything, even my other lovers." She respected his intelligence, and more importantly, Albert was her friend. "I may possibly marry him in a few years."[9]

Perhaps part of Albert's appeal was that he seemed somehow different from the other men Violet knew. While not particularly physically attractive (Jesup referred to him as "little Janin"), he had an air of cosmopolitan sophistication that others lacked.[10] At the age of thirteen, his parents had sent him to the German boarding school of Dr. Christian Friedrick Krause, the Lehr und Erziehung Anstalt, in Dresden. For Albert, his four years in Europe were "a period of almost unmixed happiness." An apt scholar with a strong desire to please, he easily accepted the restrictions imposed by the institution and thereby attained a favored and privileged status. At the same time, he was a leader of his fellow students in promoting "deviltry" and "mischief." After taking his baccalaureate at the Academie de Paris, Universite de France, Albert had returned to the United States.[11] That exposure to a different culture at an impressionable age had a significant and enduring influence in shaping his personality and outlook. Albert later claimed that his European experience had given him "freedom from race and national prejudices, a knowledge of languages, a keen appreciation of music and art, and a sympathetic understanding of cosmopolitan modes of thought and action."[12] He was a sophisticated gentleman whom Violet must have found more than a little fascinating.

Although not a Washington native, Albert Janin's father was a well-known figure in legal circles in the city. Louis Janin, a native of France, had come to the United States in 1828, settling in New Orleans. Admitted to the bar in 1831, Louis became a naturalized citizen in 1835. Building a distinguished and lucrative practice based on land law cases involving French and Spanish titles, Louis appeared frequently before the United States Supreme

Court. Albert's mother, Juliet Covington, was the daughter of Harriet Baldwin and General E. M. Covington of Bowling Green, Kentucky. Their sons were all well educated: Louis, Henry, and Alexis were mining engineers; Eugene, Edward, and Albert were lawyers.[13] While not, in Violet's estimation, the equal of the Blair family in eminence, the Janin family was respectable, intelligent, and full of promise for the future.

Sometime between mid-April and mid-May 1871, Violet promised Albert that she would marry him. He had found the key to eliciting her promise in his appreciation of her learning, and she thought him "in that respect" her equal. "I am so accustomed to refer to him that he is almost necessary to me."[14] Trusted friend, honest advisor, witty, clever, tender, kind—"almost necessary"— Albert had succeeded in winning Violet's esteem. Most significantly, Violet wrote, "He obeys me."[15] She well knew that absolute submission to her was essential. Describing herself as "haughty" was an understatement. More accurate of her self-image was her pronouncement, "I am a Queen & I will be obeyed."[16] More perceptive of the future was her comment, "I am a thistle, & woe to the ass who tries to pluck me."[17]

Although her promise to Albert was their secret, Violet had finally committed herself. Having made her choice in the spring of 1871, she faced opposition that may have helped her to a firm commitment. Her sister, Jimmie, who had taken a dislike to Janin, influenced their mother's opinion. Mary Blair was unwilling to allow Albert to spend the weekend with the family in the country, although Jimmie's beau had been invited. Their objection to Albert kindled the possibility of rebellion in Violet: "I am afraid I will marry Janin if they make me very angry."[18] Although she continued to flirt with other men, her mother suspected that Violet's romance with Albert was getting too serious. Perhaps it was for that reason that Mary decided to whisk her daughter off to Europe. Violet did not want to go, but she could not disobey her mother.

On November 4, 1871, the Blairs sailed on the *St. Laurent.* James O'Kane, Paul Dahlgren, and Albert Janin all traveled to New York to bid Violet goodbye on the deck of the steamer.[19] In his first letter to Violet, Albert explained that he could not be angry with O'Kane, who knew nothing of their secret engagement. In terms that flattered Violet's ego, he explained that since O'Kane did not know of their understanding, he had "the same right to love and adore you that pagans have to bow down together before the idol of their worship." It was another matter, however, with Dahlgren, who somehow knew of their promise yet persisted in urging Violet to break her pledge and marry him. Albert contended that his anger ("it makes my blood boil") was not based on his own jealousy but on the insult to Violet—that Paul should assume she could break her word. The usually "calm and phlegmatic" Albert was totally distraught: "I am rendered almost frantic by the mere thought of the possibility of losing you. My whole emotional being seems merged in yours; robbed of you I should be poor indeed. Though sad and lonely now, I esteem myself rich and blessed with the promise of future happiness, without you I should be but a wreck to mock at human hopes & aspirations."[20]

While still in New York, the love-sick suitor sought solace in the companionship of her brother, Jesup, and her aunt and uncle, Lucy Ann Jesup and Lorenzo Sitgreaves. To Violet he sighed, "My sweet angel, I never knew before how dear you were to me. Oh, how I love you and how I hate all who would try to separate us." After his return to Washington, he hastened to her cousin Minna, who became his confidante and sympathetic listener. Yet, even with Minna, Albert did not feel completely free to discuss Violet's expressions of affection for him. His attitude was one of complete subservence. As he explained to Violet in terms that especially appealed to her, "I do not want to present you, even to her, in any other light than that of the all conquering beauty who deigns to accept my homage."[21]

Minna, of course, kept Violet apprised of her conversations with Albert, assuring the belle that her lover did indeed feel wretched: "Your poor Jane Ann did not look well at all and we talked of you all the time." His words and demeanor were convincing proof to Minna of his total devotion to Violet: "I don't believe any man ever loved me as he does you."[22]

Violet's first letter to Albert contained a sweet expression of her affection for him: "I feel how much I need you every day, you do not know how I look to you for advice & comfort all the time. What will I do all this winter without you to talk everything over with."[23] Albert did not, however, receive this letter first. The vagaries of transoceanic mail brought him another which let loose a barrage of what she came to term her "thunderbolts." Beginning her letter to her downhearted lover with "I am provoked with you mon ami," she upbraided him in no uncertain terms. Because she had received no letter, she assumed he had failed to follow her instructions about mailing his letters in time to catch the next steamer. The imperious Violet threatened, "If I do not hear from you soon there will be a grand row & smashing of things especially engagements."[24]

From the beginning of their correspondence, the couple had agreed to continue their policy of complete honesty with each other. Albert implored his love, "Do not treat me with reserve and want of confidence—I mean, do not employ toward me the caution that you use in your correspondence with others. You know that you can trust me thoroughly."[25] Violet promised to "tell [him] everything," and she did.[26] With remarkable frankness, she described in great detail every man she met and flirted with, who was falling in love with her, and what other men wrote to her and she to them. Their emphasis on honesty was not unusual. For most American couples, candor was the essential quality necessary for a successful relationship. Openness was essential for the nurturance of trust and to ensure that one's particular individuality was the object of love. More importantly, honesty helped bridge the gap between men and women in a world which had increasingly compartmentalized them into separate spheres.[27]

During courting, it was not unusual for young men and women to urge each other to share all feelings and thoughts. What is unusual in Violet's case is the degree to which she adhered to the unvarnished truth. Shortly after her arrival in Paris, Violet recounted to Albert the results of a friendship with a Frenchman, a Mr. Thuries. They had met on the steamer, and he had followed her to Paris. After many protestations of his devotion to his absent wife and acknowledgment of her attachment to Albert (which had seemed innocent enough to Violet), Thuries suddenly professed his love for the American belle and wished, she exclaimed, to "carry me off to his plantation in the West Indies & begged me not to marry for two, or three years as by that time he could get free to offer himself to me." While she was shocked by these declarations from a married man, she admitted to Albert that he was "so gentle & sweet tempered" and confessed that there was "something fascinating about him." Nothing was hidden from Albert; she had been absolutely honest. But her letter did nothing to reassure him, ending on an ambiguous note, "Albert I am not in love with you but I will try to be good & I miss you worse than you can imagine."[28]

That letter was the first that poor Albert received from his beloved. He described to her how he felt when it arrived, holding the unopened letter: ". . . drinking in the joy that I anticipated from its perusal. I had just been dreaming most delightfully of you; the whole current of my being was set towards you and my heart was fairly panting for some balm of comfort, some word of cheer. Alas! I was soon awakened from my blissful state. The first thing I read was a scolding for my assumed failure to write; the next, a threatened breaking of our engagement—my only anchor of hope; the third, a rebuke for what I had said of P. D. [Paul Dahlgren]; the fourth thing was an account of Thouries' shameful conduct towards you."[29] Her "thunderbolts" had struck home. He was saddened by her doubt of him, sorrowful at her rebuke, and infuriated by Thuries.

On the next day, fearful that he had offended her, he wrote to explain himself more fully. His anger at Paul Dahlgren and Thuries came not from jealousy but a desire to protect her from the insulting behavior of both men. Unwilling to risk a break with her, he emphasized that his sole concern was her welfare, not his feelings. He admitted that his anger had overwhelmed him, and he asked for her indulgence and pardon. "Violet, my life is in your hands and I am completely at your mercy. The slightest rebuke from you is torture. If I have offended you in this matter, I implore your forgiveness. . . . If I have done wrong, do not judge me in anger, but in a spirit of compassion and pity, for the condition of excitement into which I am thrown by what I cannot help considering as an insult to you. Do not be angry with me. It would break my heart."[30]

For the next two years, the courtship of Violet and Albert followed the "dominant motif" described in Karen Lystra's *Searching the Heart:* "women setting and men passing tests of love."[31] It was common for a woman not only to issue pleas for honesty and candor but also to admit to faults in her character and confess to flirtations with other men. Her lover's appropriate responses to these challenges reassured the woman that she had made a good choice in accepting his proposal. Because women had become increasingly confined to a separate domestic sphere and were ever more dependent on men, they felt compelled to seek confirmation of avowed love by creating a series of crises through which they could assess the degree of commitment of their men. "The warp and woof of Victorian courtship," according to Lystra, "was a series of crises, created by the participants themselves, which led to the altar if successfully resolved."[32]

Violet Blair's testing of Albert Janin is one example of this phenomenon, unusual only in its excess and rigor. For Albert, a willing participant in this process, his love ("the arbiter of my destiny, the best part of my nature") was great enough to overcome any obstacle: "Now judge, oh ruler of my heart, what power you possess over me, and put me to the test if you doubt me, but if you have any pity in your soul, do not deny me the one blessing I pine and crave for—your affection; I dare not say your love as yet."[33] That reluctance to acknowledge the existence of her "love" was prerequisite to any testing, for Violet repeatedly made it clear that she did not love Albert: "Albert I am not in love with you"; "Don't think that means that I am in love with you for I deny it"; "It is the fondness of a friend, not what you wish from a wife"; ". . . the calm sisterly affection I give you"; and "I am fonder of you than any man I know, but I like to be loved by a great many."[34]

Violet made flirtation one of her most severe tests for Albert. Warning him that he might find her "caprices, vanity & flirtations hard to bear," she then proceeded to detail her very active social life, including extensive descriptions of the various men who walked, talked, danced, and flirted with her. She seemed to relish telling him about meeting a new gentleman, the French Count Albert de Very, "a charming man" who became much infatuated with her. In a long passage she described another who had proposed to her and had become angry at her refusal, accusing her of "breaking his heart" to gratify her vanity.[35] And Thuries was not altogether out of her thoughts, as she made clear to Albert: "I wonder if you love me as madly as Thuries. Do you know that terrible & sinful as it is I cannot help feeling an interest in it?"[36] Pushing her test of Albert to the extreme, she limited his options for response, telling him that he should not be upset when other men fell in love with her: "It would not be any fun to win a girl who never had any other lover. You ought to be proud of winning me when so many others have failed."[37]

It was not unusual for men and women to continue to participate separately in social activities after a formal engagement. When couples were apart, men often encouraged their fiancees to attend parties and balls, even in the company of other men.[38] Since Violet and Albert were only secretly promised, her behavior was not beyond acceptable practice, although it stretched that boundary to the limit. Even after her engagement had been made public, Violet continued to receive proposals. On January 20, 1874, James O'Kane still hoped to win Violet, asking her, "Tell me finally, if an engagement, *without any conditions,* it *can* or *cannot* be—*shall* or *shall not* be?"[39]

Knowing Violet's great love of society, Albert met her tests with a degree of panache, writing, "You must not imagine, my love, that I am going to be in your way in the matter of flirting and enjoying yourself. You will see that I shall prove myself a model lover in that respect." Although he admitted that he could not be "indifferent" to hosts of men "pouring flattery into [her] ears," he pointedly reminded her that he had "always had too much respect" for her to stoop to mere flattery.[40] On the other hand, he still chafed at the thought of Dahlgren and Thuries. Without criticizing her directly, and turning his example toward himself, he pointed out, "I do not consider, as you say you do, that it would be perfectly honorable and fair for any girl, knowing me to be engaged, to try and win my love from you."[41]

When Albert questioned whether his love was not enough to end her flirtations, Violet frankly replied, "That is just what I don't know." In a perverse way, she reassured and at the same time challenged him: "When I get into a flirtation it is not because I care for the man any more than if he was a dog, but I must be amused you know & it is only for want of something better & then I have such a thirst for admiration & flattery that I cannot be happy without it."[42]

While acknowledging that he had no right to interfere with her flirtations, he warned her of the risk: "A woman's heart is apt to be touched sooner or later; serious flirting, accompanied by constant companionship, is a dangerous game, and as your heart is still free, it is at least possible that it may yield when you least expect or desire it." Although she thought herself able to control her emotions, Albert honestly told her, "You are mistaken." Denying that he was a particularly jealous person, he thought her intense flirtations challenged the frailties of human nature and cautioned her, "Vivie, believe me, it is not safe to defy nature; the only safety is in caution."[43]

Not content to let these exchanges suffice for the test, Violet let loose another thunderbolt on February 1, 1872: "I have received your insulting letter. . . . You dared to think me guilty of loving a married man. I have never been so insulted in my life. How dare you think it." That Albert could ever suspect her of such "a crime" shocked her beyond words. "Do you expect forgiveness after this? . . . You certainly insulted me by your suspicions."[44] That letter struck panic in Albert: "Oh, Violet, Violet, you say that I have insulted you—I who worship the ground you tread upon, who hold you as pure as an angel, who can only live by your favor. . . . Never, as long as I have known you, have I for one single moment thought of you as other than the very quintessence of purity & holiness. I am almost paralyzed with horror. What shall I do? There is some fearful misunderstanding here."[45]

Minna confirmed Albert's pitiable state, writing to Violet that the grief-stricken man had come to see her: "His eyes were full of tears & several times his voice failed while he was talking." His words and actions convinced Minna of his "perfect & unselfish love" for Violet.[46] Chastising Violet for her "thunderbolts," Minna sympathized with the devastated lover: "I would not like to be in your Albert's place. One day you write something sweet & he is happy, the next day he is miserable for you have written something cross."[47]

Eventually, the crisis passed, and Violet again wrote tenderly to her lover, "Why Bertie I think you might have known that I like you to call me darling & such things even if I am mad with you." Calling him "foolish" to think that she could not control her feelings, she reminded him that she would always do just as she intended and would never hide behind the excuse of lack of control. "You know," she told him, "there is nothing mean or sneaky in me, though I am a cross proud disagreeable girl." Without apologizing, she made amends as best she could: "My poor child I had no idea I would hurt you so dreadfully by what I said. I never think much about other people's feelings when I am angry."[48]

One of Violet's most persistent methods of testing Albert was her insistence that she was unsuited for marriage, that she was too selfish, vain, and independent to be a good wife. "Negative self-images" were, according to Lystra, a common technique that women used to test their potential mates. Women were not fishing for compliments but considered their critical and unflattering self-appraisals exercises in honesty to which their lovers could demonstrate their love by making appropriate responses. Moreover, such honesty was a means of tightening the emotional bond between a man and a woman.[49] Repeatedly, Violet starkly pointed out her own deficiencies and warned Albert against marrying her: "My dear Albert I am such a true friend to you that I advise you to let me off, I hate to see anyone I am so fond of trying to make himself unhappy for life. You have no idea how miserable a life would be spent with such a discontented vain woman as I am. . . . I am the meanest love a man ever had."[50] In another letter, she told him, "There is more danger of your being unhappy by marrying me than anything else, I am so hard to please & so variable in every way & so vain, proud & sensitive. Oh! Bertie, I may make your whole life miserable, a spoiled belle can't make a good wife."[51]

Playing on her vanity, Albert gave responses which Violet found acceptable. "I declare to you, Vivy, that you appear to me to be, without a single exception, the most superior woman I ever knew."[52] He confessed to her, "You are my world, and a more precious one than I ever expected to enjoy before I met you."[53] Knowing that mere flattery could not convince his beloved, Albert cleverly framed his appraisal of her faults: "Will you let me tell you, Vivy, what I consider to be the only defect[s] in your charming and most remarkable character? They are a little want of charity for the infirmities and human errors of others, and a little too much love of flattery." Softening even that gentle criticism, he continued, "But what a small offset these are to your many noble and striking qualities, which fill me with more sincere admiration than any mere words of flattery could express."[54]

During Albert's persistent and regular courting of Violet, Mary Blair had developed an appreciation of, even affection for, Albert and consented to his joining the family in Europe. Arriving in late April 1872, he traveled with the Blair family throughout the summer. In June, Albert wrote his mother that he and the "incomparable Violet" were thoroughly enjoying their visit to Dresden. Strolling through the scenes of his school days, they often stopped "on the Terrace" for lunch, "which consists generally of cheese, black bread & butter and an enormous glass of beer, all of which is not only romantic, but exceedingly healthful." More enchanting was breakfasting together "in a sort of bower in the midst of flowers and singing birds." Whether eating, walking, reading German, chatting with the family, or sitting alone on the balcony after dark with Violet, Albert was smitten. Violet, he told his mother, was more than simply a beautiful and lovely woman: "Her mind is a perfect storehouse of information, and I have never seen a more intelligent appreciation of things than she shows. It is perfectly delightful to go about with her."[55] Many years later, at age seventy-nine, Albert recalled, "The happiest days of my life were those that I passed with you at Wiesbaden."[56] It was a glorious, sweet time for the lovers, and Albert had the satisfaction of Violet's reaffirmation of her promise to marry him. Enclosed by a heart-shaped drawing was a written declaration, dated July 13, 1872, which stated: "On the honor of a Blair I promise to marry you Albert C. Janin, if you continue exactly the same in *every respect* that you are now. Violet Blair." Below her signature, Albert had written, "In character, disposition, and devotion to you?" And Violet had answered, "Yes! V. B."[57] Together they discussed engagement rings, china, and crystal; Violet began to plan her trousseau.[58]

Returning to the United States in mid-October, Violet and her family stayed for several weeks at Silver Spring with her grandparents and her aunt Lizzie Lee, who commented that her niece "had grown even handsomer than ever."[59] It seemed obvious to Lizzie that Violet intended to marry "the little lawyer." Commenting that Albert had "intelligence," she was somewhat ambivalent about his family background: he had "a Europeanized Kentucky mother who however [was] the mother of six well educated self sustaining sons."[60] Before he left Washington in early November, Albert had placed an engagement ring on Violet's finger. When her girlhood friend Kate Ramsay heard of the engagement, she wrote to express her surprise that Violet, who had refused so many "with a shrug of [her] pretty shoulders," had finally been won. Even though she knew Albert Janin only slightly, Kate conveyed the attitude of many people, "The bare fact of his being your choice stamps him at once to all minds as being fully worth[y] in all respects of your sweet self. He certainly has served—almost as faithfully as Jacob."[61]

Albert had won public acknowledgment of their promise, but he could not convince her to set a date for their wedding. She continued to propound all manner of objections to their marriage and suggested that it might not occur for "two or three years."[62] To counter all her arguments, Albert marshaled his lawyer's logic: "My dearest Violet, why will you torment yourself and me by conjuring up all sorts of imaginary dangers for the future? You know how deeply and exclusively I love you; you know how similar our tastes are, how admirably we suit one another in disposition, how agreeable our intercourse during the last four years of our great intimacy has been. . . . You ought by this time to know me well enough to feel assured that I am devoted to you heart and mind, that you are ever uppermost in my thoughts and that I have every motive and reason in the world to labor to make you happy."[63] With lovesick regularity, he repeated his vows of devotion, finding, on occasion, opportunity for gentle teasing: "If I had leisure for literary pursuits, I should like to compose a work entitled: 'Violet's Reasons' or 'The Sophistries of Celibacy,' accompanied by a *pendant* to be called 'Albert's Answers' or 'The Triumph of Logic and Love.'"[64]

For more than another year, Violet continued to delay their marriage. Repeatedly, she warned him that he would not be happy married to her and asked him to release her from her promise.[65] Violet was experiencing what historian Nancy Cott has termed "marriage trauma." Because marriage was her ultimate decision in determining her future life, a woman shrank from making that commitment. Moreover, Cott suggests that many women reacted as Violet did, by "a withdrawal of emotional intensity from the too-burdened marriage choice."[66] It was one thing to handle proposals of marriage, which Violet had done with great skill and aplomb; it was an entirely different matter to set the date for marriage. Many women did as Violet did and staged a "holding action."[67] Although women experienced less anxiety than they had in earlier decades of the century, they continued to show signs of "marriage trauma." As Rothman explains, "Men tended to see engagement as the time before they *could* marry, while women viewed it as the time before they *would* marry."[68]

For Violet, as for many others, marriage meant the loss of control that she had wielded during courtship. The demands of "True Womanhood" and wifely duties meant giving up her autonomy and independence.[69] Violet recognized that as a belle, she had power; marriage, she feared, would end her independence and authority.[70] Becoming a wife, in her view, required her to step down, "down from my pedestal, where I am reigning belle," and it meant that she had "to descend from being the supreme ruler & beloved of several fellows to being nothing but a married woman."[71] For Violet, marriage signified the loss of power and identity: "I am almost bitter sometimes at the thought of all I am giving up." She considered the advantages of remaining single, allowing, "An independent old maid's life has a great charm for me."[72] Known as a popular belle and also as an intellectual, she feared that marriage meant the sacrifice of her "liberty."[73]

Violet proclaimed her solution for marital happiness, and it was simple and direct: "Nothing but *absolute obedience* can satisfy me. I reign now over my lovers & do you think I am willing to marry any man & bend my will to his? No! No! Never! . . . I was born to command not to obey."[74] Albert's rejoinder was constant: "The yoke of matrimony will sit very lightly upon your neck."[75]

Albert was well versed in how to handle a difficult woman. During his school days, his mother had lived with him in Europe, and at a young age, he had developed the skills necessary to placate and advise a woman far from home and husband. When only nineteen years old, he had reassured his mother that the family's finances were secure and that his father's business dealings were sound. Accustomed to advising his mother and perennially optimistic, he had counseled her: "You must therefore not allow yourself to be troubled by useless anxieties, nor conjure up difficulties which do not exist, but be convinced that everything will be for the best, especially now when fortune seems to smile upon us."[76] Having honed his skills through years of mollifying his mother, Albert was well prepared to deal with Violet's fears and objections.

Knowing that Violet took great pride in her scholarly attainments (which included the study of numerous languages, among them, Greek, Italian, Dutch, Latin, German, and Spanish) and that she resented the restrictions placed on women in their pursuits of vocations and education, Albert fed her voracious ego by extolling the extent of her knowledge and capacity for learning. "You incomparable creature," he wrote, "you are remarkable in every field of mental activity into which you enter."[77] More than merely appreciative of her mind, he made it clear that he considered her his equal. His idea was, he asserted, "We are to be partners in life. I propose to act upon the principle of a division of labor, and encourage you in these literary studies for which I have no time, so that the firm of V. B. & A. C. J. may be armed at as many points as possible." Pointing out, "Most men, I believe, would be jealous of so learned and accomplished a wife, for fear of being dwarfed by her superiority," he claimed he was free of that fear and, "I intend to go to you for information as often as necessary, and shall not hesitate to make that fact known."[78]

Violet's sense of independence was remarkable in that Victorian age. Unwilling to acknowledge the traditional wifely role, she told her betrothed, "I don't cling worth a cent."[79] She insisted and he agreed to relinquish his right to control her property.[80] As a woman's rights advocate, she thought it a "cruel wrong" that a wife must take her husband's name, contending that the partner "who has the most distinguished name ought to keep it & send it down."[81] Much earlier she had made clear to him that she did not intend to move to New Orleans. "You can live where you choose & as you choose & I do not wish to prevent it, but I will live where I like." Although Violet was "very fond" of Albert's company, she told him, "[You] would not be obliged to stay in the same city with me all the time. . . . You can always regulate your own movements & I mine."[82] Declaring that New Orleans was the "outer darkness," she thought it unreasonable to consider moving from Washington: "Why should not I stay where I wish—you say that you are happy when you are with me— I don't see why getting married should rob me of Mama's company, of a handsome fashionable home & comforts that I might not have elsewhere."[83]

Albert had no intention of opposing her decision to stay in Washington. His own life experience had accustomed him to frequent and extended separations of husband and wife. During the first years of the Civil War, his father had remained at home while his mother had followed her sons to Europe. Juliet Janin had chosen to remain abroad until 1869, and when she had returned to America, financial uncertainties had forced her to live apart from her husband. It was not until 1873 that the couple finally resided together in Washington, D.C. Thus, Albert's family had provided a model in which the wife, either by choice or necessity, had lived separately for extended periods of time. Albert was willing to live in the home of Mary Blair when he was in Washington, and he continued to reiterate his total submission: "What I have always told you is literally true: it is my earnest desire to conform to your wishes in all things."[84] As they moved closer to the time of marriage, Albert found it increasingly necessary to prostrate himself before his queen, and his ever-so-gentle teasing seemed to hint of at least slight impatience: "I shudder sometimes to think what my fate would be if I would undertake to resist your imperial sway, and so have resolved to disarm you by proclaiming my submission at the outset. You see, I am practical and shrewd in some things. I cannot do without you, while you can do perfectly well without me. . . . But seriously, that is not near so strong a reason for my deferring to you as is my unbounded love and admiration for my darling, for whom I am ready to sacrifice everybody, including myself."[85]

It was well that Albert had written in such a manner, for Violet's testing of his devotion began to reach toward a climax in early April when she wrote him a most extraordinary letter, filled with "thunderbolts." Telling him that she had devoted considerable thought to their marriage, she commanded him, "Pay strict attention & profit by what I say." Brutally frank, she told him, "I marry you simply & entirely because you say you cannot do without me & I care more for your happiness than for any other man's so I have a right to make my terms." Violet's ego and self-assurance were never more clearly demonstrated than in this letter of April 9. She described herself as "unconquered & unconquerable," and without a flicker of humility, she asserted, "I am a beauty—I know that I am young, graceful, intellectual, refined, spotless in reputation, fashionable & attractive, that I have a splendid name & most glorious blood & live in a big house & for a Washington girl am a sort of heiress."

According to Violet, the success of their marriage depended entirely on Albert. Her letter was filled with imperious orders: "Now you ought to know that a woman who has reigned over as many men as I have does not bear contradiction well"; "Be careful not to offend"; "Never pretend that ancestors don't matter"; "Don't say that I am prejudiced because I pride myself on my impartiality—Never try to work on my feelings for I know men too well not to see through that & it provokes me—Never treat even the most trivial remark I may make with disrespect."[86]

Once again, Albert found the appropriate response to "the terms and conditions," remarking, "I suppose there is hardly one man in a hundred who could truthfully say that he would accept such terms in entire good faith and without mental reservations, and yet I know that you will believe me when I say that I do." Once again, appealing to her vanity, he claimed, "I admire beyond measure your independence of spirit and frankness; I am very glad that you point out clearly what you expect our relations to be, and you will find that I am fully as incapable of proving false to my oft-repeated assurances of entire devotion to you, as you are incapable of breaking your promise to marry me."[87]

It was still not enough. In subsequent letters, Violet expressed further doubts and reiterated many of her reasons to put off the wedding. She hated to leave her mother; she was better suited for single life; she was reluctant to give up her independence. Most devastating of all, Albert had not distinguished himself in his profession or accomplished any great thing. On April 21, she reluctantly confessed to him, "Someone said you were only a clerk in your father's office." Although she knew it was untrue, it was devastating to her: "Everyone thinks I am throwing myself away to marry you." Trying to maintain her confidence in him, she added, "I think you may make me happy." Despite that modest attempt at optimism, Violet had been shaken by the opinions of others and gloom dominated her outlook. "There will be no more victories for me," she lamented. "I can never know again the glorious pleasure that I have known." Rather contritely she asked forgiveness for hurting him, but she had to admit, "I feel angry with you sometimes for putting an end to my triumphs & giving me no equivalent—I do wish there were some way for you to distinguish yourself so that people here might hear of it—But I can't see any yet."

If that letter had not been sufficient to crush Albert's spirit, on the very next day, there was yet another fearful blow. Violet wrote that her uncle Montgomery had voiced his objections to their marriage, telling Mary Blair that Albert had "absolutely *nothing*" and forecasting a life of poverty for Violet. In addition, Montgomery believed, "If a man is ever going to distinguish himself in anything he ought to begin before he is thirty." Violet's doubts flooded to the fore, and she admitted to Albert, "I was wrong to accept you when I did—I should have told you to prove that you were worthy to be chosen by me before I said yes." Earlier, she had told him, "I want you to appear absolutely perfect to everyone—I have made my choice from among such lots of men that I want people to see that I showed good judgment." Now, she demanded, "You must work to make a name worthy for me to bear—If you cannot prove before very long that you have talent & can be something you will find no happiness with me for I will be a cold stern discontented worldly woman. . . . don't let me be ashamed of you."[88]

It was more than even Albert's great patience and self-confidence could bear. Stung by her words, he conceded defeat, "In your present frame of mind, you can hardly marry me without a sense of self-humiliation." He released her from her promise: "It becomes my imperative duty towards you to offer you an avenue of escape from it." Because of his great love, he would, he said, feel only "contempt and hatred if I should conduct you to the altar under circumstances calculated to make you and others feel that you were being sacrificed." Repeating his vow that he was "willing to wait almost any length of time," he suggested that they postpone their marriage.[89] Now it was Violet's turn to be tested; it was up to her to decide their future.

In the first week of May, Violet decided to honor her promise to marry Albert. In St. John's Church on May 14, 1874, the Reverend John V. Lewis conducted the marriage ceremony. Submitting to conventional tradition, Violet Blair took her husband's name and became Mrs. Albert C. Janin.[90]

Although there is no documentary evidence to show why Violet finally, at that particular point, decided to set the date for their marriage, there is enough to justify some speculation. For Violet, it was not a question of bending to Albert's will. It was, however, a matter of power. When men had courted Violet, she had always been well aware of the power she had wielded over them.[91] Certainly, she had been reluctant to lose that power, as her letters abundantly illustrate. When Albert finally gave up his quest and suggested postponement of the marriage, Violet may have felt she had finally won the power struggle. At that point, she knew the decision for marriage rested entirely with her, that the power to decide their future was hers, that their marriage would be founded on her terms, not his. Rather than bending to his will, she may have felt that she had gained the ultimate triumph.

There are other possibilities. Violet may have thought that she had gone too far—that she was in danger of losing the only man she had seriously considered accepting. The humiliation of rejection was unacceptable. Moreover, despite her need for independence, she felt the pull of her culture's customs and accepted the centrality of marriage to a woman's life. As historian Nancy Theriot has pointed out, only 8 percent of the women born between 1845 and 1849 remained unmarried, and deciding in favor of spinsterhood "was not a choice easily made or easily lived."[92] Nearly twenty-six, Violet watched her former beaux find other mates and her girlfriends, one by one, relinquish their lives as belles. However much Violet had protested against the confinement inherent in the marital institution, she did want a husband. Marriage lay at the core of the meaning of true womanhood, and Violet wanted it all—but on her own terms. She had been the leading belle; she wanted to be the ideal woman. Probably all these factors played on Violet's mind and heart when she decided to marry Albert.

Chapter 4

A Bride

"You know you have my life happiness &
I may say very reason in your hands—I do
love you so, my darling." ⚜

Violet tried not to cry when her mother left her at the railroad cars, but she could not help it. Although her honeymoon was only to be a few weeks, she had never been separated from Mary, "my own dearest of all upon earth." Despite her unease at leaving her mother, Violet thoroughly enjoyed a week in New York where she and Albert were comfortably situated in a three-room apartment at the Everett House. Albert proved to be the perfect husband. "He thinks," Violet told her mother, "of every little thing likely to amuse or please me." Traveling on to Niagara Falls, they stayed another week at a romantic small hotel where they were the only guests. The German owner gave them "the greatest attention & excellent food," providing the newly-married couple with the appropriate setting to devote themselves exclusively to each other. While her husband was "as good & sweet as a *man* can possibly be," Violet reassured Mary, "He is not you my own precious Mama." It was important to Violet that Mary know she had not lost her daughter; it was equally important that nothing interfere with Violet's devotion to her mother. Although Mary told Violet her husband "must be first with you now," Violet made it clear to her mother that Albert understood their profound attachment to each other: "Don't think Bertie will ever be jealous that I put you before him, he says you have done more for me than he can ever hope to do in a lifetime of devotion & that you have a right to my deepest & best love."[1]

A strong maternal attachment was not unusual for young women in the middle decades of the nineteenth century. In her study of mothers and daughters of that period, Nancy Theriot demonstrates that "the mother-daughter

relationship was the core experience of nineteenth-century feminine accul-
turation and resulted in an intensely close bond.[2] In diary and letters throughout her life, Violet proclaimed her devotion to her mother. Typical is her
assertion in 1885: "She is my all—I don't want to live without her."[3] And Mary
reciprocated the feeling, frequently telling Violet that she had given her
mother "all the comfort she has in her children."[4] Mary indulged all her children, but it was Violet who religiously devoted herself to her mother's welfare: "I stand to defend Mamma against every worry & trouble."[5] Advice
literature, ministers, and the popular press all exhorted mothers and daughters to maintain their closeness, and in *The Anchor of My Life,* historian Linda
Rosenweig presents ample evidence documenting the powerful connection
between mothers and daughters.[6]

After the newlyweds returned to Washington, Albert could only remain
with his bride another two weeks. To prove himself to Violet, he had determined to win nomination to Congress from Louisiana as a conservative
Democrat. Before their marriage, he had promised to distinguish himself, he
had told Violet somewhat bitterly, "in such a way as to silence forever the
disparagement of myself in which my enemies and ill-wishers seem to take
so keen a delight."[7] Equally important, becoming a congressman would
ensure that the couple could live together. The only barrier to election, Albert
confidently claimed, would be not spending enough time in the state.

Violet encouraged his ambition by continuing to prick at his resentment
of others' opinions: "I am so anxious for you to succeed, because I know that
certain people think I have been a fool & thrown myself away on you, so I
am crazy for you to distinguish yourself either in law or politics."[8] Beyond
gratifying her personal pride (which was a heavy load), she also placed upon
Albert the burden of satisfying the demands of her family name: "Bertie you
must not forget that you married a *Blair* & therefore you must push forward."[9] Ever optimistic, Albert insisted that his chances of success were good,
and he toiled diligently in the tumultuous field of Louisiana Reconstruction
politics, telling Violet, "I know best how great a prize you are and how many
sacrifices of pride, independence &c I ought and am willing to make as a
token of my gratitude to you for having married me."[10]

In addition to appeasing his wife's demands, Albert was also responding
to the gender ideal described by historian Anthony Rotundo as the "Manly
Achiever."[11] Driven by ambition to work hard, the "Manly Achiever" meas-
ured his worth by his ability to gain fame and fortune. The ultimate validation of manliness was economic success, but if that goal proved illusive,
enhanced status could serve as an equally important measurement of manli-

ness. Wealth, prestige, and independence were the rewards for an aggressive, hard-working, and energetic man.[12]

Early in his life, Albert had formed definite opinions and attitudes about money. At the tender age of ten, he recognized that his vacation pocket money of a half dollar a week was "a great deal for a little boy like me." Full of good intention, every week he tried to save half his allowance but admitted, "I have not done it yet and I do not suppose I ever will do it."[13] Five years later, he commented, "It is funny that money should have so much to do with one's enjoying himself. If I have money I will enjoy myself, if not, I won't." His immediate solution to lack of funds had been straight forward: "I think I will borrow some from the boys, to repay them some other time."[14]

Raised in a strongly patriarchal family, Albert expected his father to decide his vocation. Although the boy expressed some interest in being a farmer or merchant or banker, he preferred, he wrote, "the one by which you can make money the soonest."[15] That initial emphasis on making money was undoubtedly further influenced by his father's fluctuating fortunes in Union-occupied New Orleans during the Civil War. Unquestionably, Albert felt great pressure to succeed. His own life experience, society's expectations of manliness, and his wife's outspoken requirements—all spurred him to action in his search for validation as a "Manly Achiever."

Except for a brief visit to Washington in late July, Albert remained in New Orleans throughout the first summer of their marriage, and Violet found that she missed him a great deal: "I am surprised to find how much, for such a self contained individual as I am, it is quite wonderful especially in the evening I miss you."[16] She may not have been in love when she married Albert, but she quickly came to love him, admitting, "I almost think I must be getting spoony about you."[17] Years later, she confided to her diary, "I always thought I was ice until June 10th 1874," doubtless a reference to the time of consummation of their marriage.[18] After his visit in Washington in July, there was no doubt that she was at least feeling romantic. Telling her husband, "I always sleep on your side of the bed now," she claimed that she did not know why she did it except, "I like to think of resting my head on your shoulder & having your arm around me."[19] Regretting the celebration of her birthday in August without him, she wrote: "Oh, if you were only here to take me in your arms—I do long for you so—My heart aches to be with you again, my own beloved." Unaccustomed to such feelings, she was somewhat bewildered by them, confessing to him, "My own darling husband I don't know what makes me so spoony this evening, but I am so, & I don't mind telling you so though it may not be in keeping with my severely dignified character."[20]

Not that Violet had altogether let herself turn to mush. There were serious disagreements, and she was still perfectly capable of hurling "thunderbolts." The first of them came shortly after their honeymoon had concluded. In an otherwise congenial discussion between Albert's mother and Violet, the elder Mrs. Janin had let slip her desire that her son's marriage be a traditional, patriarchal arrangement in which the husband ruled. Violet saved her rage for Albert. Such a marriage might be agreeable to many girls, but it did not suit Violet, "a belle . . . accustomed to trample men under her feet." There must be no misunderstanding, proclaimed Violet, "You are my husband & I love you as both husband & friend, but not as a master. Violet Blair never had a master & never will have one." In her usual style, she threatened her new husband, "One single attempt to control me in anything & we part forever." Provoked to white-hot anger, Violet forecast, "If we are divorced in a few years it will be directly or indirectly your Mother's influence over you— Can't you understand that where I wish to reign supreme I will suffer no interference."[21] While Violet usually demanded equality in her marriage, on occasion, as Karen Lystra has pointed out, she "turned the patriarchal assumption upside down," insisting that she be the ruler.[22]

Accustomed by now to these violent outbursts, Albert replied with soothing reasonableness, "Vivie, why do you allow yourself to be troubled by anything that my mother may say?" Pointing out that her own mother held similar views of proper marriage relations, Albert assured her that his judgment was in no way affected by his mother's opinions: "One thing is certain, *no one,* either father, mother, brother, nor friend, can influence me in the least degree in my conduct towards you."[23]

Within weeks came another blast from his bride. Violet may have fallen in love, but she had not lost touch with reality, and Albert's continual optimism and fanciful visions of a successful future wore thin very quickly. Accusing him of "castle building," she told him, "Never again try to make me see things in brighter colors than they really are." Only two months after her marriage, she had some sense of a character trait in her husband that would cloud the happiness of their marriage for years to come: "I begin to fear that I have married a dreamer."[24]

These "thunderbolts" pale by comparison to the one Violet let loose on August 26, 1874. When she received Albert's telegram informing her that he had withdrawn from the congressional race, she was furious: "As soon as I read it I tore it in pieces & trampled it under my feet." Castigating him for withdrawing, she told him, "You have offended me more deeply than I imagine it possible for you to do—It is almost impossible for me to think ever of forgiving you." A few hours later, she added to her letter, admitting that she had been in "a tremendous rage" when she had begun her letter, and on reflection, she thought, "Perhaps you did what was best." Her anger stemmed from her disappointment that he had failed to do something that could impress her friends and family, and she tried to goad him to further exertion: "Now Bertie, I will forgive you on one condition, which is that you appear in cases in the Supreme Court this winter," something she thought his father could easily arrange. Remarkably, Violet concluded this emotion-filled letter which swung from harangue to concern to lecture by telling her husband, "I am excessively fond of you."[25]

Pained and hurt by her letter which was "so hard and cruel," Albert responded with sorrowful resignation: "Well, well, I suppose it is only just that I should have my share of the miseries of life." Stung by her implication that his withdrawal from the race had demonstrated "moral cowardness," he replied simply, "No one else does." Far from feeling demeaned, he thought he had acted "honorably and courageously," and because of his conduct, he had "gained respect and reputation and every prospect of being successful the next time." Albert was all the more wounded by his wife's condemnation because everything he had ever done had been for her: "God knows that all the energy I display, all the work I do is prompted by my one ruling aim in life—to please you."[26]

In his following letter, Albert reiterated his belief in his chances for future political victory. He had been unable to garner sufficient votes, he claimed, only because he was not considered a resident. His success depended, he told Violet, on residing in New Orleans for "several months" in each of the next two years so that he could not be considered simply a carpetbagger. "Your presence," he told her, "would be of immense advantage to me." If she wished him to succeed, he needed her help and presence, and he put the question to her directly: "And now, Vivie, you must make up your mind whether you think it worth while to make some sacrifices for the sake of the future." Knowing the intensity of her desire for his advancement, Albert had already rented a house, anticipating her consent to come to New Orleans. He added, however, that if she did not wish to come, he could rent the house to someone else. He ended his letter with his wonted vows of submission: "My darling, I am going to do just what you desire. If you wish me to abandon New Orleans and politics, I will do so."[27]

Angry with him for presuming to rent the house and still irritated that he had given up his election chances, Violet greeted her husband with a cold reception when he came to Washington in September. Somehow, Albert was able to turn aside her wrath. Perhaps the advice of her dearest friend Minna had made an impression. Telling Violet that Albert was still very young, Minna reminded her, "A politician's wife must get used to disappointments for it seems to me political life is very full of ups & downs."[28] Whatever changed her attitude, after Albert's departure, Violet wrote very tenderly to him, "I miss you so much my Bertie—day & night—. . . I love to sleep with your arm around me—Are we not happy when we are together? Don't you want to come back to me?"[29]

Early in the summer, Violet had said, "I want to do anything to advance your political interests," and in August she had even suggested that she might come to New Orleans but had concluded that letter by admitting that her health would not allow it.[30] By late October her illness became the basis for not leaving Washington. Gynecological problems had plagued Violet for a number of years and had become worse during the summer and fall of her first year of marriage. She had decided to go to New York to see a female homeopathic doctor who had also treated her cousin Minna.

Several of the Blair women—Minna and her mother, Violet and her mother—had turned away from conventional allopathic medical treatment and embraced the less heroic and less extreme methods of homeopathy. Founded in the early nineteenth century by the German physician Samuel Hahnemann, homeopathy was based on the theory of minute dosages. According to Hahnemann, the best way to cure disease was to give small amounts of drugs that in large doses produced the symptoms of the disease being treated. It offered an alternative to the heroic treatments of conventional medicine such as blistering, bleeding, cupping, and purging. In the 1870s homeopathic and allopathic doctors were locked in an unpleasant struggle over proper and appropriate treatment of disease. By the 1880s, advocates of both schools of medicine had modified their procedures; homeopaths had begun to adopt some orthodox procedures and were accepted into orthodox hospitals, and allopaths had begun to forego the use of their most radical methods of treatment.[31] In this period of turmoil in medical practice, many homeopaths became eclectic in their methods and both professional and lay people held them in high esteem. For example, Tullio S. Verdi, William Seward's homeopathic physician, also treated many members of the Blair family and served as president of the Board of Health of the District of Columbia.[32]

In November 1874, Violet had her first appointment with Elizabeth Voorhies, who determined that she suffered from uterine displacement and "a terrible state of inflammation."[33] It was not an unusual diagnosis; homeopaths and allopaths alike attributed many female illnesses to problems related to the reproductive system. According to the medical profession, most female complaints could be traced to that unique part of the anatomy; a woman was, as Jane Stephens has aptly stated, "A body wrapped around her uterus."[34] The exact nature of Violet's ailments is unclear, but she claimed that other doctors would have operated on her. She willingly underwent extremely painful treatments rather than have surgery, because, as she explained to Albert, "an amputation would interfere with certain possibilities that neither you or I want to have interfered with."[35] While Voorhies was certain that she could cure Violet, she recommended abstinence from sexual intercourse until after the first of the year. But, as Violet reported to her husband, the doctor had said that it would be best for Violet's health to have a baby as soon as she was well enough—perhaps in a year.[36]

Albert played the part of dutiful husband with sincerity and obvious concern. Trying to bolster her spirits, he commented that a displaced uterus must not be too serious if it could be cured in only a short time. He encouraged her to "religiously follow" the doctor's directions and assured her that he would gladly wait to resume normal marital relations until Mrs. Voorhies said it was safe. Anxious to be absolved of any complicity in her illness, he asked, "I hope I am not responsible for any of the suffering you have undergone. Did Mrs. V. say anything about that?"[37]

Ever optimistic, Albert assumed that his wife would soon regain her health, and he continued to press her to come with him to New Orleans. "Now Vivie," he wrote, "I wish you would make up your mind to return here with me." Offering what he naively thought was an added inducement, he mentioned that he wished his mother to come also, "So that you would not be alone while I am attending to business."[38]

Once more, Violet let loose a torrent of anger: "I *will not* go to New Orleans in the winter—You know very well that I told you before I married you *that I intended to live in Washington every winter* & I will keep my word." Although she had thought he had planned to stay with her in Washington for the winter, if he chose to go to New Orleans instead, she wrote, "I can not help it, though I would be sorry to have you away." Reminding him that she was willing to go to New Orleans in the spring and fall, Violet absolutely refused to leave Washington during the three-month social season. Repeating a thought she had often expressed, she wrote, "You are your own master—but you are not mine."[39] As to his idea of her living with his mother, Violet saved her most honest opinion of that arrangement for her mother: "Now I would see her hanged first—I would not live in the house with her if she were going to die & leave me ten millions—She is a selfish old thing & wants everyone to wait on her—I did not get married to wait on any one or to be buried alive either." She also made it perfectly clear to her mother that she refused to go to New Orleans during the social season: "I have not the remotest intention of going there."[40]

Albert responded to Violet's "fiery letter" with his normal acquiescence. Disappointed that she refused to come to New Orleans, he accepted her decision: "You say that you will not come here during the winter months. Very well, n'en parlous plus." If she did not wish him to be away during that period, he was willing to sever his connections with his father's legal firm. He refused to enter the quarrel, stating simply, "In order to live constantly with you I am quite ready to give up anything." Because he had pursued the congressional seat only in an effort to please her and since the sacrifices necessary to achieve that goal had not been agreeable to her, he did not find it difficult to give it up. Still driven by the desire to prove himself, Albert contemplated other avenues for success and suggested that he could bring her happiness by "making a fortune."[41]

There matters stood for several months. In the meantime, Louis Janin died, and Albert had to remain in New Orleans to settle his father's affairs. Violet, trying to regain her health, continued to see Mrs. Voorhies in New York. Albert was finally able to come to Washington in February 1875 and spend a month with his bride. It was a most satisfactory reconciliation. Albert thought their days together "were about the happiest of [his] life," and in his judgment, Violet was "so well suited to matrimony, at least with me, that I almost believe that our marriage was predestined by fate."[42] Violet, too, regained her "spoony" feelings, writing to her husband, "I miss you of course as I always do . . . but I think I feel it more now than ever—I am fonder of you now than I was even when you last came back."[43]

As well suited to marriage as Albert thought Violet might be, she was deeply afraid of the consequences of married life. Especially in her delicate state of health, she feared becoming pregnant, and that fear became an underlying theme in much of their correspondence. They may have spent most of their first year of marriage apart, but after each reunion, Violet was most anxious for the arrival of her menstrual period. After their honeymoon, she became "very uneasy & uncomfortable" when her period was a few days late. She told Albert that she dreaded the pain and suffering of childbirth and felt that it might cause her death. At the same time, the thought that she might never be strong enough to have a child, "would crush [her] very heart with sorrow."[44]

After his February 1875 visit in Washington she wrote him that she was "scared to death" that she was pregnant.[45] Albert cheerfully offered his opinion that she ought not to fear having a baby since she was "as well physically fitted for that emergency as any one could well be." Still, he hoped that her suspicions were untrue because she did not wish it.[46] There is no doubt that he took responsibility for whatever manner of birth control they practiced, and he tried to reassure her, "I cannot believe that I relaxed my accustomed caution at any time during my last visit."[47] Probably the couple relied on abstinence and *coitus interruptus* to avoid pregnancy. At least part of the time, Albert used condoms which he had "managed to procure" in November 1874. At that time, he wrote Violet that he had "often wished since the 14th of May that [he] had some of them."[48] Despite the Comstock Law of 1872, the French *baudruche* could be obtained in New Orleans.[49]

During the last months of their first year of marriage, Violet and Albert had to face what became the major point of contention between them for most of their wedded life: his business acumen. As quick to pass judgment as she was, Violet came rather slowly to appreciate her husband's lack of ability in the financial world. In January 1875, she had taken a conventional, even submissive, approach to his business affairs, telling him, "Of course dear, you know more about your own affairs than I do." Acknowledging that he had every right to do what he wished with whatever money he made, she gently suggested that perhaps some of his ideas about making a fortune from speculation in Minnesota lands or investments in ice machines or patent medicines might not be altogether sound. "I am sorry to see you have a little of Col. Sellers in your character." With uncharacteristic humility, Violet tried to influence Albert's decisions: "I am so stupid that I have a decided preference for good bond or morgage [sic] above all manner of speculation." Although she had confidence in his talents, she cautioned him, "Perhaps you may not have the kind required to run the business part of the thing."[50]

How much Violet knew about Albert's business experience before their marriage is unknown; nevertheless, her suspicions that he might not be the ideal businessman were well grounded, considering his prior actions and attitudes. After Albert had returned to the United States in 1863, his father had ordered him to Virginia City, Nevada. There, in the boom-town atmosphere caused by the discovery of the Comstock Lode in 1859, he was to act as his brother Edward's clerk and assistant as well as study law. Within months, Papa had decided that Virginia City was no place for Albert and had sent him on a dangerous and exciting trip to Mexico with another brother, Louis.[51] Albert then took up residence in San Francisco to continue his legal preparation.

His father's reasons for shifting his son from place to place are explained in a long and very serious letter of March 13, 1864. Since Albert's final years in Europe, his father had felt a "good deal of uneasiness" about his son's "habits of self indulgence" which had only increased with his return to America. His father had discovered, he wrote Albert, "You slept late, and spent your evenings in idle conversation." Albert's efforts at legal studies, his father wrote, "amounts to nothing." Worse was that Albert had become "possessed with a marked mania for speculation" in Virginia City. The trip to Mexico had been an attempt "to develop the habit of exertion" in his profligate son. Laying down a strict regimen of work and study under Edward's direction, Louis Janin had hoped to "fit [him] for usefulness." Admonishing his son to develop "habits of steady application and good hours," Papa castigated Albert for his "peculiarly American notions that whatever parents do for their children is to be received by the latter as their birthright, to be received with no more thanks than life." Papa ordered, "You must give up the idea of smoking 20 cent cigars, . . . as for *speculation,* you must give it up altogether until you are independent of me."[52]

The move to San Francisco did not improve Albert's extravagant ways. He had indeed borrowed money in Virginia City (for speculative investments). While he recognized that he had a keen desire to make money—"so that I may not have to hesitate before indulging in the Italian Opera, or a good dinner, or carriage-ride &c"—he denied being self-indulgent.[53] His own testimony, however, makes clear that pleasure and entertainment dominated his life in San Francisco. Acknowledging that his "progress in law ha[d] not been very rapid," Albert summed up his first ten months in the Bay area by stating, "I have led a life of pleasure & profit, combining recreations of society and the various amenities of social life with a conscientious study of the law."[54] His diary for those months finds precious few mentions of legal studies and constant references to billiards, dinners, balls, theater, wine, women, poetry, and novels.[55] Ultimately, Louis Janin's solution had been to bring Albert to Washington where he could personally supervise his son's conduct. Ostensibly, his justification was that his son's "social qualities and knowledge of languages fit him immanently for Washington business."[56] Practically, Albert's work consisted of being an errand boy for his father—"to make myself useful to him when he is here, and to act as his agent when he is absent."[57] Satisfied to play a minor role without much responsibility, Albert devoted himself to Washington society, and it was in that milieu of Washington balls, teas, and receptions that he had met Violet Blair.

Suddenly, after his marriage, Albert Janin faced the manly duties of providing for his wife. It was all very well to be a chic and clever bachelor, but a husband had serious responsibilities, and Violet's demands added to his sense of urgency. As he later told her, "I had the ambition to pay to you a tribute of wealth as a token of my love and admiration for you."[58] And thus, with abundant energy and high hopes, he had set off in numerous directions to claim financial success and public esteem.

Violet was especially enthusiastic about one of his dreams: his interest in the newspaper business. Since her grandfather Blair had been a founder of the Washington *Globe,* she admired newspaper men who stood for right and justice, fighting the good fight for principle and honor. For an entire letter, Violet displayed unwonted diplomacy, ending with the mildest of recommendations: "I do hope you will not be reckless about anything—but you know more about your own affairs than I do—only don't talk like Col. Sellers."[59]

Although she willingly agreed to allow him to invest the money derived from the sale of some gold belonging to her ("do what you please with my money"), she angrily rejected his idea that he buy property near New Orleans. Her objection probably was based as much on his buying the land in partnership with his mother as on any business principles. Whatever her true reasons, she reacted with vehemence, vowing, "*When you buy that place I cease to be your wife*—. . . I am in earnest & will consider such a thing as a defiance— & we Blairs don't back down."[60]

As always, when faced with her refusal, Albert quickly abandoned that project. He did, however, try to justify his apparent lack of success and to convince her that he had the potential to be a good businessman: "I am inclined to believe that I am one of those persons whose powers mature slowly and who do not achieve real distinction in the earlier years of their professional or public life."[61]

A few days' reflection on the matter brought Albert to stronger conclusions, unlike any he had ever before voiced. Beginning his March 30, 1875, letter to Violet as he often did, with assurances that she had complete control over his actions, he told her, "There is not the least necessity for threatening me. No subject ever more readily and unhesitatingly obeyed his sovereign than I do you, and if blind obedience to you should lead me to utter ruin, I would nevertheless yield to it, because I so promised." Having proclaimed his servility, Albert then adopted a different tone, more assertive than he had ever been, claiming that he was more experienced in business than she, that no one uninvolved in Louisiana could judge opportunities there, and that he was in a position to know what investments ought to be made.

Issuing his own subtle threat, Albert told Violet that if she continued to keep him "in leading strings," the results would be disastrous: "My natural strong self-reliance, which is the secret of success in life, and my independence of spirit would soon break down . . . I should soon feel contempt for myself and become utterly worthless." Repeating his determination to obey her in everything and acknowledging her "complete power" over him, he was compelled to warn her "of the consequences of humiliating me in my own esteem. If you cannot respect my judgment, I cannot respect it either, and when a man loses self respect he loses all." Issuing his own challenge to her, Albert wrote, "It is for you, and you alone, to determine, how far you wish to guide and control my business actions." Pledging to "cheerfully submit" to whatever her decision required, he concluded on an ominous note, "Of course, if I cannot guide my bark I cannot promise to reach the port of success and distinction."[62]

Violet responded to this remarkable letter calmly and logically. Displaying no anger, she systematically explained herself. Addressing his major contention, that she exhibited "a want of confidence" in his business abilities, she countered, "I gave the best proof of the contrary by putting that money in your hands to invest, for you know I am very fond of money." Reminding him that he had married a belle, "& above all a BLAIR," she told him that he should not expect unthinking acceptance of his decisions. "Now Bert," she cajoled, "I have never tried to control you or your money except by advising you to be economical." Violet did not want her letter taken as "a concession" to him, yet she did desire to clear up any misunderstandings that they might have had. Her view of their relationship had not changed, and she repeated what she had said before, "I claim no authority over your movements, nor shall you over mine."[63]

Having experienced her violent outbursts in the past, Albert was elated by her reply: "I admire your answer immensely. You take up my complaints seriatim and answer them as logically as a lawyer would." Having expected that she might carry through on her threat to end their marriage, he was delighted with her calm reaction: "The fact is, you are not only a lovely creature and a charming wife, but also a woman of splendid intelligence." He gladly accepted her letter as the basis "of articles of partnership."[64]

The immediate crisis passed, but Albert's self-assertive letter marked a significant change in their relationship. By challenging her absolute authority, Albert had adjusted the balance of power in their marriage, and Violet no longer issued imperious orders or extravagant threats. Indeed, she assumed a more traditional, if not submissive, tone. Taking advantage of his new-found sense of authority in his marriage, Albert quickly suggested that Violet plan to spend two months in the fall (from mid-October to mid-December) in New Orleans with him. He followed that bold proposal with an admonition: "No flirting, if you please, madame, when I am away." Far from his premarital acquiescence to whatever behavior made her happy, he now stated, "I would not mind it much if I were present to regulate it and to say: 'this far, and no further.'" Inspired by his recent success in self-assertion, Albert playfully queried: "Do you admit my right to do that, Mrs. A. C. J.? If not, remember that there are judges who do and who would gladly assist me in enforcing it."[65] His solution to their financial disagreements was to adopt the following rule: "All of your money to be invested according to your plan, and mine to be employed by me as I deem wisest."[66]

Violet accepted this arrangement, and for the rest of 1875, their relationship was a happy one. During those periods when they were apart, she regularly expressed her desire for him to come to her. When she was particularly anxious after an attempted burglary of her home, she wanted to see him very much because, she confessed to him, "You always seem to quiet my nerves sooner than any one else."[67] She allowed that they were able "to talk about things so much better than write them," and she had a great many items to discuss with him.[68] Describing herself in less than flattering terms ("I am in my proper place with an old dress, old shoes & ink on my fingers, & a Greek dictionary in my hand") she wondered how he could be content with her. Although she could admit outright, "I love you," she could not be altogether optimistic, predicting, "I doubt if we always get on as well as now."[69] For his part, Albert, always sensitive to her needs, was able to find the most appropriate words to please her: "I do want to gratify your ambition and love of distinction, and since you are shut out of the race by reason of your sex, I want to do what I can to please you, my darling wife."[70] Arriving in Washington in late June 1875, Albert spent most of the summer at the Moorings with Violet, and in the fall, she fulfilled his wishes by spending two months in New Orleans.

Beginning in the fall of 1875, unlike their first year of marriage when they were separated most of the time, Albert and Violet arranged to spend the greater part of each year together. Succeeding years followed the same pattern: Albert tended to his New Orleans business for most of the first two months of the year, joined Violet in Washington, and at the end of the social season they traveled together to New Orleans where they remained until mid-May. After bringing his wife back to her home, Albert went back to Louisiana, returning to Washington in August where he remained until they departed for New Orleans in October. Each year they managed to be in the nation's capital to spend Christmas with the Blair family.

During her first trip to New Orleans, Violet was understandably lonely for her mother and home. With Albert gone all day and having no friends, she had no one to talk to but the servants. Although a neighbor sent her "an immense bunch of the most exquisite cut roses & jasmine" and she found the weather "delightful," she yearned to return home. Significantly, she did not tell Albert of her unhappiness. Sensitive to her every whim, however, he recognized, as she told her mother, the need to "make everything pleasant & agreeable for me."[71] Albert succeeded by appealing to Violet's love of learning, asking her to translate Spanish documents for him. Delighted by the prospect of helping him and finding useful employment to justify her studious habits, she eagerly took to the task, happily anticipating, "I will be able to brag that I have earned some money, & my studying is not unprofitable."[72] Albert, of course, praised her efforts as "first rate, & better than any he ha[d] had done by men."[73] That first trip to New Orleans was as successful as Albert could have hoped and meant that his wife was willing to return the next spring.

In her subsequent trips to New Orleans with Albert, Violet met many people and found some of them to be real and valued friends: "I could not have found such congenial people in hardly any other city."[74] During her spring visit in 1876, she regained a taste of social victory reminiscent of her Washington belle days. Participating in a Martha Washington public tableaux at the Opera House, she was a striking success. Appearing before two or three thousand people, Violet received innumerable compliments, and she relished them: "I looked better than I ever did in all my life."[75] Generally, Violet enjoyed her visits to New Orleans, accepted her responsibility to help her husband promote his political career, and assumed a more traditional role as wife and helpmate than she (or Albert) had ever thought possible. It was always with a sense of duty that she went to New Orleans, and she was always reluctant to leave her mother and home in Washington. But she did. For two months each spring and fall, from the fall of 1875 through 1877, Violet willingly submitted to her husband's wishes.

After Albert's rebellion against Violet's "leading strings" in the spring of 1875, Violet's demeanor had dramatically changed. As she wrote to him, "It seems as though my whole character & disposition had changed since my marriage— . . . you, my own dear husband are the very light of my life."[76] Perhaps it should not be surprising that a woman of such strong feelings and opinions should throw herself into an utterly thorough remaking of her attitude. One capable of feeling and expressing the hateful, selfish extreme of the emotional scale can also move to the other pole. At least in the case of Violet, a self-centered, vain, cold woman became, for a time at least, a romantic, tender pawn of love. Before their marriage, Albert had warned her of that possibility: "I will bet you that I shall succeed in making you love me more than you would perhaps care to."[77]

Both partners were deeply in love. Albert continued to write lovely paeans to his wife: "The more I know you and the longer I live with you, the greater is my admiration of your rare qualities and the deeper my love for you."[78] Violet responded with equal devotion: "You know you have my life happiness & I may say very reason in your hands—I do love you so, my darling." After his departure in the summer of 1877, she tried to tell him how much she missed him: "You dearest old fellow, you don't know what a blank you leave in my daily life when you go away from me. . . . you are not for a moment out of my thoughts."[79] On occasion, Violet was even more ardent than Albert, hinting at her sexual passion. While describing the social events of the season in Washington, she told Albert that she wished he were with her, not so much to attend the balls, "For I want you still more later."[80]

Albert clung to his hopes of political success, considering himself a viable candidate for the Democratic congressional nomination in 1876. In January of that year he was appointed to the Central Executive Committee of the Democratic party which he considered an indication of "a recognized and high standing in the party."[81] In addition, Albert had become associated with a new newspaper, the *Democrat,* through which he thought he could promote his political interests. Ever optimistic, Albert told his wife proudly that the board of directors "seems to be willing to leave everything to my judgment." Acting as an unofficial editor, he claimed, "Everybody treats me as the real head of the paper."[82] He was, in his own estimation, "gradually pushing . . . forward and winning favor and appreciation."[83] It was not to be. In July 1876, he informed Violet that he had not been nominated for Congress, indeed, that his name had not even been put in nomination. But he was not discouraged, bragging, "I have come out of the affair with great credit for wisdom and good sense."[84]

Throughout the first half of 1876, Violet had been supportive of his political aspirations, yet she had continually reiterated that she would not be disappointed if he did not succeed.[85] Recognizing that his chances for elective office were not very good, she made a gentle suggestion: "Don't you think Bertie dear, that you had better give up politics for the present?" Wishing to avoid an angry confrontation and not wanting him to think that she was issuing orders, she quickly followed her question with, "*Mind you,* I am *not* advising you, I am only asking your opinion."[86] Unlike the past, when she had demanded and exhorted him to triumph, she now did not expect victory and philosophically accepted defeat when it came. Consoling him in his loss as she had never before done, she calmly wrote, "Darling, don't you worry yourself about the nomination—You are very young yet & I can stand the disappointment very well if I have you with me."[87] Her attitude was not due entirely to her new-found infatuation with her husband. Undoubtedly she had changed from the days when she issued imperious orders, but she had also gained a sense a realism, even admitting to him without a hint of rancor, "I have learned by experience not to be as sanguine as you are, dear."[88]

At the same time that Albert was pursuing a political career, he was also striving to make money. With his accustomed enthusiasm, he told Violet that he had been retained to represent a very important client before the Southern Claims Commission. Established by Congress in 1871, the commission heard claims for reimbursement for commissary and quartermaster stores supplied to the Union army by loyal citizens during the Civil War.[89] Sure that his suit would be successful, he anticipated that his fee would amount to $50,000. Always presenting himself in a favorable light, he boasted, "It is a big triumph to have got this claim without begging for it, as so many other lawyers have been doing."[90]

In addition to his law practice, Albert became involved in several speculative ventures, among them building a canal in St. Bernard's parish, south of New Orleans; buying farm land in Minnesota; recovering shell to sell as road material; and buying bonds and dealing in scrip. He was, in short, a small-time operator with great visions of future profits, something of a Colonel Sellers, as Violet had suspected. "I am," he proclaimed to Violet, "determined to make a fortune and certainly shall do it." His only motivation, he asserted, was "the desire to lay at your feet what wealth can purchase and what will be agreeable and acceptable to you."[91]

In his pursuit of wealth, Albert had one major drawback: he lacked capital. Undaunted by that obvious weakness, he began to call upon Violet and her mother for financial assistance, and they were quite willing to help him. In February 1877, Albert borrowed $2,500 from Violet to buy a one-fourth interest in the newspaper, the New Orleans *Democrat.* Painting a rosy picture of its prospects, he told her that he was certain that the paper would soon be named the "Official Journal" of the state legislature, thus "public patronage will pay all of the expenses." The future always looked bright to Albert, and he predicted, "In a year's time we can make it the best paper in the south." More important, as an investment, it would "yield a handsome income." To impress his wife with his importance, Albert confided to her, "Of course I could not get such a large interest for so small a sum except as a matter of favor because of my connection with the paper."[92] Violet agreed to this first request to borrow money without giving it any thought. Her surrogate uncle, James Alden, had died on February 6, 1877, and she was deeply distraught. Distracted and uninterested in anything but her sorrow, she told Albert, "As for the money you write about—you can do as you choose with it & if it is lost it doesn't matter."[93]

In a matter of days, Albert was back again asking for additional assistance, this time for his ice-machine manufacturing business. Telling Violet that they had sold a 5,000-pound machine but that payment for it would not begin until it was operating successfully, Albert asked Mary Blair to endorse a note for $3,000 in order to pay some of their start-up expenses. Explaining that the national financial panic had left him and his business associates short of ready capital, he assured Violet that they would be "perfectly able" to make the payment in another month. Since it would not involve any outlay of money on her mother's part and the note was only for one month, he did not hesitate to call upon her good credit rating.[94] Although Violet reported that her mother had gone to the bank immediately to endorse his note, she pointed out that the economic outlook was not good and voiced her real concern: "I do hope you are not engaged in any speculation."[95] Within a few months, Albert was even more sure of their eventual success, predicting to Violet, "I have no doubt that next winter, after people will have had an opportunity to witness the successful working of the three machines which will be in operation during the summer, we shall receive a good many orders."[96]

Even if Albert's ventures could generously be called reasonable speculations, it was a difficult time in which to make money in Louisiana. Since 1873, Louisiana in general and New Orleans in particular had felt the effects of the national economic depression. In the view of historian Joe Gray Taylor, "probably no city in the nation fared worse than New Orleans."[97] The unsettled national economy, coupled with the onerous economic burdens of Louisiana incident to Reconstruction, boded ill for any business ventures in New Orleans. Nevertheless, the ever optimistic Albert, anticipating an economic upturn in the near future, pressed ahead. In June 1877, Albert again called on the resources of Mary Blair. Having inside information that interest on state bonds was to be paid, he wanted to buy more. It was another one-month endorsement that he asked for, and he assured his wife of the soundness of the investment: "There cannot possibly be any loss in the speculation and there are ten chances to one that I shall make a handsome little sum by it."[98] Once again, the Blair women acquiesced.[99] For the time being, Violet resisted any temptation to tell Albert how to handle his money. Although she detested speculation, she remained silent and supportive, ostensibly happy that his business affairs were apparently doing well.

Of greater importance to her at the time was her desire to become pregnant. In January 1876 Violet had worried that they could not afford to have a baby and that she might not be strong enough to endure a pregnancy, but by summer she had begun to change her mind. Writing in a very guarded manner, she hinted that she was sorry she had not been willing to try to become pregnant during their time together in the spring. In July, she acknowledged her willingness to begin their family: "About that matter you can have your own way as far as I am concerned."[100] For nearly a year, they tried to have a baby without any success. In May 1877, informing Albert that her menstrual period had begun, Violet admitted that she was "right blue about it." Although she faced the prospect of pregnancy with great fear, she wanted to have a child and was "so much disappointed."[101]

It was not until the fall of 1877 that she became pregnant. While in New Orleans, they kept their secret, but friends had begun to suspect, and after Violet had returned to Washington, Albert finally "let the cat out of the bag."[102] Violet did not mind that their New Orleans friends knew of her condition, but she admitted that she would feel "very uncomfortable" if those she saw were aware of her pregnancy.[103] Complying with her doctor's orders, she took regular walks, but she did not enjoy her pregnancy. She was disconcerted by the movement of the baby, who was, she said, "entirely too active for my comfort."[104] Dejected by her changed appearance, she complained, "I am getting horribly awkward & clumsy, & my walk is elephantine—it is disgusting."[105]

In mid-January 1878, Violet had begun to feel movement, and both she and Albert tried to calculate when the baby might be born. She determined that the birth could not occur "before the 2nd of July, or after the 13th."[106] Confused by feeling movement so early, she visited her doctor, Tullio Suzzara Verdi, a respected homeopathic physician who had practiced in Washington since 1857. He allayed her anxiety by assuring her that although quickening generally did not occur until four and a half months, it was not unusual for it to happen a month earlier. Comforted that her pregnancy continued to be normal, she nevertheless was still uncertain as to when she could expect to deliver: "I do not know whether it will be the 2nd, the 7th, or the 13th of July."[107]

Despite confusion over her delivery date, Violet did not experience any major physical problems in the early months of her pregnancy. Walking sometimes more than fifteen blocks a day, she reported that Dr. Verdi "thinks I am doing finely, & says that the movement coming so early may be because I am so finely built which allows so much room; he thinks I need give myself no uneasiness about anything."[108] Albert was at his best in encouraging and praising her, writing, "I am lost in admiration at your feats as a pedestrian." Working on her ego, he flattered her: "I feel quite sure that you are looking splendidly. If my dreams are a true index to the real state of affairs, you must be."[109] Uncomfortable as she was, Violet could still on occasion comment humorously on her situation. Mentioning that the baby's movements had become "violent," she remarked, "If I were a dancer still, I would understand it, but perhaps that one of my particular talents will be inherited."[110]

Unhappy over her physical appearance, Violet gave regular reports of her increasing size. By late April, her shoes and gloves no longer fit, and she had been forced to move her wedding ring to her little finger. Nevertheless, she had to admit, "I never thought I would get along the hundredth part as well as I am doing."[111] Filled with sympathy and love for his wife, Albert wrote tenderly to Violet, "I wish I could keep you free from all kinds of suffering. You are such a sweetly and delicately fashioned darling that you ought to be protected from the rude touch of physical pain."[112] Ecstatically satisfied, he extolled their relationship: "I don't believe there ever was a fitter or happier marriage than ours. How I long for the coming of the time when my occupations will permit me to pass my whole time with you!"[113]

In early May, Violet could still report that she was doing well and receiving many compliments on her health and ability to walk an hour a day. Albert, pleased that his wife was not suffering too much and hoping that she would not have too difficult a delivery, suggested, "I guess we shall have to repeat the business." Delighted with the thought of an expanding family, he boasted, "I shall feel very proud in the future when I shall be able to write in a hotel register: 'Mr. and Mrs. A. C. J. and family.'"[114] Violet responded favorably to his suggestion, laying down only one condition: if this time she did "not suffer too much for human endurance." [115] Both prospective mother and father were overjoyed with the expectation of their future family, and Albert allayed Violet's fears that he would be disappointed if she produced a girl. On the contrary, he contended, "She will probably take after you, and I can ask no thing better than that."[116]

Despite her seeming happiness at having a child and her willingness to undergo another pregnancy in the future, Violet was truly frightened by the prospect of her possible death. That fear formed an underlying motif in many of her letters to Albert. "Death fears," as Judith Leavitt and Whitney Walton have shown, continued to be the fundamental concern of pregnant women throughout the nineteenth century.[117] Violet was no different from thousands of others. She did, naturally, draw a distinction, considering herself a "nervous intellectual woman," who was more likely to suffer during childbirth and die. She repeatedly told Albert of her anxieties: "Oh Bert, I am still very young to die, & I love you so much & there is so much I want to do." Never far from her mind was the tragic death of her cousin Betty Blair Comstock who had died in childbirth in 1872. As the months went by, she continued to worry about her future: "Oh I hope I will not die. I am not prepared or reconciled to it—I love you, Mama & Minna too much to wish to go."[118]

Albert naturally tried to buoy her spirits, assuring her that she was perfectly suited to have children and reminding her that "millions of women" survived the ordeal each year.[119] His greatest concern, he told her, was not "fear of your body failing to stand the ordeal," but rather emotional strength, "the probable state of your mind and the suffering it will cause you." He counseled that her nervousness over death was her biggest obstacle to overcome.[120]

It was not so much that Violet dreaded the unknown of the afterlife, but that she was unwilling to give up what she had in this world. As she confided to Albert, "My greatest reason for wishing to live is because even Heaven has not charms enough to make me willing to leave you."[121] Her dependence on and love for Albert had only increased as the years had passed. Repeatedly, during these months of pregnancy, she reiterated her devotion to him. After he made a two-week visit to Washington, she wrote, "Oh Bertie, I don't believe any woman ever loved as much as I do—I feel dead without you—Were we not happy the little time you were here?"[122] If she were to die, she told him that he must not blame himself. She had been a willing partner in conception and the fault would lie entirely with herself, "my nervousness &c. . . . Oh Bertie how I love you."[123]

Although she confessed her fears to Albert, it was only in her diary that Violet showed the depths of her conviction that she would not survive childbirth. She bemoaned her fate, dreading separation from her mother, her cousin, and her husband. Facing death, she recognized the extent of her love for Albert: "He is so sweet & I do love him so—I never believed that I could care so much for any man."[124] When he left her to return to New Orleans, she thought, "It seems as though the very sunshine were darkened for me."[125] She felt like "a man who is condemned to be executed." Whatever her feelings had been when she married Albert, now while facing the possibility of death, she knew that she truly loved him and hated the thought of ending her earthly pleasure: "Life is so happy with him."[126] She analyzed her ability to educate her child and considered what that child might be like: "Bert is clever & so am I, so we ought to have a clever child."[127]

All went well for Violet until May 12. On that Sunday she and her mother set out for an afternoon walk. Not far from their home, Violet stumbled over a loose brick but kept herself from falling by clinging to Mary's arm. They immediately returned home. When Violet began to experience some slight pain and seepage of fluid from the amniotic sac, they called Dr. Verdi, and he ordered her to bed. Writing to Albert the next day, she told him only that she thought she had a cold and that the doctor had said, "A day or two of rest will bring it all right."[128] Hoping that all would come right, they told Lizzie Lee and their other relatives that Violet had a cold and was to keep very quiet.[129] That evening Violet went into labor, and for over twenty-five hours she suffered great pain. The doctor finally had to use instruments to assist the delivery, and just before eight o'clock on Tuesday evening, May 14, a daughter was born. Violet named her Mary after her mother. Premature by two months, little Mary was very weak, prompting the new grandmother to baptize her namesake herself. Violet, however, did not realize the danger and spent the night imagining future bliss: "I lay awake all night listening for her little cries & thinking how happy Bertie & I would be with her, & what I could teach her & how many pretty things I had that I could give her—Oh I was so happy!" By the next morning, the baby was very weak and little could be done. Keeping her warm by the fire in Mary Blair's room, they fed her milk and brandy. It was not to be. Before noon on May 15, 1878, after living less than sixteen hours, the frail baby, Mary, died.[130]

Violet was desolate, and she later poured out her emotions in her diary: "It almost broke my heart for I loved her as much as if she had lived for years. I think I could have borne it better if she had lived a month or even a week— but to go so quickly before I could kiss her enough, before her father could see her, Oh it is so hard." Unable to leave her bed, she could not attend the funeral services for her child, who was placed in the Montgomery Blair family vault at Rock Creek Cemetery. Although they had telegraphed Albert immediately after the birth, he could not get to Washington before his baby was buried. Without husband or child, Violet shed passionate tears, unable to accept her terrible loss meekly: "My heart rebelled & I felt bitterly almost crying out blasphemously that our dear Lord was hard & cruel to take my baby." Although she had had the joy of holding her child, the time had been too brief. All she had in remembrance was a lock of her hair, the nightgown she had worn, the cup used to feed her; there was no photograph, and Violet was "haunted" by fear that she might forget what her baby had looked like. Devastated by her loss, she cried out, "There seemed no consolation for me, & I know that this sorrow will never leave me." Her religious beliefs offered little consolation: "she would be alone even in Heaven without me."[131] Albert's arrival helped her, but she was filled with an ineffable sorrow: "I cannot get over my sadness—I cannot forget what might have been."[132]

Violet Blair.

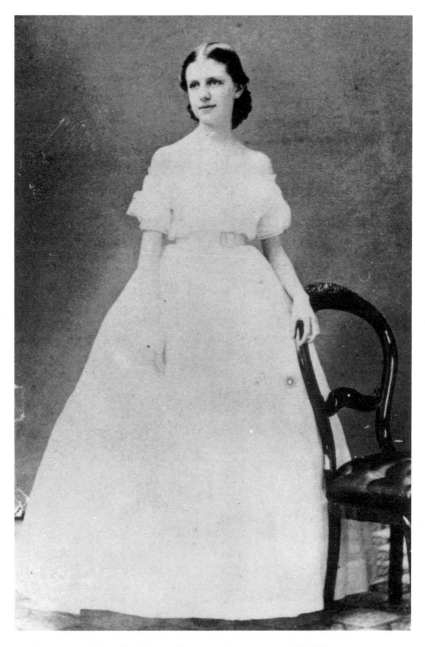

The young belle, in Bethlehem, Pennsylvania, during the Civil War.

Violet Blair, Bethlehem, Pennsylvania, during the Civil War.

Violet Blair, 1865, Washington, D.C.

Violet Blair, 1865, Washington, D.C.

The belle at Nice, 1867–1868.

Violet's mother, Mary Jesup Blair, in Nice, 1867–1868.

Grandparents Francis Preston and Eliza Gist Blair.

Aunt Elizabeth Blair Lee and her son Francis Preston Blair Lee, 1861.
COURTESY OF BLAIR LEE FAMILY.

Uncle S. Phillips Lee, 1863.

Uncle Montgomery Blair.

Aunt Mary Elizabeth (Minna) Blair.

Grandfather Thomas Sidney Jesup.

Jackson Place, west side of Lafayette Square, Washington, D.C. The Blair home is to the left of the light-colored house in the center of the block.

The Moorings, the Blair summer home near Silver Spring, Maryland.

St. John's Episcopal Church, on Lafayette Square, Washington, D.C.

Eliphalet Nott Potter.

Paul Dahlgren.

George DeLong.
COURTESY OF THE U.S. NAVAL HISTORICAL CENTER.

James O'Kane.

William Emory.

Albert Covington Janin.

Albert Janin.

National Board of Management of National Society of Children of the American Revolution. Violet is second from right, front row. The photo appeared in the June 1914 issue of the *DAR Magazine*.

Violet at the entrance to the Memorial Wing of the National Cathedral Library.
Photo appeared in *Cathedral Age,* Michaelmas, 1931.

Chapter 5

Marital Crisis

"My life is not what I had a right to expect." ⚜

Remaining in Washington with Violet for the month following the death of their child, Albert did his best to comfort his wife. As always, simply his presence brightened her spirits, and after he returned to New Orleans she was able to think positively about the possibility of having another child. She was, nevertheless, devastated by her loss and constantly had to fight against her sadness. Her feelings for her "Bertie" were increased, as she told him, "You have now a double title to my love." And that added love made it harder to be apart from him: "The longing for you seems to intensify my longing for her."[1]

Their mutual grief spurred Albert to greater efforts to win fame or fortune. Once again, he became involved in Louisiana politics, striving to win the Democratic congressional nomination. Although he promised not "to delude myself with the notion that I shall have plain sailing," his optimistic nature could not resist offering an enthusiastic portrayal of his prospects. Advising her that his political strength was "constantly growing," he thought she should prepare to become a congressman's wife. Not wishing to be seen as unrealistic, he added, "I am not going to halloo until I am out of the woods, but I want to keep you informed about the progress of the contest."[2] Violet had learned to be more cautious than he in anticipating favorable outcomes; because the powerful Lottery faction opposed him, she knew he faced a difficult battle.[3] Violet tried to relieve some of the pressure Albert felt by assuring him that she would not be disappointed in him if he were defeated: "I know your talents & good qualities."[4] Once again, Albert's dreams had overreached reality. There is no evidence that he was ever considered a major player in the contest for the congressional nomination.

After his inevitable defeat, Albert left New Orleans, dividing his time for the rest of the year between Washington and New York. Stymied in his political aspirations, he turned again to attempting to make a fortune. Whether speculating or investing mainly in Louisiana bonds, Albert spent a great deal of time on Wall Street, leaving Violet lonesome and wondering if she were no longer "indispensable" to his happiness. His absence made her more aware of how much she loved him and needed him. "Strange to say," she confided to her diary, "I care more for one of Bert's caresses now than I would to have all my social triumphs back again."[5]

As the first half of 1879 passed and Albert continued to be apart from her more than he was with her, she began to think his love for her had diminished while hers for him had increased. Trying to explain her feelings to him, she wrote, "Before we were married & for the first two years after it, you cared much more for me than I did for you but now it is exactly the reverse."[6] Surprised by her revelation, Albert vowed that his love was "much more tender and deep-rooted than ever." Thinking their feelings for each other typical of most married couples, he wished her to be "comfortable and happy in every respect." Complimenting her in his usual easy fashion, he told her, "If any one deserves to enjoy all of the blessings of life, you certainly do, for, wherever you go, you diffuse about you an atmosphere of pleasure and happiness. In short, you are a darling and a blessing to all who are connected with you."[7]

Other matters contributed to Violet's unhappiness. It was in February 1879 that she and Albert's mother had their most dramatic confrontation. When Mrs. Janin raved at Violet for stealing her son and for what she considered an improper attitude toward bearing children, Violet was mightily insulted and spilled her indignation in her diary, haughtily deciding that she, as a Blair, was "socially, morally & mentally" the superior of almost everyone and that her "equanimity" could not be shaken by the dreadful outburst of her mother-in-law.[8] While Albert came to his wife's defense, the incident stayed with Violet; although she loved her husband and knew he loved her, she began to doubt once again her fitness for marriage.[9]

In June, Albert's financial setbacks began to weigh on Violet's equanimity. Albert had first become involved in the development of a canal in St. Bernard Parish in 1877. Year after year he persisted in that venture but consistently failed to find profit.[10] When he went to New Orleans in 1879 to look after his canal business, his New York associates managed to amass a substantial loss in Albert's investments, "selling when the bonds were low and buying when the price advanced."[11] Now seriously in debt, Albert looked to his canal investment, his "big thing," which he thought by good management could extricate him from his difficulties.[12] Eventually incorporated as the St. Louis, New Orleans and Ocean Canal and Transportation Company, the canal, something over seven and a half miles long, was intended to run from the Mississippi River to Lake Borgne in St. Bernard's Parish.[13] Although two years earlier he had had a chance to sell it for a $5,000 profit, he had claimed then that it was "a pretty good speculation" but that he "didn't buy to sell."[14] He should have; the canal continued to be a major drain on his capital for many years. In later years he admitted that he had "sunk over $100,000" into the canal.[15]

It was all rather a mystery to Violet, who could not understand—"how it is that a man who has seen so much of men as he has & is as intelligent as he is can be so fooled by people." Through the years she had suggested that he should not be so trusting of people, but he had never taken her advice. Provoked by his dealings, she thought she could "manage business matters much better than he," although she did not complain to him.[16]

The year 1880 saw further financial disaster for Albert. He had been cheated by another associate out of his portion of the proceeds from the sale of land scrip; he lost more on his Louisiana bonds; and his partners in the newspaper, the *Democrat,* had sold the paper and cheated him of his share.[17] Always hopeful, Albert determined to make money from his canal by cutting and selling timber to planters in the area. He also had prospects of selling the canal to Florida investors and at the same time began to investigate the possibility of building a lock in the canal. All these schemes and dreams worried Violet whose appraisal was much more realistic: "I guess it will be like everything else he takes a hand in—he will spend more money than he will make—'Col. Sellers' is a true character."[18]

Concerned over his financial affairs, she was even more frightened by her own losses. She knew she would never see again the money (about $7,000) that she had already lent to Albert; and his additional requests to borrow from her came at a time when her income was reduced. Her father's estate, if prudently managed, had been sufficient to support the family, but it was not large enough to sustain significant speculations, especially in a year when their income had dropped. Her California receipts were much less than in previous years, and taxes were higher. She had used what money she had to pay interest on Albert's loans and other of his business expenses; she had not been able to help her mother with their household expenses.[19] Mary Blair had explained her reduced circumstances to Elizabeth Blair. Property values in California had dropped precipitously while taxes had increased.[20] All around, Mary and Violet had to watch every expenditure.

Anxious about Albert's growing indebtedness, Violet was relatively gentle in her admonishments: "Oh Bert, my heart sank when I came to what you said about the cost of digging the mouth of the canal deeper." Pointing out to him that she never objected to having to be economical and that she willingly practiced self-denial to reduce their liabilities, she begged him, "Don't get deeper in debt." Reminding him that he had lost money in all his speculations, she counseled, "Be prudent when you have not the money to undertake anything." Without a trace of bitterness, Violet tried to curtail his Colonel Sellers attitude: "Don't think that I mean one word of reproach by this letter—I only want to warn you against getting deeper into debt—My poor dear old Bert I would not say anything to hurt you for the world but there is only one sure way of making a fortune & that is by working hard & saving."[21]

Albert was appreciative that she wrote so "kindly and sympathetically" about his financial situation, and he optimistically forecast, "I don't think my pecuniary embarrassments will last very long." Trying to prove that the future would be different, he analyzed what had happened to him: "I have had a pretty hard experience, but it has taught me lessons that I shall never forget and that are likely to be of immense advantage to me. One can hardly pay too dearly for such experience, provided it is acquired while one is still young. The main mistake in my life has been in trusting everybody."[22]

While Violet agreed that Albert had been in error to trust others, she did not think it his "main mistake"; continuing to increase his indebtedness was his major fault. She pleaded with him, "Bert, oh Bert, for Heaven's sake, don't think of getting yourself involved in any more wild schemes."[23] When on April 11, 1880, he requested her to sign another note for $2,000, she confided her apprehensions to her diary: "He is so sweet natured that I hate ever to hurt his feelings by telling him he knows nothing about business—but yet he will ruin himself, & me too, if I do not say something." Frightened by the prospect of increasing the amount of her liability, she worried that she could not cover it if it had to be paid off.[24]

Certain that further investment in the canal was a wise decision, Albert wanted his enthusiasm to rub off on Violet: "I wish I could within the limits of a letter explain to you all that is going on at the Canal. My object has been to develop its resources so as to make money out of it in the event of its not being purchased by the Florida people."[25] If he did sell, the additional improvements could only increase its value and his profits. When Violet replied to Albert's request, she pointedly wrote, "I don't think you can lay the blame of your want of success in all business matters entirely on those who cheated you." Reiterating that she did not wish to hurt his feelings, she charged that part of the reason he was in his present precarious position was his "obstinate disregard of the advice of those who knew better than [he] did."[26]

And others did try to advise him. After having advanced Albert $10,000, his own family refused to give him any more money, urging him to abandon his hopeless project. Juliet Janin wrote her son that his brother Louis had stated, "I think he had better give it up," and Henry had said, "[I] would sooner pay your debts than advance money for speculations—as the canal must be considered." Reminding him that his father had lost his money because of overconfidence, she pointed out that Albert shared some of his father's traits: "a determination not to give up" and "indomitable energy." With motherly affection, she told her tenacious son, "Now my dear Albert you have no better friend in the world than myself." Then she spoke plainly, "I am persuaded that you are making desperate efforts where there can only result failure."[27]

All their importunings were to no avail. Albert industriously, energetically, and with single-mindedness pursued his dream; yet success eluded him. Only six months after his mother's appeal, Albert railed at his brother Louis for refusing to give him more money: "Why will you persist in telling me that I must give up and begin afresh. Why should a man's spirit be broken and pride and honor crushed, when there is really no reason for it?" If only he could be relieved of his pressing liabilities, he foresaw "the road to fortune and distinction open."[28]

Albert framed his justifications for his speculations in terms which echoed the ideals of the "Manly Achiever." Insisting on independence from any interference and stressing his industriousness, he could only imagine a future filled with financial and personal success. Convinced that the canal would make him "a small fortune," Albert tried to persuade Violet, "The opening of this Canal will divert the trade of the Mississippi Sound (lumber, oysters, charcoal, cotton, bricks &c) from the Old & New Basins of New Orleans to the Canal. That trade will give a splendid revenue in Canal tolls." As if to affirm his judgment, he told her that his brother Louis, a successful mining engineer, had agreed to invest in it.[29] Brimming with optimism, Albert claimed, "Now, I tell you that I have here not only a chance, but a certainty of extricating myself from all of my difficulties and coming out far ahead, and I must prove it."[30] What he envisioned, Albert told Violet, was grand: "If I am let alone, I shall make a quarter of a million out of my canal."[31]

In June 1880, Albert's straitened financial situation became even more precarious, and he wrote to his mother-in-law asking to borrow securities worth over $13,000 for six to twelve months. Explaining away his past reverses, he prophesied, "Within a year I shall be worth over $100,000 if I am not hampered in my operations or my energies paralyzed by the humiliation of not being able to make a settlement with those who have a right to demand it." To prove the worth of his canal, Albert offered the evidence of participation by Antoine Carriere, a prominent New Orleans banker and insurance company executive. Carriere had, according to Albert, agreed to become president of the company and had also advanced him money, accepting stock in the canal company as payment. Unfortunately, Albert explained, Carriere was in Europe; the final organization of the company could not occur until his return in the fall.[32]

At the same time that he outlined that bright prospect of the future to Mary, Albert wrote his wife in more desperate terms. Contrite for the "trouble and worry" he had caused her, he claimed, "I hate myself and feel like committing suicide." As much as he regretted it, he had no alternative but to call upon her mother for help. Despondent, Albert was reduced to suggesting that perhaps Violet should have married someone else. Still, his optimism could not be totally eradicated, and he clung to his faith in his canal: "I am certain to make a fortune out of it, if I can hold on to it. Don't hurt me by suggesting that it is all in my imagination."[33]

But Violet did hurt him with a reply that he found "very severe" and that "cut deep."[34] Telling him that she had wept bitterly after reading his letter, she coldly gave her judgment: "Of course I do not expect you to make anything out of that canal, & I think if you have used good money to buy out the other men you ought to be ashamed of it." Angry because she felt that Albert would only lose more of her mother's money, she ordered him, "You must never ask Mama to endorse any more notes for you."[35] By the next day, her anger had subsided somewhat, and she wrote again, telling Albert that he had her mother's approval to use her securities. Her mother's only condition was that the money be used to pay his clients who had suffered losses because of his mismanagement. Violet's condition was absolute: "*Not one penny of it* for that wretched canal." If he did so, she vowed, "I will *never* forgive you." While she repeated her order that he never borrow from Mary again, she tried to cajole him: "Now Bert, try to look at things reasonably & don't let your mind run on millions to the exclusion of hundreds."[36]

Although he had received so many thunderbolts in the past from his wife, Albert still suffered from the sting of her words, admitting, "Sometimes I am almost afraid to open a letter from you as soon as I receive it, for fear of being hurt; so I wait a while to prepare myself for a possible shock." Having portrayed himself as a pitiable, wounded man, he then proceeded to justify his worth, telling Violet that plenty of people in New Orleans who knew of his circumstances still trusted him, implying that she should too. He concluded, "I have but one aim in life now and that is to get out of my difficulties so that those whom I love may no longer be troubled on my account."[37] Albert's failures were a heavy burden for him to bear. Not only did failure cast a shadow on his manly worth, it also directly affected the lives of those who should be able to depend on him. His failure meant failure for the entire family; it meant not only financial hardship but loss of status as well. For one caught by such adverse circumstances, "there was," as historian John Demos has pointed out, "a bitter legacy of self-reproach—not to mention the implicit or explicit reproaches of other family members."[38]

The exposure of Albert's financial disasters was only a prelude to the couple's greatest crisis, which was precipitated by Albert's brother and sometime partner Edward. On June 18, 1880, Edward had told Violet that Albert was "entirely ruined," that his indebtedness exceeded $200,000, that he had speculated away everything belonging to his mother, that he had lost money given him by his brothers (Edward and Henry), and that he had used his clients' monies for his own purposes. Claiming that Albert was "a liar and a cheat," Edward advised her never to endorse another note for her husband. Shocked by these revelations, Violet barely managed to return home from Edward's office. "It seemed," she wrote in her diary, "as though my life was over, . . . that all the happiness of life has really gone from me forever." Over the next few days, Edward continued to weave his stories of Albert's dishonesty and unreliability, and Violet was in no position to "indignantly deny" any of Edward's charges.[39] After she and Albert had come to their 1875 agreement that he would decide how to invest his money while she would look after her own, she had very little knowledge of his business dealings. Resenting any questions (which he considered interference in his affairs), he had stopped confiding in his wife, telling her only what he wished to.

Unable to refute Edward's vicious charges, Violet wrote a desperate letter to Albert asking, "Why have you deceived me, Albert? Why did you not tell me honestly what you had done?" Unable to believe that he was capable of cheating clients and family members, she told him, "I will not condemn you without hearing what you have to say in your defense—I believe that you meant to do right & in some instances are far more sinned against than sinning." Torn by her loyalty to him and her inability to refute Edward's charges, she demanded answers. She was unable to believe that he could have acted as Edward said, yet she knew his propensity to neglect details. On more than one occasion, he had left her and her mother to pay his interest on loans. Such nagging thoughts impelled her to demand, "*Now You must* make a full clear statement of all your indebtedness & let alone your wild speculations." As his wife, she told him, she had every right to know his true situation: "*If* you have fallen, you must confess it to me, & I am willing to believe that you hoped to benefit me—I do not wish to hear any more by accident." She tried to encourage him to make a full disclosure by telling him, "I am disposed to judge you leniently, if you deal frankly with me—But do not conceal anything from me."[40]

Albert's first explanation came to Mary Blair. Ignorant of Edward's exact charges, he nevertheless labeled them "the product of his own imagination." Refuting the allegation that he continued to speculate, Albert claimed that he had long since given up any speculation and informed his mother-in-law, "I am engaged now in as legitimate a business enterprise as ever existed and one that would speedily extricate me from my embarrassments if I were not harassed to death by pressing claims." Justifying his position, he told her, "I have tried my best to shield others from blame and have taken upon myself the reproach that belonged to others." His losses, he asserted, were the result of "being robbed in some instances and by my property, which was in the custody of others, being seized by banks &c for the liabilities of the latter." Allaying her fears about her money, he told Mary that her liability was limited to one loan held by Riggs' Bank in Washington. As to her suggestion that his brothers should assist him, Albert said that Henry's advice had been to "let my creditors manage as best they may." For Albert, that suggestion was not a viable choice. To abandon his debtors would be dishonorable and disgraceful; he continued to struggle to pay them all.[41]

To his wife, Albert had to make a more difficult and astounding confession. Edward's charges against him, he said, "compel me to say what I hoped I would never have to say." Not wishing to hurt others, he had kept secret the reality that Edward was an alcoholic: "There are two entirely distinct personalities in Edward. When he is himself he is an earnest and hardworking man. When he is under the influence of liquor he is the most reckless person I ever knew and does and says things that he forgets all about afterwards." For years, according to Albert, he had been looking after and covering up for Edward: "I have literally dragged him out of the gutter. I have hunted him up in gambling halls. I have cramped and pinched myself to pay gambling debts." He had been his brother's keeper. Although his mother had some knowledge of Edward's problem, no one else did, not even Edward. "Edward sober knows nothing about Edward drunk and would not believe one tenth of what I might say of his doings."[42]

Although it is impossible to determine if his accusations against Edward were altogether true, Albert had never before told outright lies about anything. Moreover, four years later, Juliet Janin worried about "Edward's illness."[43] Although she insisted at that time that he was capable of working if he had any business, she admitted that "his dwelling upon certain topics which are supposed to be hallucinations" had prevented him from attaining any legal clients.[44] Whatever the exact nature of Edward's problems, it is reasonable to conclude that he was not a reliable judge of Albert's situation.

In subsequent letters to Violet, Albert tried to explain the intricacies of his financial dealings. Pages of complicated transactions, promises, actions, and inactions came down to his summary: "The simple truth is that through blind confidence in agents and improper carelessness, based upon a sort of fatalistic faith that everything would be done by friends and agents that ought to be done, I got into pecuniary difficulties, out of which I am trying to extricate myself with every prospect of doing so successfully." Disheartened that she might believe any of Edward's stories, he concluded, "If anybody who knows me thinks me capable of committing any dishonest act, then my character is not worth defending."[45]

Trying hard to make sense of all the conflicting accounts, Violet cried out, "Oh Bertie, if I could only see you & hear from your own lips what to believe— . . . I cannot & will not believe that you have done anything wicked—Oh Bertie, tell me they are not true—My Bertie, I am so miserable."[46] Each day that went by and she did not see her husband only increased her misery. At the end of July she wrote, "So many things look badly that can be so easily explained, if one asks the right person about them—I do wish you would come back—I am sure you could explain everything."[47] Understanding and supportive as she was in her letters to Albert, she was suspicious and angry in her diary. There, she admitted that she found Albert's attempt at justification through Edward's alcoholism "very unsatisfactory." His subsequent attempts to explain his situation did not allay her worst fears, and she concluded, "I cannot help feeling that he is not the man I thought him when I married. . . . An enemy reading his letters & comparing things would say that he was either a knave or a fool. He considers himself a martyr to his generosity & confidence in others—I know that he has been cheated on every side, & I think he has been foolish & excessively weak."[48]

Despite her attempts to offer supportive words, Violet continued to question him about specific financial matters. Albert recognized that her faith in him had been deeply shaken. Explanation followed explanation, but he knew that their relationship had changed, perhaps permanently. Her occasional comments, reminiscent of passages in their premarital correspondence, suggested that she had returned to her old consideration: that she had made a mistake in marrying him. Depressed at the thought that she could think him capable of dishonesty, distressed by his financial straits, and forlorn at the possibility of losing Violet's affection, he wrote, "My love for you is not and never has been a passing fancy. It is deep rooted and will abide with me, however unworthy you may think me of your love and even though we should never meet again."[49]

Indeed, Violet was unhappy. While telling him that she and her mother had faith in him and did not believe him capable of cheating, she revealed her ambivalence in her diary. Although he may not have broken any law, she felt, "He has not acted according to the strictest rules of honor as I consider it." Most importantly, "He was not open & square with me." Because of her reduced income, his financial difficulties weighed even more heavily on Violet. Not wishing to burden her mother, she had some resentment that Albert had not been able to contribute to her support for more than a year. Since she had been teaching neighborhood children in the country for years, she considered the possibility of teaching for pay, but she quickly rejected that idea: "I cannot do anything of the sort without causing a talk & injuring Albert which I do not want to do." Social convention was more important than whatever help she could give in paying bills. That, too, discomforted her: "It would not do me any more harm to teach for money than to teach for charity."[50] It was a difficult constraint on one so independent.

Although they continued to write to each other, the frequency of their letters fell off. Albert, ill for much of the fall, could excuse himself by the press of business. Generally, Violet wrote in answer to his letters, encouraged him to come to Washington, and fretted that she did not know he had been sick. Polite but somewhat distant letters passed between them, with only occasional references to their great crisis. Neither was happy. Violet epitomized their feelings when she wrote: "Everything is depressing—I look in vain for something to feel happy about—even the horses are sick."[51] Determined to make his canal pay, Albert ventured to explain the difficulty of making money without adequate capital. Stating that it required an expenditure of "$600 for cutting, hauling and transporting" three hundred cords of wood, he attempted to show how hard he was working to get out of debt so that he could provide for her comfort. In the past, he admitted, "Instead of making, I have lost; but I am not made of the stuff that yields. I do not give up."[52]

Rather than take heart in his determination, Violet saw only the mention of expenditure of more funds, which she felt meant only that "expenses cover all possible profit."[53] On her birthday, August 14, she summed up her feelings of the past year: It was "the end of the saddest year of my life."[54] Doubting that he still cared for her as he had in the past, she knew that their crisis had affected her attitude toward him: "I doubt if it is possible for us ever to feel towards each other as we once did, for though if we ever see each again we may have a satistory [sic] explanation of a great many things, still I can never feel that he had acted well towards me, & I cannot feel any respect for his opinions again knowing him to be weak & obstinate."[55]

For the remainder of 1880, Albert did not return to Washington. Violet had anticipated such a turn of events as early as August when she noted in her diary, "I do not know whether he will care to come back to me again."[56] She suspected that their disagreements had made him not want to be with her, and she hinted as much in her letters: "I have thought sometimes that you did not want to come."[57]

Albert could cite all manner of business reasons for not coming to Washington, but his motivation was never that he did not wish see her. In fact, he wanted her to come to New Orleans, a suggestion that infuriated her. Bluntly Violet told Albert, "You cannot support me," and she refused to live on the charity of their friends. In utter exasperation, she wrote, "How in the world could you keep me in New Orleans?"[58] When Christmas came, Violet was all alone in Washington, without even her mother. Mary had gone to New York to help nurse her other son-in-law, George Wheeler. Although her aunts (Minna Blair, Lizzie Lee, and Lucy Sitgreaves) continually invited Violet to dine in their homes, and her cousins (Gist and Woodbury Blair and Blair Lee) regularly called on her, showing their solicitous concern, she missed her mother desperately.[59] For Violet, a wretched year ended on a woeful note: "I feel so utterly blue & miserable all alone this Christmas day."[60]

As the beginning of the new year of 1881 came and went, Violet remained uncertain what her and Albert's future relationship could ever be. Disconsolate at the direction her marriage had taken, she told Albert that she felt he had made "a very great mistake" in marrying her, a "sick helpless & perhaps morbidly sensitive" woman. Too delicate to risk having any more children and useless except as a scholar, she thought he could have been happier with a different sort of woman. Because he did not write as regularly as in the past, she thought that he no longer loved her. "If this is true," she wrote, "tell me so honestly & I will not be in the least angry, & will not expect any show of an affection you may have ceased to feel—All that I want is the plain truth."[61]

Albert's less frequent letters did not reassure her. Filled primarily with his quotidian activities, he did not often deal with their personal relationship. When he did, it was not altogether satisfying to Violet. Although in early January 1881 he had referred to "the perfect faith that two people who really love and respect each other can feel at times with regard to one another," the context of that remark came when he dilated upon his lack of jealousy of other men's love for her. Responding to Violet's mention of a visit she had had from one of her old suitors, Eliphalet Potter, Albert contrasted his views with those of "this conventional world." He allowed, "Some husbands would be astounded at the coolness with which I discuss the visits to you of a married man, who was once your lover and still loves you deeply."[62] Albert's attitude is reminiscent of that found by Ellen Rothman among courting couples who thought their relationship was exceptional and better than that of others: "*we are not like most people.*"[63] Whereas Rothman's examples illustrated the uniqueness and the superiority of the special love between two people, Albert's expression at this particular time was more an indication that he felt their relationship was simply different from others and not subject to conventional standards. Whether he intended to convey that attitude may be debated, but the fact was that Violet was not comforted by his letters and wanted to see him in person. "It will be a year," she reminded him, "since we parted—I wonder if you have found it long."[64]

When Albert finally did return to his wife in March 1881—after an absence of nearly fourteen months—he was able to assuage the worst of her fears. Despite whatever worries and concerns she had, Albert always had the ability to brighten her outlook and make her happy. This occasion was no different. After a long talk, she reported to her diary that they "came to an understanding." He convinced her that Edward's charges had been lies and that he had avoided telling her about the loss of her mother's money because he had thought he could quickly make up the loss and had not wanted to give Violet undue worry.

Greatly relieved to know certainly that he had not been dishonorable in any way, she nevertheless recognized that he had not been a good businessman: "I am convinced that Bert has done nothing wicked but he has been very very foolish."[65] Foolishness she could deal with; dishonesty and cheating were unbearable. After he left in May, her letters exhibited much of her old affection. Happy that they had cleared up their misunderstandings, she returned to using her old salutation, "Sposo Mio," when writing to him and told him, "I missed you so much last evening & this morning, & in the night." Wishing he could be with her all the time, she knew that she would never tire of his company.[66]

Although relieved of a terrible burden, Violet was not entirely free from worry. Her own and her mother's financial situations were not good. Still struggling to make ends meet on their reduced income from investments, they were attempting to sell some of their unimproved property in St. Louis and California so that they might increase their monthly income. Taxes, insurance, repairs, servants, and horses took all they had.[67] She even considered ways in which she could earn money: "I wish I could write well enough to write for the papers or magazines."[68] Another possibility that she considered was selling translations that she had made. By that means she had made a little in the past. When she had been in New Orleans with Albert in 1875, he had paid her for translating documents, and in recent years, she had made some small amounts doing similar work for her brother-in-law George Wheeler. Frustrated by the lack of opportunities for women to earn money, she told her diary, "I want so much to do something for my support."[69]

For the next few years, Violet and Albert returned to their more accustomed routine, with Albert making periodic visits to Washington every few months, although he stayed with his wife for ever shorter periods of time. Because of her pinched circumstances, Violet continued to fret over Albert's financial situation. Worried about the money she had lent to Albert and more worried about her mother's loans to him, she continued to press him for an accounting: "Are you really paying off your debts? I wish you w[oul]d tell me what I have asked so often, a rough calculation of the amount of your debts & a list of your principal creditors."[70] Her greatest desire was that he pay off the $2,000 note on which Mary had signed. It had always been an especial irritant to her. For years, Albert had borrowed money from Mary to make his interest payments on the loan she had guaranteed, and he always had waited until the last moment to take care of that note. For two women who felt that any indebtedness was nearly sinful, his lax handling of that note had caused them untold worry. Knowing that he might never be able to pay back the large amounts that he had borrowed from Mary, Violet harped on this small loan, bringing it up time and again, as she did on June 3: "I want you to pay off that note with the very first money you make, it has given me so much worry & unhappiness."[71] Irritated by her constant pricks at that sore, Albert tried to explain that extending the note through payment of interest was not a dishonorable or bad business practice; it was what bankers expected, and they did not think less of their clients who regularly renewed notes. "It cuts me to the quick," he told Violet, "to have you constantly referring to this matter as one that gives you great unhappiness."[72]

Violet was convinced that Albert's most realistic opportunity for making any money was through his legal representation of clients with claims before the French and American Claims Commission. Created by a joint French-American convention in 1880, the commission was empowered to hear appeals against either government arising out of the French war with Mexico, the Franco-Prussian War, or the American Civil War. The cases dealt with confiscation of property, mainly cotton, when Union forces occupied New Orleans and the surrounding territory. Albert's most important case submitted to the commission involved the attempt to reclaim a payment of $405,483.08 made by the Confederate government to Alfred and Jules LeMore for the purchase of gray military cloth. Between the time of delivery of goods and receipt of payment, Union forces took New Orleans and refused to allow the LeMores to collect their money. This case and others entrusted to Albert were complicated and consumed a great deal of Albert's time both in New Orleans and Washington.[73]

Violet pinned what little hope she had for Albert ever to be able to support her on the outcome of these cases. Desperately interested in his progress, she harped at him to concentrate his attentions on them, with periodic reminders such as "You had better stick to your cases" and "I hope you are not neglecting your French Cases."[74] At the same time, she wanted to encourage him and offered her help: "I will try to cultivate my friends in the French commission." She also reported to him on the favorable comments she had heard, "It was said at the commission that your cases were the best prepared that had been presented."[75]

Albert responded with pledges to succeed: "I don't want to lose a single one of my cases. It is a matter of pride with me to succeed before the commission better than any one else and I think I shall do it. At least I hope so, for your sake and mine."[76] Succeed he did, but not on the scale he had anticipated. The final settlement for the LeMore brothers amounted only to $14,000.[77]

Another possible source of income from his law practice was Albert's suit against A. C. Gilmore, a Washington land agent and attorney. When some of his New Orleans clients had sent him land scrip to be sold in Washington, Albert had turned the scrip over to Gilmore who sold it and then refused to turn the proceeds over to Albert or his clients.[78] Although he won the suit for $24,000, he was unable to collect because Gilmore had no money.[79]

Albert clung to the hope that his canal could extricate him from debt. By directing "considerable energy" into the canal business, he wrote with certainty, "I shall be able to contribute regularly to the expenses of our household." He excused his current lack of success with the canal on his inability to oversee it on a regular basis because of his absences while attending to his French claims cases: "Everybody notices the difference when I am there."[80] While physically improving the canal, he also devoted considerable time to finding other investors or even buyers. Always optimistic, he looked favorably upon the various opportunities presented by Florida investors, an English lord, his New York contacts, and the Mississippi, Terre aux Beoufs and Lake Railroad Company.[81] When Violet objected to his continuing to invest more money in the canal, he tried to explain how it would eventually pay off and why he expected it to be successful, predicting, "You will discover your mistake one of these days." Persisting in building fine castles in the air, he boasted to Violet, "I knew what I was about when I first took hold of this place and others are now beginning to understand that while they were asleep I was awake."[82] Inspired by visions of success, Albert told his wife that his canal could become "an important channel for commerce, particularly for the bringing to the Mississippi river of the coal of Alabama and the lumber of the Gulf coast."[83] With obvious bitterness, he insisted his canal was "destined, in spite of your doubts and sneers, to furnish you the means with which to gratify any and all reasonable tastes."[84] He confidently predicted that by the end of 1884, she would no longer have to worry about money matters.[85]

While Albert sang his fanciful song of success, Violet provided a contrapuntal rhythm of caution, pessimism, and unhappiness. She was no longer taken in by his quixotic visions. "I wish I could control him in business matters for I have a great deal more common sense & prudence & knowledge of the world than he, though he is remarkably clever in many respects, he is really one of the most brilliant men I know—but he is reckless & visionary & I am too practical to feel sympathy or respect for that—if I had managed his affairs since we were married he would not have them now in such a muddle."[86]

When his excuses and explanations did not satisfy his wife, Albert occasionally struck back at her. Tired of her wounding remarks, he complained, "It is exactly as if you should meet me on the ocean in a foundering boat and should stop, in your efforts to rescue me, to reproach me with having been imprudent, foolhardy &c. You are always harboring suspicions against me." Angered by her carping, he suggested another "understanding," "You will cease your reproaches and tearing open old sores."[87] Recognizing that she must "seem rather unkind to him," Violet nevertheless thought she had every right to continue to remind him of his obligations: "He is so careless about money matters that I feel obliged to be a little sharp with him sometimes."[88]

Throughout the 1880s, Albert struggled to get himself out of debt and provide fame and fortune for Violet. In 1882, he once again had "Congress on the brain," and ran as an independent candidate. Violet ridiculed his effort, thinking it was a foolish waste of time: "I am afraid he will act the part of the dog crossing the stream with the meat in his mouth—neglect his law cases for the shadow of a nomination."[89] When he received the nomination of the Greenback-Labor party, she had to admit that she "was never more astonished."[90] Amazement followed astonishment when he also received the endorsement of the Republican party.[91] Even though he did not believe in "any greenback nonsense," he thought his chances of winning were good, although he promised his wife that he was, he said, "not counting my chickens before they are hatched."[92]

This time, Violet hoped for his success more for his own sake than hers: "It would be such a triumph—then he would be no longer 'the young man Violet Blair married,' but a man of some note & I would be only his wife."[93] She saw no particular benefit to herself in his victory: "My position as a wife is so different from most women's." She genuinely wanted this victory for him, for, she confessed to her diary, "I love him more than I care to say sometimes."[94] It was not to be.

Once again, Albert failed to obtain his goal, and once again he had what he thought was a perfectly legitimate rationale: "I have reason to believe that I was elected and counted out, and I propose to have an investigation of the matter." Rationalizing that he had been cheated in the election, he envisioned himself as another Sam Tilden who would gain "national reputation" from the scandal.[95] Nothing came of it.

While Violet accepted Albert's defeat gracefully, she continued to worry about his financial situation, especially after he convinced her to endorse another note. Unable to deny him but knowing that the money would most likely be lost, she felt frustrated and fearful. Their crisis caused by Edward's accusations still haunted her, and she recognized that their relationship would never be quite the same: "I don't know that I could ever feel just as I did before the troubles came, but I could try to forget what does not come up to my standard."[96]

Albert persevered in developing his canal and working on his French claims. To prove his industriousness, he described in detail a myriad of activities designed to improve the canal: providing a rail connection for it, meeting with possible investors or buyers, and drawing up documents for incorporation. At the same time, he labored at his legal practice and gave the impression of vigorous and manly effort to succeed. Naturally, he was certain that such hard work would produce good results, boasting to Violet, "I think I am quite safe in saying that one year from to-day you will no longer have occasion to worry yourself about the cost of repairing house-property."[97]

Despite her love for Albert, Violet was profoundly disappointed in her marriage. "My life," she wrote, "is not what I had a right to expect." As "the great belle" of Washington who had had her pick of so many men, she had made a foolish choice. She thought that she had found, she said, "a man in sympathy with me on most subjects, full of energy, unselfish, scrupulous in all matters of importance, & who placed me & my happiness above all things." Although he was "affectionate" and "demonstrative" and she still loved him, she was not satisfied and could no longer deceive herself: "No woman ever had a more devoted lover than Janin was or seemed to me—but I now believe that if he had plenty of cigarettes, coffee, newspapers, rich food & a comfortable sofa or chair, he would never miss me."[98] Regardless of her realistic appraisal, she was still quite fond of him. "He has such a gay happy nature & always feels so hopeful that nothing depresses him—I am afraid he will never learn hard, practical worldly wisdom—perhaps he would not be so sweet & attractive if he did."[99]

Chapter 6

Separate Lives

". . . society is my Lethe to forget what might have been." ❧

To distract herself from constant financial worry and discontent with her marriage, Violet devoted ever more time to society during the 1880s. She joined the St. John's Woman's Auxiliary of the Board of Missions, the Society for the Prevention of Cruelty to Animals, and the National Woman's Suffrage Association.[1] Trying to supplement her own income, she submitted her translation of an Italian novel for publication, but it was rejected.[2] She was successful, however, in earning a modest amount of money from the federal government by translating documents for her brother-in-law George Wheeler.[3] These diversions, coupled with added attention to teas, luncheons, dinners, chaperoning young friends to dances, and other social functions, filled Violet's days and nights. Unhappy in her marriage, she found pleasure elsewhere and regained her sense of humor and fun. At a dinner in the home of David Yulee, former Florida senator, she had stated her support for woman's rights. "I think I could hardly have shocked them more had I proclaimed myself an atheist or a cannibal," she wrote in her diary. Her hostess, Nannie Yulee, did what she thought any good hostess should do for such a radical guest; she asked Violet if she wished to smoke a cigarette. Violet immediately sensed the absurdity of the question and had the perfect rejoinder: "I said no & asked if she smoked."[4]

As much as she might shock her friends by her radical support of woman's rights, Violet was conservative in her views of social rank and her belief in the superiority of the Washington resident elites. At the reception after the marriage of Simon Cameron's daughter, Virginia, she was pleased but not overwhelmed that the illustrious General William T. Sherman escorted her into the dinner. More important to her was her ability to look refined. She was "never so glad to be thin," than on that evening when the excessive heat of the crowded rooms was a trial for the fat women; reddened faces, drooping hair, and oily complexions gave them a vulgar and coarse look. Always aware that she was part of the most exclusive, oldest class in Washington, she disdained the pretensions of Henry Adams whose claim to society rested on "the fact of having dead presidents in the family." She haughtily rejected any Adams's claims to equal social standing with her: "Of course it may be nicer to have had your great grandfather & grandfather presidents than to be one yourself, still as those who went before the greatgrandfather were very plain people, we of older blood do not think him [Henry] such a great aristocrat."[5]

Her snobbishness affected her opinions of the younger women in society. Maud Davidge, the daughter of the distinguished lawyer Walter Davidge, became one of her favorites, and Violet enjoyed chaperoning her to various functions and attending her parties. Part of Maud's attraction was her bold style: "She is full of life & spirits & loves dancing & beaux & says so honestly." But Violet also cared that Maud was descended from the Father of the Country: "Her mother is a Washington & I do like people of really good blood."[6]

On April 10, 1883, at a tea at the Yulee's, Violet was introduced for the first time to the counselor of the legation for Austria-Hungary, Count William Lippe-Weissenfeld. In his mid-forties, Lippe was physically attractive to Violet: "He is about 6 ft., broad shoulders, blond, blue eyes, light hair, mustache & whiskers, not fat but well filled out as is proper for a man of his age."[7] Their tête-à-tête, involving only a conversation on philology (which happened to be a particular interest for both of them), was pleasant and entirely innocent. When Count Lippe called on Violet a week later to continue their discussion, she found him rather fascinating: "He is one of the few people I meet who teaches me." During the rest of the month, Lippe and Violet saw each other occasionally at afternoon teas, and she commented, "He is so cultivated that he is delightful."[8] Lippe very quickly became a frequent visitor to her home, and on the last Sunday evening of the month, he stayed until 12:30 in the morning, reading poetry in German and talking about various languages. Again, it was a "delightful evening," and it allowed Violet, at least temporarily, to forget about her troubles and worries with Albert.

From that innocuous beginning a deep and lasting relationship developed between Lippe and Violet. The Austrian called regularly on the proper (and married) Washington aristocrat, often staying into the early morning hours. Conveniently for the budding affair, Albert was in town only periodically and usually only for a few days at a time. Between attempting to raise money for his canal and taking testimony for his cases before the French and American Claims Commission, Albert had little time to spare for socializing in Washington.

It was not uncommon or even improper, according to Henry Loomis Nelson, for a man to call on a married woman. Describing the habits of the period "when Washington was in the comfortable habit of relapsing into a village," he commented that "there was a delightful freedom about life" for the man and woman "of sympathetic nature & abundant leisure." In that bygone era, "a man might then profitably waste a whole afternoon on a bench in Lafayette Square, listening to the music of the birds and of a feminine voice, and lazily discussing love or art, or other people, or any subject that is dear to a woman's inmost thoughts." Nelson maintained that in that innocent day, "it was not improper then to sit on the stoop through the warm evenings, and to continue there the flirtations of the season that was passed, innocuous from their very frankness."[9] With her home facing on that very Lafayette Square, Violet had for years wiled away afternoons and evenings in flirtations, but this time was different. Rather than sitting on the stoop, Lippe came in. While her mother ostensibly chaperoned from another room, it is likely that Mary dozed off when the hour became late. Moreover, Violet did not discuss her late evening visitor with her friends and was very careful not to be overattentive to him at more public gatherings.

Violet ended the year of 1883 in a more contented state than she had been for some time. Whether the diversion provided by Lippe was more important to Violet than Albert's modest successes in winning a few cases before the claims commission is uncertain. Whatever the reason, Violet could admit that she began a new year "in much better spirits" than the last and that she and Albert had been "very happy together."[10]

Although Lippe usually did not call when Albert was in town, the two men did meet, probably in January 1884, and occasionally thereafter. Naturally, in her letters to Albert, Violet mentioned her new friend and their common interest in languages. In the past, Albert had always been quite understanding of Violet's flirtations, feeling somewhat sorry for the poor fellows who were so obviously smitten by his wife. This friendship, however, was different, and Albert recognized the danger. The tone of his letters changed significantly, taking on a sharpness that he had never before displayed. In April 1884, he wrote, "I give you fair warning that my suspicions are aroused." And in May, he cynically wondered why he had not received a letter from her: "I suppose you are pursuing the even tenor of your ways, laying in a heavy store of philological learning and information for use during the summer vacation. I wonder if you are so ardent in your studies that you disapprove of the custom of summer vacations and would willingly continue your studies during the hot weather provided you had the same erudite instructor."[11]

Violet did nothing to allay Albert's suspicions, telling him that Lippe, "supposed to be a lady killer," had suggested that afternoon "buggy driving" could be "of great benefit to me philologically." Coyly, she asked her husband's opinion, "Do you think my health & the development of my mind requires the fresh air of Soldiers' Home on pleasant spring afternoons?" Violet was undoubtedly testing her husband's devotion when she added, "I am afraid he could be induced to be flirtatious with very little effort."[12] Albert immediately shot back, "I cannot say that I am at all convinced by your plausible reasoning in justifying buggy riding on the part of married women with single men. Dans le doute, abstiens toi."[13] When Violet suggested that her friend might be upset with her, Albert sarcastically responded, "What a pity it would be if 'Bill' should be angry or displeased with you. What a loss it might prove to the philological world if such results as might be produced by the joint studies and labors of two such devotees of the science should be doomed to failure by an estrangement between you."[14]

From the beginning of their relationship, Violet had always written very honestly to Albert about all other men in her life. Accustomed by habit to describing her flirtations, she continued the practice, but with regard to Lippe, she was not quite as open as she had been in the past. Her diary reveals a deeper fascination with this man than with any other. While she told Albert that "mon ami" did not come to see her "very often," her diary shows that he called quite regularly. While she told Albert that Lippe had stayed until one o'clock in the morning, her diary records occasions when he stayed until after two.[15]

Meeting an intriguing, cultivated, and educated man at a time when she had begun to doubt whether Albert still cared for her placed Violet in a rather vulnerable circumstance, a new situation for her. She was uncertain if she still had any power over her husband or if he had been happy during their married life. After Albert had spent two nights on the railroad cars in order to be with her two days, she thought, "He must be fond of me."[16] Still, she felt the need to test him, and her new companion provided the means. As the months progressed, she told Albert about the increasing frequency of Lippe's visits:

that he had come to the Moorings three times in a week (no casual drop in, considering that she was six difficult miles from the city); that he had spent a weekend with the family in the country; that they had spent the late evening on the lawn, she in the hammock and he in the rocker. Despite the romantic setting, Violet assured her husband, "Conversation was lively, but for the most part very literary, & on the purest platonic basis throughout." Only a few days later, she modified her judgment, stating, "I don't think him as entirely philological & platonic as I did—He is however a perfect gentleman."[17]

Albert understood that this relationship was different from Violet's previous flirtations and gave sharp warning to his wife: "I wish you to understand that I consider your philological 'masher' to be quite as human as other people and that he will bear watching."[18] As to the cozy evenings on the lawn, he sardonically remarked, "You seem to take things easily, you and your teacher. He is more indulgent as a teacher than you are, since you do not place your pupils in hammocks."[19] Albert's unwonted cynical tone made it clear that he did not approve of Violet's activities, and he said so bluntly, "What you need, I think, is rather a moral than a physical tonic."[20] Having briefly been in Lippe's company during one of his short stays in Washington, Albert was certain of the danger: "I know perfectly well how he feels towards you. I could read his feelings in his manner, tone of voice &c." Yet Albert felt unable to do anything about it. The terms of their marriage did not permit him to give orders to his wife, and he could do no more than warn her of the hazards and express his displeasure. "I have nothing to say about the matter, so long as you are amused and entertained," he told his wife, adding insolently, "for you can certainly take care of yourself."[21]

But in this flirtation, it was not certain that Violet could take care of herself. This time, she could not read her suitor; she was not sure of his feelings or intentions. Perhaps she was simply not sure of her feelings or intentions and thus refused to recognize his. Throughout the summer, Violet was in something of a dither over Lippe. When she invited him to spend the weekend at the Moorings, she admitted her nervousness. In their plainly furnished country home, she needlessly worried that he would not be comfortable: "I am in rather a state about it."[22] Unable to decide how he felt about her, she suspected that he was "ever so slightly smitten," but she used her supposed fading beauty to deny the possibility. She had lost, in her opinion, "the intoxicating charm of youth," and she tried to convince herself that "men do not lose their heads because a woman studies Greek, Hebrew, Sanskrit &c & political economy."[23] In earlier days, she admitted, "I enjoyed flirting & counting scalps," but now that she was "older & a married woman," she found pleasure in learning from men. And Lippe was a perfect companion: "He has read so much & lived in so many places & known so many people you read about & has seen so many interesting things & appreciates everything whether of noble sentiment or just amusing."[24]

Not everyone was so taken with Lippe-Weissenfeld. Henry Adams's wife, Marion, had entertained him and offered a subdued evaluation: "He is not an *esprit fort,* but well-mannered and full of small talk."[25] Her opinion of Lippe, however, must be weighed against her generally low opinion of the foreign diplomats whom she described as "little secretaries with handles and spouts to their names." With their ancient lineages, they reminded her, she told her father, "of T. G. Appleton's cook when he showed her his three-thousand-year-old pottery. 'Lor, Sir! What improvements we have made since that day.'" While she thought Lippe more intelligent than most of the diplomats, she still described him as "the simple-minded Austrian."[26]

For Violet and Lippe, afternoon walks to Violet's Spring and to the grottos of her grandfather's gardens gave way to evenings on the Moorings lawn, with Violet resting in the hammock and Lippe close by. On one occasion, she drove him in the carriage to the railway stop. Her aunt Lizzie Lee did not approve of her niece driving with another man on a lovely moonlit night. Violet discounted her aunt's concerns, contending, "The name of *Blair* is as safe in my hands as in hers." The thought that anyone might think her "fast" was abhorrent to Violet; it was "so underbred," and to her there was no question that she was "certainly a thoroughbred."[27]

However much she called on her breeding, her cold nature, her fading beauty, and her love of learning to discount the intensity of her infatuation with Lippe, she could not entirely control her desire to know his true feelings: "Does he care for me, or does he want to make a conquest?" Violet admitted, "Either would be very wrong & possibly it is wrong for me to think of such a thing," but she found excuse for herself in her circumstances: "I have had so much sorrow & worry & so little real pleasure for so long & I have so much anxiety all the time & have had such a load of worry & disappointment to carry for at least 4 years. . . . What have I to look forward to—what hope of happiness."[28]

After a two-week hiatus to Bar Harbor, Lippe returned to Washington and resumed his visits to Violet. Still unable to admit that their relationship was anything more than platonic, Violet expressed her uncertainty in her diary, beginning with "I cannot quite make him out." Although he was "sentimental" she thought he was "not exactly flirtatious." Although he was "respectful always, almost reverent," she could not decide how much he felt for her. Yet she wondered if "his feeling amount[ed] to a sin." Knowing that she should stop seeing him if that was the case, she refused to name Lippe's amorous inclinations. Rather than admit the nature of their relationship, she once again fell back on her usual excuses: She was no longer a "radiant belle"; he was a foreigner, accustomed to flirtation, and "too much a man of the world to be disturbed by any grande passion."[29]

On August 23, 1884, Lippe came to the Moorings and stayed with the Blair family for the weekend. During that visit, he told Violet his feelings, and she wrote in her diary, "He can do nothing but think of me & long to be with me & yet when he is where I am I set him nearly crazy." Even those words could not convince her, and she pretended, "I don't think he is really in love with me," and persisted in claiming, "I do not understand it."[30]

Because of the illness of his father, Lippe returned to Europe in October 1884, leaving Violet with time to consider their friendship. Still reluctant to face the seriousness of her involvement with another man, Violet persisted in claiming ignorance: "It is a curious thing that I cannot judge of his feelings." At the same time, she questioned, "Does he care enough for me to make it a sin for him." Mentioning a bit of poetry he had written to her on his departure, she admitted that it "might sound rather startling in prose," but she excused its "exaggerate[d] feelings & compliments" with a reference to literary license, which made it "different." Yet she had enough realism to admit, "Some people might think it dreadful, if they knew the things he says." As a proper lady, Violet resisted any admission that Lippe might love her. Love between a married woman and a single man was sinful, and any respectable woman, especially a good churchwoman like Violet, would never see the man again. Unwilling to face the possibility of ending their relationship, Violet could only admit that her dalliance with Lippe had been "a delightful break in the monotony of [her] life," and she sought refuge in her accustomed arrogance: "I am vain enough to be pleased with having held him so long, whatever his feeling may have been."[31]

On only two occasions did Violet come close to acknowledging the reality of their affair. In mid-October, she confessed in her diary, "I have enjoyed very much my philological affair this summer, but I do *not* approve of the part I have played in it."[32] At the end of the year, she allowed that her conscience bothered her: "I could not feel sure that I was truly penitent." For Violet, "sins of thought," rather than of deed, were "not so easily overcome & repented of."[33]

Throughout this intriguing interlude, Violet continued to express her concern for Albert. In her letters to him, she encouraged him to come to

Washington, telling him, "I get quite upset at the idea of your being away so much longer."[34] Her affectionate greetings to him on his birthday were followed in the next month by another plea that she was anxious to see him but was willing to wait longer: "I would rather have six weeks of your company later than three sooner."[35] Regardless of the distress that Albert's schemes and dreams had caused her, and despite her lack of faith that he could ever be a successful businessman, she still appreciated him: "He has magnificent ideas, but they do not work out practically."[36] Never one to mince words, Violet told her husband, "It has turned out very badly, this marriage of ours." Yet she also honestly conceded, "I believe if all my ex-lovers stood in a line to be chosen from I would be silly enough to choose you again."[37]

And what of Albert? He continued to assert his love for Violet, as he told her in April: "I speak seriously when I say that I think you are the most beautiful woman I know, in addition to being the most attractive in other than physical respects, and that I have been singularly fortunate in securing you for a wife."[38] His less frequent letters, his more extended absences, coupled with fewer paeans of devotion, were indications to Violet that he cared less for her. Albert, however, did still love his wife, even if their relationship had changed since their marriage. In November 1884, he urged her to come to New Orleans, hinting at the possibility of continued intimacy: "You may think that I no longer feel towards you as a lover, but it is quite possible that you may be mistaken. We will see about that."[39]

At the end of 1884, Violet considered her relationship with Albert, wishing they "could be happy again." Still "very fond" of her husband, she thought of her love for him as "the tenderness of a Mother towards a weak willful child." Because he had "done so many foolish things," she could not "have much respect for his opinions." It was not simply his failures, she contended, but the fact that he had "concealed everything from me." Since the time she had discovered the true nature of his business affairs, Albert had confided even less in her, which only compounded her distress with him. The result was that since 1880, there had developed "a sort of wall" between them.[40]

That "wall" had convinced Violet that she had "very little hope of domestic happiness," and she vowed to "get what I can out of life."[41] The usual rounds of visiting, teas, and parties occupied a great deal of her time. While Albert had cases before the French and American Claims Commission, she dutifully sought gossip and influence by entertaining the French and American secretaries to the commission, Jules Boeufvre and Washington Peddrick, respectively.[42]

In addition to social events, Violet found time to attend and take great interest in the Woman's Suffrage National Convention at which Susan B. Anthony presided.[43] She also immersed herself, almost religiously, in her linguistic studies, devoting nearly every morning to reading and translating various languages. Her schedule was quite demanding, as she recorded in October 1889: "I try to read or study nine languages every day, & the others twice a week each." In addition to English, she studied German, Greek, Latin, Russian, Icelandic, Swedish, Anglo-Saxon, Spanish, French, Volapuk, Hebrew, Flemish, Italian, Walachian, Chinook, and Danish.[44] Weekly, she gave German lessons to her cousin Sallie Lee and Italian lessons to Mary Henry, daughter of Smithsonian secretary Joseph Henry. Miss Henry became one of her favorite friends, and her lessons became "a joy" to Violet. She loved teaching such an apt pupil, but there was an added attraction: Mary taught her much that she did not know, particularly about electricity and scientific subjects.[45]

An added intellectual pursuit was the Shakespeare Club which Mildred Hazan, wife of the army's chief signal officer General William B. Hazen, had asked her to join. Not expecting to learn a great deal ("I almost know Shakespeare by heart"), Violet joined the group as "an intellectual amusement."[46] The reading group provided her with a pleasurable diversion each Friday morning, for the women were "bright & interesting." More significant to Violet, however, was the effect on her ego: "My vanity was rather pleased," she bragged. The women appreciated the depth of her knowledge of Shakespeare "& other authors—Greek, German, Latin, Italian &c, not to mention Marlow, Ben Johnson & the other great Elizabethans."[47]

Lippe returned from Austria in time to enjoy Grover Cleveland's first inauguration day with Violet. March 4, 1885, was a warm, May-like day; for Violet, it became "a glorious day." Friends began to congregate early to watch the parade from the Blair home on Lafayette Square. With plenty of food, conversation, and laughter, it was a festive, happy day. Interested in seeing her old suitor Fitzhugh Lee, Violet searched the marching military units and was rather amused to find that instead of a "red bearded man" Lee was now "so fat & grey." Thrilled by seeing "Pennsylvania & Virginia regiments marching together," she was deeply moved by the thought that the Civil War was over at last: "I hope all bitterness is forgotten." That night, she and Lippe joined a number of others to view the magnificent display of fireworks. Her uncle Gus Nicholson had arranged for them to watch from an office window in the Navy Department. After the fireworks, they all returned to the Blair home and, because the evening was so lovely, sat on the front steps to see the final rockets set off from downtown. The perfect end of the evening came when all the others had gone, and Violet and Lippe made "a jolly little supper" from the leftovers of the day.

For Violet, not only had the day been glorious, but so too was Lippe. Although he was a nice-looking man and Violet was especially taken that he was "so exquisitely neat & clean," she was much more impressed that he had "a fine mind & good memory, highly cultivated." Her constant adjective for him was "charming," and she thought him "such a finished courteous gentleman." She was certain that there was "nothing of importance in the history of literature of any nation or language of Europe that he [was] not familiar with." More than academic knowledge, however, attracted Violet: "He has a knowledge of the world acquired by traveling & living at so many courts as a very observant & intelligent diplomat must have." Even if she could not admit it, she was smitten.[48]

When Lippe received word of the death of his father, he bowed to convention by withdrawing from society and determined to live in "strict seclusion for some weeks to come."[49] After Violet had written a letter of consolation, Lippe responded in terms more intimate than in any other letter. At the top of his unsigned letter was the admonition *"To be burned immediately."* Apparently she had also been less formal, for he wrote, "Your letter was a ray of sunshine in these last days of darkness. Will such further lovely rays of sunshine delight me? I hope so. I must await it. I yearn for it.—What endless pleasure your loving, heartfelt lines have given me. How can I ever repay you: you are sweet, as good as you are pure." Without crossing that fine, vague boundary marking the limits of propriety, Lippe skillfully provided ample opportunity to read between the lines: "You say that our temporary separation hurts you. But what should I say to you? The monotonous, unhappy days roll by and I count them—estimate how many hours separate me from you, which bind me to you with a thousand invisible threads."[50]

Lippe found it impossible to stay away from Violet, but because he was in mourning, he was anxious that no one know he came to her. Violet ingenuously excused this breach of propriety by saying, "I guess he is lonely with his grief in a strange land away from his own people."[51] Albert had anticipated such a result and had written his wife: "I haven't the least idea that he will cease his visits to you. On the contrary, he will probably visit you oftener."[52]

Albert was right: Lippe kept calling. As the summer progressed, Violet continued to try to decipher his motives. Before he left on vacation to the North, Lippe made the unpleasant journey to the Moorings four times, and Violet queried, "Is it possible that he cares so much for me?"[53] Two weeks later, she returned to that thought, asking, "Is he in love with me or not? I am not sure." Almost admitting her real dilemma, she concluded, "My vanity would be flattered, but it would trouble my conscience."[54] More perceptive than his wife, Albert had no difficulty in assessing the situation, explaining to her that her philological lessons were accompanied by "the unconsciously enacted but unspoken romance that forms the under-current of your intercourse." He refused, however, to try to order his wife to end the relationship. Instead, he subtly reminded her of her responsibilities to social convention. Assuming a detached attitude, he claimed that no husband need be jealous "if every married woman who inspires admiration and even love in a man other than her husband would or could conduct the 'affair' with the same self-possession, prudence, and propriety that have characterized your intercourse with your friend."[55]

While the extended Blair family refrained from comment on Violet's affair, her sister, Jimmie, was not so discreet. Subject to raging fits of temper, Jimmie, on several occasions, confronted Violet and "said nasty things" about the friendship. Violet and Jimmie had never gotten along, and after Jimmie's marriage to George Wheeler, their relationship was even worse. During one loud and rancorous argument, Jimmie struck Violet, nearly knocking her down.[56] Evidently, Jimmie's insinuations went beyond the family circle, for Minna reported to her brother that Jimmie talked "in the most scandalous way . . . circulating compromising stories."[57] Violet, however, felt certain that her conduct was above reproach and attributed Jimmie's accusations to jealousy.

When Lippe returned to Washington, Violet was disturbed by his demeanor: "He seemed restless & emotional, looked at me passionately—I think he has fallen in love with me."[58] She dismissed such thoughts by claiming that he was "a real sincere friend" and that it was only her vanity that made her think he loved her.[59]

Albert certainly did not present any obstacles to his wife's continued flirtation. In November 1885 he left the country to pursue collection of his fees granted by the French and American Claims Commission, not returning until mid-June 1886. At that time, he had only been with his wife "a day or two over two weeks in the last thirteen months." And when he was in Washington, he declined to linger in the room when Lippe called. As Violet put it, "Bert excused himself & got out of the way."[60]

For nearly another two years, Violet continued her infatuation with Lippe. Thoroughly enjoying his company, she pulled back when he became too intimate. In January 1886, she "did not enjoy his visit as much as usual—he was too personal."[61] Her greatest concern was that they would become the subject of gossip. At parties, she made a conscious effort not to spend too much time with him and to devote herself to other men. Her fear of "l'opinion publique" required circumspection. It was a small price for Violet to pay for the reward of Lippe's regular twice-weekly calls to spend "a quiet evening" with her. Those visits were not generally known, and significantly Violet admitted, "If people knew *that* I would have to stop it."[62]

Rather than admit her infatuation, Violet found all manner of reasons to justify her dalliance with Lippe in her generally unhappy life, "He is so bright & charming & makes me laugh." "He is a brain stimulator & he finds me one too."[63] Still, her fear of what others thought was ever present. When another man boldly asked Lippe if he loved Violet, the Austrian nobleman replied in most gentlemanly fashion that all her friends were devoted to her. Violet was extremely embarrassed and called the incident "too horrid."[64]

It was only after Violet suspected that Lippe might be leaving the country that she began to admit the true meaning of their relationship. With the announcement of the appointment of a new Austrian ambassador, she knew that Lippe might lose his position, and that knowledge seemed to affect her ability to judge his feelings. After a late evening visit, she was sure that she could read his face as she had so many others, and what she saw disturbed her: "There was strong passion for me." Her worry passed, however, for on his next visit, he reverted to his calm, dignified ways. Still, for the first time, she had admitted his love and considered its consequences: "I am sure, if I were free, he would wish to marry me, & though I think he is fine & noble & interesting I know that I could never be happy away from my Country & my own loved ones."[65]

After that burst of honesty, Violet returned to her protective stance of coy uncertainty. The frequency of Lippe's visits increased, and Violet progressively came closer to acknowledging the truth. In October 1887, she gushed, "We had *such* a pleasant evening—I feel sure that ——— even if only a little & temporarily." A week later, after several late evening trysts, she wrote, "I wish I knew surely if ——— or not." In another week, she was sure: "I scarcely doubt."[66]

With orders to return to Austria, Lippe had come to take leave of her on November 6, 1887. Violet recorded, "We have parted perhaps forever." Their final tête-à-tête was bittersweet: "It was a precious evening, if somewhat painful." Deeply saddened by the loss of her favorite admirer, she took heart in the knowledge that he did indeed care for her and she for him: "How flat life will be without him. No one can take his place—He has been my favorite dictionary, encyclopedia & anthology— . . . I am unnerved today, & have not quite recovered my balance—I have never had just such a man friend."[67] And he reciprocated her feelings; Lippe never married.

Violet never recovered from her liaison with Lippe. While never conceding that anything improper occurred, she did allow, "For some men & women this intimacy of ours would have been dangerous." But after he had gone she could resume her habitual pose as a cold woman, claiming, "No man is dangerous to me."[68] Nevertheless, when she reflected on her behavior, she admitted, "I do not get rid of my extreme conscientiousness which makes me dissatisfied with my life." Although others considered her "a good woman," she thought differently: "I see & know my sins as clearly as if I were judging another in whom I am not interested—I make no excuses to myself." Violet wished that she felt repentant. "Yet I know that I am not penitent & that in all probability under the same circumstances I would do again the very things for which I condemn myself."[69]

Lippe had been only one, although the most important, diversion in Violet's life. Dispirited and disappointed in her marriage, she had looked elsewhere for happiness and consistently pursued her goal to "snatch the pleasure society gives."[70] She was encouraged to do so by her dearest friend, Minna Blair Richey. Telling Violet that Albert "has done exactly what suited him without regard to you," she urged her cousin to stop worrying about a husband who "does not add to your pleasure & life in the slightest."[71] Throughout the 1880s, Violet doggedly tried to avoid her troubles, flatly declaring, "Now society is my Lethe to forget what might have been."[72]

Albert understood the importance of society to Violet, and because of his dismal performance as a businessman, he could only encourage his wife to find what pleasure she could. While he did not enjoy society and had to spend his time trying to shore up the fiasco of his finances, he assured his wife, "I know you so well and understand your feelings so thoroughly that I can appreciate the delight you take in society."[73]

When Grover Cleveland assumed the White House in 1885, the New York *World* ran an article on "The Ladies Who Are Expected to Lead in Washington." Naming Violet "the most beautiful resident here," it commented particularly on her eyes: "If the heavens are blue, she has a great deal of heaven in her eyes."[74] Although she was pleased and flattered by the notice, Violet no longer considered herself beautiful: "I am surely faded & passee." Not altogether ready to give up her vanity, she added, "Pretty—well, yes—a number of people think that." Surprised to have been mentioned in the article, she discounted its accuracy: "I have about as much idea of leading society as of going into a convent, besides I have neither the wealth, health or influence for it." Conceding, "I am acceptable when I go into society because I have good blood, good manners & brains," she did not think of herself as a social leader: "People talk of my charm sometimes & that means that I am polite to them."[75] She was proud enough of the article, however, to tell Albert about it; and he took "great pleasure" in the compliments, adding his own: "That you are the prettiest woman in Washington society, is no news to me."[76]

Despite her disclaimers, men still found Violet irresistible, and she still gathered flocks of them at social events. Eliphalet Potter, the first man to propose to her, called on her whenever he was in Washington and always professed his abiding love for her.[77] When he vowed that he had never gotten over his love, Violet was "flattered & shocked at the same time." Although she did not encourage him, she was not angry: "[I am] pleased to see the passion of the man for me, that has lasted all these years, & disgusted that he will not admit that he is wicked to feel so."[78]

Other former beaux appeared at Violet's side with some regularity. In her diary Violet wrote that Pierce Young professed "never to have recovered from the blow of my refusing him or as he put it 'rejecting his love' &c— never has loved another woman &c." She did not take him seriously, attributing his sentimentality to "facon de parler."[79] James O'Kane flirted with her, attempting to convince her that he had "never cared for any other woman as he cared for [her]." Again, she questioned the sincerity of her former lover, but she thoroughly enjoyed the attention.[80]

At all the social events of the season in 1887, Violet eagerly grasped at pleasure and found respite from her troubles: "I have very rarely in my life gone to a party, tea, dinner, luncheon or any other affair where I did not have a good time—People seem to like to talk to me & I like people, men or women, & my spirits rise with pleasant society."[81] Sometimes she was even a belle again. At an evening reception in January 1887, she found herself surrounded by admiring men and sought out by the renowned John Hay. Wearing a new white silk dress, she knew that she looked lovely: "For I saw myself in a long mirror & was not as pale as sometimes & being in high spirits the blood came up a bit & gave me a little color." It was a memorable evening for Violet, who recorded, "I do not see why I should have been the belle, but I certainly was." It had been some time since she had been such a sensation, and the experience was exhilarating: "I scarcely slept at all that night, I was too excited—nervous, almost intoxicated with the pleasure of it—gratified vanity—I felt myself a happy girl again—What they call my joyous temperament had full swing—Will it last? I am not old yet."[82]

Albert wrote in great admiration, encouraging the feeling of satisfaction that her social triumphs gave Violet: "If ever I catch you bemoaning your 'lost beauty' and faded youth, I shall remind you of your experience this winter. You won't admit it, but I verily believe you are the belle of Washington this season."[83] Without money or position or time to devote to maintaining his marriage, Albert fell back on his only resources: his ability to flatter his wife and the continuation of their practice of openness and honesty. As he wrote her, "You know, the condition of my refraining from jealousy is that you confide to me all your little womanly pranks . . . in which I take a vicarious interest." Asserting that he was not vain, he did not delude himself that her continued affection for him was based on anything "but the outcome of habit and sympathetic companionship and, perhaps, of something more" that she could "hardly define" herself."[84]

To repay her social debts, Violet concentrated on her weekly receptions and teas and luncheons, less expensive forms of entertainment than dinners.[85] Always careful to invite congenial guests and meticulous to include only the most elite of Washington, Violet took great care to present the most exquisite table possible. Her luncheons became notable occasions: "My pretty silver, china & glass make a lovely table, & I think I have the sense to get the right people together—That is everything at a lunch—I do not have them too elaborate, only three wines, sherry, claret & champagne but the best—I would rather not have champagne than not have the best—No flowers—but the food of the best & well cooked—It was quite gay."[86]

Her tea in February 1889 was a complete success. She invited a large but select group, which she said included "our own old Washington set," in addition to "such of the newcomers as are sufficiently wellbred & pleasant to suit my exclusive taste, not many of them, & none of the nouveaux riches." Wearing a long black velvet gown, Violet was proud of how she looked, commenting, "I think I was almost beautiful." Many spoke admiringly of their "fascinating hostess," and Violet reported that, according to her aunt Lizzie Lee, "I had a positive genius for society."[87]

Always conscious of her social standing, Violet was particularly discriminating in choosing which parties she deigned to attend. One of her favorite homes to visit was that of the chief signal officer of the army, General Adolphus Greely. There, she could depend upon finding especially agreeable company, on one occasion commenting, "The conversation was ahead of any I have heard at a dinner." Her judgment was not an exaggeration, considering that the guests included Daniel C. Gilman, first president of the Johns Hopkins University, and Samuel P. Langley, the new secretary of the Smithsonian Institution.[88]

A special treat for Violet were the regular Friday evening soirees at Mary Henry's home. The members of the "club" played charades or gave readings or participated in amateur musicals and theatricals. Among the cleverest members were an old friend of Violet's father and her devoted admirer, Rear Admiral Thomas Stevens, his son Rowan, and Supreme Court justice Joseph Bradley and his wife, Carrie.[89]

In 1889, during the last months of President Cleveland's first administration, Violet became acquainted with his wife, the pretty twenty-four-year-old Frances Folsom Cleveland. Having heard of Violet's many charms from their mutual friends, the young first lady wished to meet her. Violet was charmed: "Mrs. C. is so sweet & pretty & has a fascinating manner—The newspapers have not overrated her charms."[90] Evidently the feeling was mutual, for Frances Cleveland soon asked Violet to receive with her during an afternoon reception. Violet was fascinated by the aplomb with which Frances greeted 5,000 guests: "It is marvelous how she stands it—She is so charming to everyone—Her smile is fascinating—Her hair, eyes, teeth, nose, mouth, skin & figure are lovely, but it is her wonderful bright smile that makes her different from so many pretty women."[91]

Until the Clevelands left office in March 1889, Violet was a regular visitor at the White House. Impressed by the woman, not the office, she felt it appropriate to call frequently since Cleveland had been defeated, and no one could think she was trying to gain anything. In fact, she claimed, "I would not go if it was the beginning of the Administration, instead of the end."[92]

A new presence among Violet's male admirers was the Swiss minister Alfred de Claparide, whom she met for the first time in November 1888. "A tall handsome man, with beautiful brown eyes & grey hair & beard, courteous manners & pleasant conversation," Claparide quickly became a devoted and regular visitor.[93] When "Clap," as Violet nicknamed him, became "too spooney," Violet knew exactly how to handle him; he "had to be snubbed."[94] It was all great fun for Violet; it was a relationship in which she was in total control; it was reminiscent of her belle days when she coldly and calculatingly played with men's emotions. When Claparide invited her to a dinner party, ostensibly in honor of another woman but featuring violets as table decorations, she knew she had made a conquest: "He is in love with me—no mistake about it."[95] She delighted in making Claparide jealous, thinking him "a fool to carry on so about a married woman." Certainly she felt no remorse: "I really do not think I am wicked, for I do not care a pin for him & do not encourage him."[96]

Another new conquest was Henry Kingsbury, a young captain in the cavalry. After their initial meeting in March 1889, when Violet thought Kingsbury "rather impressed with [her] charms," the young man became a constant presence in Violet's coterie of male admirers.[97] Despite Kingsbury's engagement to another woman, he flirted with Violet, who believed that he was "ready to break with" his fiancée "if I give him the least encouragement to hang around me." Violet was not the least interested in stealing the young man, but she did "find it interesting & flattering to see the weakness of the man." She refused to accept any responsibility for leading Kingsbury astray, arrogantly claiming, "I have not been to blame, unless showing off my learning & talking amusingly with him was wrong."[98] Playing Claparide against Kingsbury to make them both jealous became a favorite amusement for Violet. "What business have they to be in love with a respectable married woman? But it is fun!"[99] Albert provided the most acute analysis of Violet's behavior. About an earlier but similar episode, he had written: "I understand perfectly well the role you like to play in such matters. It is an exquisite pleasure and amusement to you to witness the agitation of a man suffering from harrowed feelings."[100]

In a matter of months, Kingsbury was "quite wildly in love" with Violet and unhappily anticipating his forthcoming marriage. Violet was not overly concerned, thinking, "He will get over it after he is married—It is silly of him to be so."[101] After he left for New York for his wedding, Kingsbury continued to send letters and flowers to Violet every day and even wrote to her only a few hours before the ceremony. Violet thought the poor man had "lost his heart & head temporarily." It was extremely flattering and inflated her ego: "I am an uncommon woman, & men seem to be easily charmed by me, even when I do not make any effort to attract."[102]

She reveled in her powers of attraction and delighted in recording her triumphs. At Judge Bradley's Fortnightly, she reported, "I had, as usual, lots of attention."[103] It was not uncommon for her to be surrounded by men, as she described in her diary: "I stood for a long time in the middle of the front room with sometimes as many as seven gentlemen talking to me—not all beaux, of course—I was so glad to be in rather a conspicuous space that everyone might see what a belle I was."[104] At a dinner at the Washington McLean's, she sat next to the well-known Republican politician, soon to be secretary of state, James G. Blaine. He "was disposed to be flirtatious," and she delighted in the "chances to say saucy things." They talked of politics, but their conversation turned to more flirtatious topics when Blaine "made lots of sweet speeches." He asked when he could call on her, but she refused to see him except during her regular Monday afternoon reception time. "It would be very different receiving such a conspicuous man from receiving other fellows—people would notice it."[105]

Although Violet tried to forget her troubles by self-indulgence, she was not able to cast Albert completely from her thoughts. His financial failures and poor business practices were the root of her dissatisfaction and had brought her the most grief. It was not simply that he had been unable to support her for most of their married life; the problem was that he had lost a great deal of Mary Blair's money, that there was almost no hope of ever recovering it, and that there seemed no end to his indebtedness. More important even than the loss of her mother's money was Albert's unwillingness to discuss his business dealings with Violet or follow her advice. Money had, indeed, created a wall between them.

From the beginning of their marriage, Violet had not wanted Albert to pay for her support when they were apart. As the years went by and they lived together less frequently, she felt even more strongly that she should not take his money. Not resentful of his inability to support her, Violet felt it was only fair that a husband should not be responsible for his wife's expenses when they did not live together. Besides, after she understood his financial problems, she had made concerted efforts to increase her own income. By prudent investments and strict economy, she had been able to improve her fiscal situation and did not need his support.

At the same time, she was willing to give him her money, as she explained, "I do not refuse him anything that I can give."[106] When Albert had to go to Paris on business, she lent him what money she could. Not wanting to embarrass him, she arranged a ruse by which she deposited money in her mother's account, and Albert borrowed from Mary. She also offered possessions that he could sell: "I gave him the black lace sunshade with real coral handle given me by his mother as a wedding gift."[107] To protect her own self-interest, however, she had determined not to endorse more notes for him: "I will not be a pauper, if I can help myself, & depend on anyone else."[108]

Reflecting on her marriage, Violet sadly concluded that it had been a mistake. When she had accepted his proposal, she had been sure that they had similar tastes: "He *was* the man who was most adaptable to all my ideas & thoughts (in perfect harmony with me & I do not think it was pretended)."[109] The passage of years had proved her wrong. Although she thought him a "cultivated man" who loved books, they were different: "I love Dante, Sophocles &c—& he likes Offenback & the newspapers."[110] Knowing him to be "amiable generally, intelligent & amusing—kind hearted too," Violet had entered their marriage with high hopes, "thinking to find a true friend & companion, a sharer of [her] thoughts, studies & aspirations—a helpmeet in fact." After nearly twenty-five years of marriage, she was bitterly disappointed: "He simply wanted me for a mistress, & has treated me as such, except that he would have had to support a mistress. By force of character & my other qualities I force his respect, but he cares only for my body, if for that, now."[111]

For Violet, wedlock was a sacred institution, and divorce was an inconceivable, unacceptable solution for marital unhappiness. Besides, she did have some love for him, and they both respected each other. When Albert came to Washington, she tried to make him happy and wanted his reassurance that his visits had been pleasant. Her cousin Minna pointed out that Violet was always happier when Albert was present: "I don't know whether you realize how much brighter view you take of life in general when he is with you, . . . you are braced up mentally & physically."[112] Violet was aware of Albert's effect on her moods and had to admit, "I get on with Bert better than I would have done with any of the others, I imagine."[113]

Fundamentally, Violet was deeply unhappy. As the years had passed, she concluded, "I have not grown in grace & good deeds, but have hardened & grown cold & cynical." She knew that her failed marriage was partly her fault and conceded, "I have, maybe, only myself to blame, but I was not prepared for the disappointments in character &c of some I believed in—I have become somewhat embittered."[114]

Perhaps the greatest disappointment for Violet was her inability to control her husband. He was, she wrote, "the only man I wish to have power to bind." During their courtship, she had reigned supreme, but somehow she had lost her power over Albert. She had always demanded that he respect her individuality, but she had never accepted the reciprocal of allowing him to maintain his; without direct confrontation, Albert had simply established his own independence. Although she knew that he still cared for her, it was not enough: "He is fond of me in a way & proud of me, but I am unnecessary in his life—My future is gloomy & hopeless, my past full of regrets, my present anxious & worried."[115] Her only way to come to terms with her unhappy circumstances was to rely on her sense of self-worth and egotism. Even if she no longer had the love of her husband, she knew that others appreciated her: "I have always been the favorite in our large family connection." With inordinate arrogance, she proclaimed, "My supposed lovely character is more the result of a calm studious taste, a rather passionless temperament, a sense of fitness & boundless pride—being my own heroine perhaps."[116]

In the waning years of the 1880s, her greatest consolation was in remembering Lippe, "my lion, my kingly, knightly friend."[117] When she knew that he would never return to America, she revealed the depth of her passion for him. Lippe-Weissenfeld was the only man who elicited from her "the feeling that makes the cheeks hot & the heart beat quickly."[118] She expressed her emotional involvement with Lippe in a poem which included these stanzas:

> And the waves are chanting a requiem
> O'er the beautiful nights of yore
> And my heart, my heart is breaking
> For the words that I hear no more.
>
> I think of the joyous e'enings
> Under our old oak trees,
> With the moonlight shadows moving
> When stirred by the gentle breeze.
>
> I think how he sat beside me,
> His strong hand clasped in mine
> Of the tender words he was breathing
> As we watched that moon decline.
>
> Oh those days when my hero was with me
> When I lived in a beautiful dream,
> Nor cared for the past nor the future,
> So each happy day did seem.[119]

In 1892, when she learned of Lippe's death, she was devastated: "Oh my life, my love— . . . Mine now—no one else can claim him." Saddened and sickened, she put up a brave front, continuing her usual activities, so that almost no one knew the painful blow she had suffered. Only in private and in her diary could she mourn her lost lover: "I live over the past & dream it over—Sleeping & waking he is rarely from my thoughts—The poems he wrote me which I know by heart—It was not sinful for we broke no law— human or divine."[120] Three years later, she still cherished his memory, describing Lippe as "Jove himself." He was, she judged, "high born, high bred, learned, brave, true, courteous, tender, cultured beyond his fellows, a flawless, peerless gentleman Fine in mind & soul & body & neat as a woman— One by whom I measure all others, & find them poor mean & small."[121] Lippe-Weissenfeld was the love of her life.

Chapter 7

The Final Years

"It is sad, this unwedded married life." ✑

As the 1890s began, Violet and Albert settled into a relationship of separateness. She no longer struggled to control him, and he pursued his own interests, spending even less time with his wife. Albert, consumed with visions of making a fortune from his canal, traveled between New Orleans and New York where he hoped to raise capital. His visits to Washington usually consisted of a day or two en route to Wall Street. Sometimes he avoided Washington altogether; in May 1894, Violet recorded in her diary that Albert had not been with her for more than a year.[1] Congenial when together, they regretfully accepted their conditions of marriage and independent lives, as Violet commented: "Matrimony does not seem to hang heavily on him or me—I wonder if there is another respectable woman in this city—so slightly married as I— . . . It is sad, this unwedded married life— . . . At least we do not bore each other & we make no scandals."[2]

Despite their somewhat estranged relationship, Albert still struggled to extricate himself from debt so that he could repay what he had borrowed from Mary Blair and thus recapture Violet's esteem. When his financial negotiations in New York bogged down, he naturally took an optimistic view, boasting to his wife, "The fact is, I have made quite a reputation for myself among these bankers during this week, and among others also, as a correct businessman."[3] Indicative of his bright hopes was his arrangement to create at his canal a new post office which he named Violet's Post Office.[4] As it turned out, the men he had impressed were simply scoundrels, and Albert had once again been duped. He was forced to call on his brother Henry, who had made a great deal of money as a mining engineer. It did not take Henry long to determine that this business was not going to make a fortune, contemptuously calling it "this little canal" which had "no income, gross or net, and has no money behind it, or promised to it." Recognizing that his brother was "a very poor businessman," Henry thought that the best that could be done was "to make this little property free from all present and future shadows . . . and to give it a chance to obtain some value, for it has none now."[5] Success, however, was not to come. The financial panic of 1893 set Albert back further and caused him to lose even more of Mary Blair's bonds that he had promised as security for some of his loans.[6]

Although she felt sorry for Albert, Violet kept her frustrations to herself, only confiding in her diary. There, she wrote, "I am angry & weary of his business ways." More frustrating than the loss of money was his attitude: "He takes it so lightly—His way of treating things is to blame others or fate . . . & then he airily dismisses the subject. He has his cigarettes, his newspaper & his zither & coffee, so he is amused."[7] Sometimes, Albert's failures infuriated her, and she railed in her diary, "He calls himself a good husband because he does not meddle with me—*That* he could not do! My marriage is a very bad failure."[8] Yet, believing divorce a sin, she thought herself "bound by a chain that only death can break."[9] Only occasionally did she give way to despondency. On the anniversary of her wedding day and her baby's birth, Violet forlornly concluded, "A childless woman has no future in this life to look to."[10] Presenting herself to the world as "a charming happy woman," she continued to find refuge in society, repeating her pledge "to forget my sorrows, & live in the gay world."[11] When Albert made his infrequent visits to Washington, he refused to join her in social events; instead, as Violet expressed it, he "keeps out of people's way when they come here."[12]

In addition to her concern for Albert, Violet also bore the burden of discord within her own family. The relations of the Blair siblings had never been peaceful, and the wrangling only became worse as they aged. Violet felt herself the martyr, always supporting and protecting her mother. Her sister, Jimmie, had a terrible temper which she let loose on the family whenever she visited. Jesup was never engaged in any gainful employment, spending his time racing horses and socializing. Mary, the self-sacrificing mother, bent to their wills and gave them everything they wanted. It was infuriating to Violet that her mother had "to go without things for herself to supply their wants." Seeing herself as the ideal daughter, Violet claimed that only she paid her own expenses.[13]

Although Jesup was a kind-hearted man, gentle with children and a tender nurse to the sick, he had little purpose in life except self-indulgence. His greatest failing, according to his sister, was his lack of sexual control. In 1880,

Violet had worried about his "low moral character," commenting to Albert that Jesup was "in another scrape."[14] Again, in 1886, Jesup nearly brought the family to disgrace by his involvement with a senator's daughter. Her sudden departure to Europe ended the affair, but Violet was furious with her brother, claiming, "I would like to have him fixed so it won't happen again."[15] A surgical solution was not to be, and Jesup continued his profligate ways, giving the family another crisis only two years later. In 1896, when her son was forty-four, Mary Blair was forced to extricate him from another compromising situation by bribing the young woman's family when they threatened public scandal.[16] In each case, Jesup fled from the unpleasant scenes, leaving Violet to handle the aggrieved parties.

With her sister, Jimmie, Violet had always engaged in loud, rancorous arguments. Jealous of her sister, Jimmie rarely missed a chance to abuse her, flinging insults at will, the worst of which was her accusation that Albert kept a mistress in New Orleans.[17] The climax of their tempestuous relationship came in the late 1890s when Jimmie's husband, George Wheeler, had convinced Mary Blair to lend him mortgages valued at over $20,000. When he refused to return them after the agreed-upon time, Mary and Violet sought the help of lawyer-cousins Blair Lee and Woodbury Blair, who resolved the matter.[18] The incident was only one of many disagreeable confrontations in which Violet thought her sister and husband mistreated her mother. Surely adding to Violet's indignation was her discomfort in knowing of her own husband's indebtedness to her mother.

Incensed by her siblings, disappointed with her husband, Violet sought diversion, and she continued to amuse herself with the attentions of the Swiss minister to the United States, Alfred de Claparide, whom she had first met in 1888. Although at times she thought him "tiresome" and wished for "a new man to be as devoted as Clap," she found it easy to justify her flirtation. "Perhaps I ought to repent of encouraging C's devotion," she wrote, "but I do not, I think it is good for him to run after me rather than after a woman who might forget herself."[19] Her self-centered interest in Claparide was typical of her attitude toward men in general: "I like him & his attention, & he teaches & amuses me. . . . I enjoy seeing him jealous & I like to be admired."[20] After he had finally returned to his homeland and family, Violet privately admitted she missed him, although she said others "would not understand that I can miss attention, flattery & an intellectual companion where there is no sentiment on my side." Truthful to herself, she recognized Claparide's value to her: "I suppose it is my vanity that misses him more than anything else. No one just takes his place."[21]

Her conduct toward Claparide epitomized her treatment of most men. Cold and arrogant, she knew that she could never fall under the spell of romance, and she did not wish to. She had honed her skills of flirtation to a fine state of refinement so that she had the "power to hold men just at a proper distance." Violet reveled in her power: "I am amused by the power I have to draw & make men wish for me, while they have to be respectful to me."[22] Flirtation was a means to escape the unhappiness of her marriage, and she used it "to fill the void."[23]

Violet never wished to relinquish that power she had learned to wield as a young belle. In her fifty-first year, she rekindled the flames of an old affair. In 1899 she attended the Bachelor's Cotillion with her brother, Jesup. At that dance, she encountered her former admirer Bill Emory, who "was quite devoted," and they "talked of old times &c." He claimed that "it took him years" to get over Violet's rejection of him.[24] In the spring, she again saw Emory, and they went for a walk. Violet claimed, "It is not an elderly flirtation—I am too dignified for that."[25] With the passage of another year, however, the situation was apparently different: "I wonder if anyone could suppose I am having a mild middle-aged flirtation—*Pas si bete!*" Not a serious involvement, their flirtation was an enjoyable diversion. It was all very pleasant to receive visits, notes, and flowers from an admirer, and it brought back memories of her former days of conquest when she had been a youthful belle.[26]

As the years passed, she and her brother, Jesup, made the social rounds together. She accepted him for his good qualities and tried to overlook his faults. It was an agreeable arrangement for two who enjoyed society as much as they. Whether attending dances or teas or making calls, the two aging Blair children became a familiar sight at old Washington functions.[27] Another special joy for Violet was her close friendship with Mary Henry. Mary's language lessons and the Friday evening soirees at the Henry's provided opportunity for the development of a close bond between the two women. Intelligent, clever, and refined, Mary returned Violet's affection, calling her "my little queen among women." Mary cherished Violet's friendship and tried to explain how much it meant to her: "My Violet has a soul that has touched mine so closely that words are foolish things to tell how I love my Flower."[28]

Another of Violet's favorite women friends was Frances Cleveland. When the Clevelands returned to the White House in 1893, Violet was delighted to see her friend again, commenting, "She is perfectly sweet & lovely as ever—unaffected & unchanged." Frances reciprocated Violet's affection, arranging that any time Violet called, she was to say she "had a perpetual engagement."[29] Frequently invited to White House dinners and receptions, Violet enjoyed her association with the Clevelands. On one occasion, Violet had what she described as "the time of my life." Invited to receive with Frances Cleveland, she attended a small supper afterwards in the private rooms of the White House. The president singled out Violet to sit at his table, and she was delighted at his attention and cordiality.[30]

Entertaining and being entertained provided the center for Violet's life. As she continued her endless rounds of calling, attending teas, luncheons, and dinners while at the same time reciprocating with her own parties, Violet became ever more egotistical and exclusive in her outlook. Asserting, "I am the most cultivated woman I know," she disdained official government society, exemplifying the "Cave Dweller" mentality of her class.[31] As government expanded in size and the nouveaux riches of the Gilded Age invaded the city, the old resident society lost its place of eminence. In the final decades of the nineteenth century, beleaguered and lamenting the decline of propriety and gentility, they adopted the tactic of fighting against loss of status by withdrawal; they became more exclusive and refused to accept brash newcomers into their society.[32] Called the "Antiques" by Mark Twain and Charles Dudley Warner and the "dying snails" by Emily Edson Briggs, old Washingtonians proudly accepted the title of Cave Dwellers by the 1890s.[33]

The Cave Dwellers "wrapped themselves in the comforting mantle of genealogy," and declared their criteria for acceptance: culture, gentility, refinement, good manners, taste, and propriety.[34] Violet was forthright in stating what made "people worth knowing." Representative of the Cave Dwellers, she listed "good blood, good morals, good manners & culture as the most needful things; & have no regard for wealth or official position."[35] Marietta Minnigerode Andrews, calling Violet "Queen of the Cave Dwellers," described her way of life: "Her colonial traditions, her orthodox churchmanship, her conservative standards, her infallible decisiveness, her beautiful profile, have never changed; she lives in the same atmosphere as in her youth, under the same lofty ceilings, among the same priceless calf-bound books, even with the same venerable and unresponsive, faithful old servants! Unchanged, unchanging."[36]

The social gatherings of Washington's elite, having "quite the air of a European capital," were dignified and distinguished, including only likeminded and congenial people.[37] Violet was in the forefront of maintaining old Washington standards; she took pride in her reputation: "I have such a name for being exclusive."[38] When she gave a tea for 250, many men attended, unusual at a tea, and nearly everyone knew each other. Violet thought those factors made it a success: "It was really a brilliant reception, for all the nicest of Old Washington society turned out for me . . . & I do not admit any of the parvenus within my door."[39] Without doubt, the elegance of the surroundings also added to the pleasure of her guests. When she gave a ball in 1895, her home on Lafayette Square was resplendent. Bringing in from the country branches of wild cherry and other flowering trees, in addition to magnolia, spirea, and spring flowers, she made her home "a perfect bower." Many of her guests had sent her bouquets, and she filled every vase and numerous preserving jars ("carefully concealed," of course) to create "a beautiful effect." While others commented on the decor, Violet thought her party successful because she had invited only those whom she thought pleasant: "The mob is never asked here & people like to come who are asked."[40]

As the 1890s progressed, Violet's tendencies toward the Cave Dweller mentality increased. In 1891 her aunt Elizabeth Lee was instrumental in establishing the Mary Washington chapter of the Daughters of the American Revolution (DAR), and Violet immersed herself in her genealogy. Later in that year, her aunt, along with her cousin Minna, worked to found the exclusive woman's organization, the Washington Club, and Violet also joined that group. "That sanctuary of sanctuaries," as Violet called it, the Washington Club became a bastion of conservatism and a protector of old Washington society.[41] Although Violet was not especially active in the club, she believed in its principles and supported its goals.

Of greater importance to Violet was her membership in patriotic societies. In their Daughters of the American Revolution chapter, her aunt Elizabeth was elected regent, and Violet, registrar, positions to which they were regularly reelected for many years.[42] In 1892 Violet played a central role in forming the Washington, D. C., chapter of the Colonial Dames, and in 1895 she was an initial vice president of the National Society of the Children of the American Revolution (CAR).[43] These societies became her life work, and she devoted enormous amounts of time, energy, and effort to them for the rest of her life.

The formation of women's patriotic associations was only one part of the much larger women's club movement that began to flourish in the 1890s. At least part of the reason for forming patriotic and hereditary societies was fear of the changing social and economic conditions in the United States. The new immigration from southern and eastern Europe, labor strikes and riots, and the populist revolt were unsettling to upper-class Americans, who "watched apprehensively the black cloud of anarchism."[44] The nouveaux riches, made wealthy by industrialism, pushed aside the old families who had traditionally been civic leaders. According to Frederic Jaher, "Beleaguered patricians saw in democracy, immigration, racial degeneracy, and industrialism the essence of the modern era and the enemies of the fallen elite."[45] In defense of the old ways, many turned to organizations such as the Sons of the Revolution (1883), the Colonial Dames (1890), the Daughters of the Cincinnati (1894), and the Society of Mayflower Descendants (1894).[46]

Nativist sentiment was a cornerstone of the patriotic organizations.[47] Violet recognized and responded to the direct connection between hereditary societies and anti-immigration feeling. Her vehemence may not have been typical of most elites but, given her personality, it is not surprising: "I expect great things of the 'Daughters.' I want to see them spread the cry of 'America for Americans' & a hatred of foreign immigration. It makes me rave to think of foreigners being naturalized. It is bad enough when the foreigner is a German or Scandinavian, but worse when it is one of the inferior races: French, Irish, Pole, Italian &c. I would rather see the cholera here than the immigrants."[48]

As a younger woman, Violet had expressed a desire for "a strong native American party," and she had wished for laws restricting immigrants from voting until after "thirty or forty years residence." She also wanted to prohibit them from holding office.[49] By 1882 she had become more emphatic and specific in her diatribes against foreigners, mistrusting Germans and referring to Ireland as a "beggarly little island that I would like to have sunk in the ocean."[50] Violet's outbursts against immigrants did not moderate; they only became worse. She never retreated from her attitude of 1886, when she wrote in her diary: "These dreadful riots, strikes, socialists &c—that the newspapers are so full of worry me very much. It makes me rage furiously to think of those wretches, foreigners. . . . The very idea of their daring even to express an opinion on American affairs enrages me so. . . . I would not leave a single one of them between the Atlantic & Pacific. . . . I would stop at nothing to rid my country of these vermin." As irrational as her thinking was, Violet accurately assessed her convictions: "In the old 'Know Nothing' times there was not one of the whole party as rabid on the subject as I am."[51] While Albert had his own prejudices against immigrants, he occasionally tried to soften her rage, as he did in 1894 when he sarcastically wrote, "If you write much more in the same strain about your feelings toward foreigners, you will tempt me to murder one of them."[52]

John Higham has identified three themes implicit in all American nativist movements: anti-Catholicism, anti-radicalism, and nationalistic racism.[53] While Violet apparently felt little of the religious prejudice, she was quite fearful of foreign radical elements, becoming absolutely passionate in defense of Anglo-Saxon superiority. For patricians and old family elites such as Violet represented, the new immigration posed a threat to what she thought was traditional America.[54] Her work with the Children of the American Revolution was closest to her heart, "for that is sowing good seed of patriotism 'America for Americans'—no place for the accursed foreigners."[55]

When the DAR formed the Children of the American Revolution, they did so in direct response to "the great influx of foreign immigration." In their official statement they asserted: "There was great danger that coming generations would utterly forget the purposes and ideals that gave strength and unity to the nation."[56] Although Mrs. Daniel Lothrop of Massachusetts was the founding president, Violet, who became treasurer of the organization, felt the justification of a comment by one member who told her, as Violet later wrote, "that *I,* not Mrs. Lothrop, have made the Society what it is." As Violet explained to Albert, her value to the association was to be found not only in the performance of her official duties but also through her annual "Children's Tea" given at her home. That exposure to aristocratic surroundings, "these handsome rooms with the old furniture, portraits, silver, swords & books," was, according to Violet, beneficial to the lesser sorts. At her most snobbish, she added, "I suppose few of them have been used to meeting the *real* Washington hostesses."[57]

If ancestry and lineage were important to the Daughters of the American Revolution, they were at the very heart of the Colonial Dames' organization. Even more elitist than the DAR, the Dames were also particularly sensitive to the social standing of their members.[58] When Violet helped write the constitution for the Washington chapter, she applauded the exclusive provision: "No one can belong to it but women who had ancestors in this country before 1750 & whose ancestors founded a town or commonwealth or college or held an important position in the colonial times."[59] As chairman of the committee on admissions, she became a strident protector of the restrictive membership rules. At the 1896 national convention, she opposed an amendment which would have allowed a signer of the Declaration of Independence to qualify a woman for membership on the grounds that that act was the beginning of revolution and could not be used as the basis of a claim to membership in a colonial society.[60] More than heritage only was important to Violet. In her roles on the admissions committee, as vice president, and finally as president, she worked hard "to keep together the Old Washington families" and exclude all others.[61]

It is not surprising that Violet was especially devoted to the Dames. Her own interest in ancestry was long-standing and fervid. As a young girl, she frequently expressed her pride in being a Blair. At the age of twenty-five, she had already been recognized as being second only to her grandmother Blair in knowledge of family history. Admitting to Albert, "[My] besetting sin is pride & especially with regard to my blood," she told him of her delight in finding that she was related to Queen Elizabeth I of England.[62] In 1891, when her cousin Blair Lee became engaged, Violet was pleased with his choice, not because her family was wealthy and socially prominent (which it was), but because she was related to one who approved the Declaration of Independence, giving Anne Clymer Brooke "signer blood." To Violet, "good blood is better than good looks or money, or even brains."[63]

Using the DAR, CAR, and the Colonial Dames, along with a plethora of social engagements, Violet tried to be too busy to dwell on her personal unhappiness. Her diary was an important means for venting her dissatisfactions, but it was not enough. Violet suffered from assorted and vaguely defined illnesses. Although she had been a typically "delicate" Victorian young woman, it was only in the last decades of the century that health problems became a recurring theme in her diary. While the documents do not give evidence of a direct and consistent link between her health and unfortunate circumstances, they do show an increase in physical maladies as marital felicity lessened.

In the 1880s Violet complained of "neuralgia," problems with her eyes that kept her from reading, "heart trouble," and "inflammation of the lungs."[64] Despite a great deal of discomfort, these ailments were not so debilitating that she could not continue most of her accustomed activities, as she reported in the fall of 1886: "I suffer a great deal from neuralgia, but have managed to keep up & go around most of the time the same routine."[65] Sometimes, however, her spirits flagged, and she gave way to her illnesses: "neuralgia—cough—blues—gloom—is my week's record."[66]

Her most worrisome affliction was a nervous twitching of her right arm, leg, and eye that was sometimes so severe she was unable to function; she feared it might lead to paralysis, St. Vitus dance, or some other dread disease.[67] The doctors, treating her with oxygen and electricity, reassured her that she was in no danger of paralysis and insisted the twitching was caused by "nervous exhaustion." It was hardly a reassuring diagnosis when the symptoms struck. When Ballard Smith, head of the Washington office of the *New York World* called on Violet, she felt one of her attacks coming on as they were conversing: "I felt that I must get out of the room, & made an excuse to go—before I reached the door I knew that one side of my face was drawn down, eye & all, & my right arm & leg were as though paralyzed—I dropped into a chair & could not move or speak for some minutes."[68] In 1891 Violet admitted that her "sadness & heart ache" made her "nervous trouble" worse.[69] Learning of the death of her love, Lippe, brought on a severe attack of what she came to call "the jerks."[70] Whether it was the death of a dog, concern over Albert's affairs, or sadness at the loss of Lippe, there is sufficient evidence to conclude that Violet's nervous "jerks" were often precipitated by emotional upset.[71]

Doctors of the era did not offer definitive diagnoses of such problems and were quite willing to attribute such afflictions to the peculiar nature of a woman's physiology, influenced, as it was, largely by her womb. Sometimes using the term "neurasthenia" and at other times, "hysteria," doctors simply concluded that women were naturally prone to nervous exhaustion. While some tried to distinguish between symptoms, their descriptions are vague and contradictory. A common attitude of the medical profession was expressed by J. H. Pulte in his *Medical Guide:* "They [women] dislike extremely to be told they have the hysterics; they have nothing against it, however, to be nervous, which essentially means the same thing."[72]

Whatever the exact nature of Violet's maladies, they added to her burdens but did not prevent her from pursuing an active life. Her ailments did, however, affect her spirits. In 1902, when she was diagnosed as having Bright's disease, she pondered her future: "Much as I have enjoyed life, I do not wish a long one—I dread surviving Mother." Living only to take care of her mother and brother, she assumed, "Bert can take care of himself & my death would not trouble him as much as it would Mother & Jep—He is more philosophical in his affections." The thought of her own death was not particularly troubling to her: "I am not a bit frightened, nor have I had beautiful Christian resignation—I *know* that I am needed by my loved ones & that no one can take my place—I have not thought of it much from the spiritual point of view—I seem to be about the average commonplace Christian & trust the Infinite Mercy for pardon for whatsoever I have done amiss."[73]

As her own physical ailments increased, so did her aging mother's infirmities. In the 1890s, the two women established the habit of escaping to a variety of healthful vacation spots during the late summer. Deer Park, Maryland, the Homestead at Hot Springs, Virginia, and Narragansett Pier in Rhode Island were their favorite destinations. Beginning in 1894, Albert came home from New Orleans to look after affairs at the Moorings while Violet and Mary were away. After the turn of the century, Violet and her mother traveled to Cohassett, Massachusetts, where Mary's sister Lucy Sitgreaves had moved with her daughter Mamie. Violet always benefited from these excursions and especially loved the rugged seashore at Cohasset: "I enjoy being on the rocks so much—I love to climb far out & read with the water coming up close around."[74]

Although Albert performed a needed family function by returning to the Moorings when Violet was gone, he spent most of his time separated from his wife while he struggled to make his canal a viable business. Ever optimistic, he doggedly continued to hold to his fanciful dreams: "I have a plan for plucking victory from the nettle of apparent defeat," he wrote in 1893.[75] When his plans once again failed and he found himself "more destitute of money in hand" than he had ever been, he still anticipated success: "You know the old saying that the darkest hour is that which immediately precedes the dawn." After citing the example of his father, who had at one time lost all, he proclaimed, "I expect to make a big 'coup.'"[76]

Violet became resigned to her husband's impecunious state, regularly paying interest on his loans and sending him money. On May 11, 1895, the canal was finally sold, but Albert's financial woes did not end.[77] He had no means of support, let alone cash to pay debts. For a time, he tried writing occasional pieces to sell to the newspapers, but when he realized he could get only five dollars for an article, he gave it up.[78] By the summer of 1896 Albert, too, began to face the reality of "what a great dreamer" he was. In reply to another draft she had sent him, he wrote, "Every remittance you send me brings to my eyes tears of gratitude and intensifies the immense disgust & discontent I feel over the positions into which I have brought myself." Vowing to direct all his effort to the task of paying off what he owed, he admitted that she had been right in opposing indebtedness: "I wish I had possessed your wisdom. Unfortunately, I never had the proper training in that respect. My father made money too easily and I also at the beginning of my career."[79] When he did come to Washington, he felt thoroughly shamed and did not care to socialize, never going out except to attend congressional debates. While he did assist Violet with the paper work of her patriotic societies, he avoided visitors. As Violet put it, he "keeps out of the way when they come here." In her view, "He does nothing much but read the newspapers & smoke."[80]

In 1897, his failures seemed complete: "Bert has nothing but what he gets from me."[81] When Violet asked him to execute a mortgage on his Louisiana property in favor of her mother, to secure his indebtedness to her, Albert replied that all he owned in Louisiana was personal property which was not subject to mortgage in that state. The best that he could do to fulfill his wife's request was to sign a note promising to give her mother his property upon her demand.[82] When Albert's brother Alexis died, Violet even had to give her husband money to pay for the funeral.[83]

Despite her "disappointment & disgust" concerning her marriage, Violet felt a responsibility to provide for Albert in case of her death: "I want to be sure of my money going to those who need it, & I want Bert & Jep protected from their own foolishness."[84] According to the contract signed at the time of their marriage, Albert had renounced all claim to Violet's estate. In her will, she told him, she had left him "an annuity . . . in such a way as to protect it from [his] creditors." Because of the peculiarities of Louisiana law, whereby her estate might be probated where her husband lived, she wished him to declare Washington as his official residence.[85]

Albert agreed to make such a statement, although his sentimental nature overcame his legal training: "I don't at all like the idea of a cold-blooded preparation of a document designed to benefit me in the event of your death." Satisfied that he had no claim on her estate, he told her, "I don't see any sound reason in the theory that, because a man has induced a woman to marry him, he has a right to a part of the property derived by her from sources alien to him."[86] Nevertheless, he began preparations to move permanently to Washington, although he knew that he had "no way of making money there." Reluctant to give up hope of making his own living, he felt he could not leave New Orleans until, as he said, "I shall have provided for a more or less regular income sufficient at least to meet my obligation at Riggs' [Bank] and my small personal requirements." His attempt to accomplish that purpose was rather pathetic; he set out to organize a fishing and hunting concern to take sportsmen into the bayous.[87] Of course, that venture did not work out, and Albert himself provided the keenest insight into his financial situation: "I won't say anything about my own losses except that my horse—a fine animal that I expected to sell soon—is dying."[88]

Extricating himself from Louisiana took longer than he had anticipated. Violet did not understand the delay and thought he simply wished to remain in New Orleans. To encourage him, she inelegantly enumerated various reasons why he should come to Washington: "You have no ties there to break— no friendships as I count friends—You have no home in La. & no particular business." Discounting his feelings, she arrogantly told him, "You find the climate more to your taste perhaps, but that is a matter of no real importance." Assuring him that he could "always get away to the swamps part of the year," she put the best light she could on their relationship: "Even if you & I are not perfectly congenial, we are *not* incompatible & we have the sense not to meddle with each other—We are at times quite companionable."[89] In light of her insensitivity, Albert was compelled to be very clear about his motives: "I hate the idea of returning to Washington empty handed and practically a pensioner and therefore a burden."[90] It was not until 1900 that Albert was able to dispose of most of his remaining property in Louisiana.[91]

Violet was no longer angry with him or even disappointed; she was only resigned: "My own marriage has not been happy, Heaven knows, but I have stuck to my bargain like an honest woman—I do not mean that Albert is bad, but not every woman would have stood his business ways & neglect &c— Well I have faults too probably." She recognized that none of her old lovers would have made her happy and that at least she and Albert were congenial: "Bert at least does not meddle with me—He lives his life, objectless, smoking & reading newspapers, & I mine too busy to think & despair."[92]

Ultimately, Albert proved himself to his wife and regained his self-esteem. The vehicle for this rejuvenation was Mammoth Cave in Kentucky. Mary Blair's unmarried uncle, John Croghan, had willed the cave to the children of his siblings. The Jesup sisters, Mary Blair, Lucy Sitgreaves, Juliet Jesup, and Jane Nicholson, represented two-thirds of the heirs. For years, the property had simply been something that did not produce much income, but it had caused significant turmoil among family members. In the mid-1890s, arguments among the heirs became more frequent, and by 1900 they were acute. Albert suggested that he visit the cave en route to Washington, "to quietly observe how matters are managed there."[93] He quickly became the one in whom Violet, Mary, Aunt Lucy Sitgreaves, and Aunt Julia Jesup placed their trust. Even his brother Henry recognized that Albert had found an appropriate means to make use of his "acute intellect."[94] By spending considerable time going over cave financial records and observing the operation, Albert was able to give them sound and honest advice.[95] Opposing them were Aunt Jane Nicholson and her husband, Augustus, who was one of the cave trustees.

Violet told Albert she was delighted that the cave provided "a chance to show the family what is in you." While all the family had always liked Albert, Violet was pleased that they now depended on him. "The appreciation is very gratifying to me," she told him. "I am glad to have them all know that you are much more than just agreeable—that you can do."[96] In 1901, Aunt Lucy asked that Albert be appointed a trustee to represent her, and the fight was joined. For three more years the family feuded, until Albert was made a trustee in 1904. Violet considered his final triumph a "great victory," and she was "very proud" of the manner in which he had won control of the cave.[97] At last Albert had regained Violet's esteem, and while she noted, "[He] may not be an affectionate husband to me," she acknowledged with pride, "He has worked splendidly to carry out our will."[98]

Albert threw himself into the cave business with a will, devoting the greatest part of his time to promoting, advertising, improving, and expanding Mammoth Cave. Finally, Albert Janin was a "Manly Achiever." His efforts resulted in larger profits for the heirs than they had ever before received, and Violet was gratified by his achievements.[99] In her eyes, he had proved himself to her and to her family. It was what she had always wanted.

During the last decades of their marriage, their living arrangements did not change; they were still separated most of the time. Spending only brief periods in Washington, Albert worked at the cave, running away periodically for brief visits to New Orleans. When he did come East, he and Violet enjoyed playing croquet with the neighborhood children at the Moorings, taking them to plays, and frolicking with the numerous dogs around the place. In town, they attended together quiet entertainments given by close friends and family, but Albert refused to join Violet in her larger social world.

Neither did Albert's ability to support his wife change. Although his work at the cave produced a significant increase in income for the heirs, it did nothing for his personal economic situation. Meanwhile, through the years, Violet had wisely invested her money in new growth stocks such as electric and telephone companies, gradually building quite a handsome fortune.[100] Lack of money was no longer a problem, and Violet was always generous with her resources, never hinting that she expected anything from her husband. Economic dominance was simply not an issue to her.

Albert and Violet had always enjoyed each other's company, but they continued to live their separate lives, neither interfering with the other. Albert's success with the cave gave a balance to their marriage, and the couple, at long last, found their "angle of repose," as much out of habit as affection. Violet no longer railed against Albert. She continued her busy involvement in society and in patriotic organizations; he maintained his independence, living as he wished, coming to Washington at his pleasure. They were loyal to each other, but neither exercised control or power over the other. They did not "bore each other" and they made "no scandals." They lived, as Violet had said, an "unwedded married life."

On June 6, 1914, Violet's beloved mother, Mary Blair, died. Although it was a shattering blow, she had no time to assuage her grief. In the last days of the month, Violet learned that Albert was seriously ill in Kentucky. Quickly packing her bags, she went to him. Caring for him first at the cave and then for three weeks in a miserably dirty Bowling Green hospital, she tried to convince Albert to return to Washington.

Albert was a most irritable patient, and Violet's attempts to take charge of him revived hints of past quarrels. Central to their argument was Harry Pinson, a cave employee who had worked for Albert for several years. Violet thought Pinson manipulated Albert for his own advantage, kept Violet away from her husband, and prevented her from any conversation with other cave employees. After Violet had overheard Pinson bragging about his influence in cave matters, she tried to warn Albert about this unscrupulous character, but he refused to listen.

Unwilling to take part in an "undignified" harangue, Violet wrote her argument to Albert. Rejecting his claims that she was "silly" and "vindictive" toward Pinson, she charged that he was not "a good reader of character": "This would not be the 1st time you have thought a black crow a swan & lost money by it."[101] She issued an ultimatum; she would leave unless he promised to consult with their physicians at home.

Albert gave in to Violet and returned to Washington. There, the doctors diagnosed that he had a growth in his bladder. His condition required two operations, on July 29 and again on August 13.[102] Albert evidently continued to chafe at Violet's apparent attempt to control him. When he was well enough to travel after his surgery, he did not allow Violet to accompany him on a recuperative trip to Atlantic City even though her favorite cousin, Minna, was vacationing there.[103] Although he never mentioned the incident again, Albert became more distant. His letters in the following years, while congenial, were filled with business matters, and there were few effusive expressions of affection.

Violet, on the other hand, was very lonely. Her mother's death had left a terrible void in her life which could never be filled. At the end of 1914, she despondently wrote in her diary, "My life work is done—I lived for Mother."[104] She plunged ahead in her work for the Colonial Dames, the DAR, the Children of the American Revolution, and her social obligations, but she missed the intimacy that she had always had with her mother. When Albert came to visit, he spent most of the day apart from her, as she described: "He writes in his den or reads till afternoon, then goes for a walk & to the moving picture shows." After dinner, they retired to her library to read and talk. After forty years of a marriage in which she was proud that they did not "meddle" with each other, she was still pleased that he said he looked "forward to the evening all day."[105] Albert never lost his affection for Violet, telling her in the spring of 1923, "The happiest days of my present life are those that I pass at the Moorings when I see you." He could still find the appropriate words to appeal to her: "I have never known or seen any girl or woman who made upon me the slightest impression of the possibility of her being more desirable as a life companion for me than you with your superior charm of body and mind."[106]

In contrast to his, her letters frequently refer to her desire to see him: "I would rather be with you than anyone else in the world."[107] More explicitly, she recognized her dependence on him: "As time goes on we need each other even more, I think. When are you coming?"[108]

Beginning in 1916, Violet expressed a wish to sell the cave so that Albert could be with her all the time. Her loneliness and desire that they be together became frequent themes in her letters. Typical was her plea in 1920: "I want you here at home, we are not so young as we were 40 years ago & we are entitled to see more of each other."[109] As the years passed, her importunings became more regular, but her reason for wanting to bring Albert home changed. According to his doctor, by December 1923, Albert, at age seventy-nine, had "been confined to his room" and was "mentally unfit and wholly incapable mentally of making or entering into any contract or transacting any business at all."[110]

Albert's increasing senility became a heavy burden for Violet. Unable to recognize his disability and unwilling to leave the cave, he had announced his intention to "die in harness."[111] His obstinacy reversed their travel patterns, and Violet began making frequent trips to Kentucky. In addition to caring for him, she began to handle most of the business affairs of the cave. Harsh winter weather and rather primitive living conditions were particularly hard on the seventy-five-year-old Violet. Moreover, Albert's increasing irascibility made it impossible for her to remain with him. Upon leaving Kentucky in February 1924, she wrote him that although she thought she had "been very badly treated," she understood his illness and asserted that "no rudeness, unkindness or profanity to me matters."[112]

Despite his ill treatment of her, Violet returned to Mammoth Cave in June and remained with her husband into the fall. In the following years, she adopted the practice of spending the months of mild weather, the cave's most active season, in Kentucky and returning to Washington during the winter. In addition, she made shorter visits to Albert in early spring and late fall.[113]

When Violet was in Washington, a variety of cave employees looked after Albert, sending her frequent health bulletins.[114] By 1925, Albert had become a very difficult patient, causing his caretaker to write to Violet: "he is getting So bad that we can't do anything with him at all. There will have to be something done. I have done all I can do. he just raves all night. he will not listen to what we tell him. In fact he will not let us do anything for him."[115] It was not until the fall of 1927 that Violet was able to move Albert to Washington where she loyally and tenderly cared for him until his death on May 29, 1928.[116]

After Albert's death, Violet completed arrangements to sell to the United States government her family's interest in Mammoth Cave. On December 31, 1928, the transaction was completed for the sum of $446,000.[117] Freed of that burden and without any financial worries, she continued her work for her patriotic societies, finally retiring in 1932 as president of the District of Columbia chapter of the Colonial Dames but remaining active as president emeritus. In 1923, she had resigned as treasurer of the National Society of Children of the American Revolution but had immediately become vice president of the organization.[118] In the 1920s, Violet had begun to turn over various assets to the Washington National Cathedral to provide for the construction of a library. Although the Mary Jesup Blair Memorial Library was opened in 1927, it was not until 1931 that it was officially dedicated.[119]

After 1915, Violet no longer kept long, detailed diaries; instead she used small pocket diaries in which she made short notes. None exist after 1927. Perhaps she felt she no longer needed that outlet for her feelings. She was financially secure. Approaching eighty, she had outlived her mother, sister, and brother. After Albert's death, she was alone, and there was no one left whom she wished to control. Although her younger relatives, along with her social and patriotic friends, were important to Violet, the center of her life was gone. Her health began to fail, and on January 14, 1933, she died at her home on Lafayette Square.[120]

Epilogue

In her first diary entry in 1893, Violet concluded: "I will probably go on mentally & morally as I have done—not very bad & not very good—just about the average Christian woman's life, when in the fashionable swim." While the statement exhibited her accustomed manner of judging with an air of dogmatic finality, it also contained a good deal of truth. Violet's lifelong struggle to maintain autonomy represented "the average Christian woman's life," unusual only in its extravagance. Many women were able to choose their husbands; few, probably, turned down twelve proposals. Many struggled with financial difficulties and impecunious mates; some, certainly, had to support their husbands. Many couples lived apart for a good deal of their marriage; few left such an extensive record. Many tried to exercise control over their husbands; few struggled so diligently. Perhaps Violet's marriage was, after all, a common story writ large.

Her experience in love and marriage points out the need to redefine the concept of the southern belle. The stereotypical belle was a beautiful, frivolous flirt with no more substantial thought than what to wear to the next party. Received wisdom proclaimed that after marriage, the irresponsible coquette suddenly became a lady—a plantation mistress or a self-sacrificing worker for benevolent causes. Simplistic and superficial, this vision of southern womanhood failed to explain how such a dramatic transformation took place.

One answer lies in the interpretation of the belle. While southern girls were flirtatious and could be manipulative, they also understood and used power. Subordinated to men by laws, religion, family, and the customs of marriage, they knew that their belle years presented them with a temporary opportunity to reverse the flow of authority. They realized the high stakes involved in choosing a husband and considered their decision a serious matter. They learned the subtle art of influencing decisions without directly challenging male authority; they exercised power without seeming to dominate. As Violet told Albert, "I love power but do not care for the appearance of it" (June 10, 1905). Organizing teas and balls might appear inconsequential, but it required organizational and administrative skills, along with hard work. Generally close to their mothers, belles learned appropriate tactics through observation and shared tasks. Knowing that social mores constricted women's lives, they imaginatively found ways to expand their sphere. The southern belle was not simply a passive victim of her life. She did not suddenly become a southern lady, magically endowed with the requisite skills necessary to run a plantation household, manage a large family, organize an orphanage, or establish a Sunday school. Recognizing the cultural limitations placed on women, she resourcefully developed means to express her individuality and to establish her own sense of self, however limited that might have been. Her belle years were her testing ground, a period in which she discovered the ways and means of exercising power and the extent of her own desire to do so. Many were content with their prescribed role in marriage; few refused, as absolutely as Violet did, to compromise their aspirations. Nevertheless, Violet provides a prototype for defining the southern belle.

Violet never relinquished the prerogatives of a belle. She had developed a taste for power in those heady days of courtship and refused to settle into the expected role of subordination. Having been Washington's most popular belle, with the authority to rule over men, she was determined to retain control of her life. Within her own family, she found role models of independent women. Although most of them accepted patriarchal organization (however companionate their marriages), they were strong-minded women accustomed to voicing their opinions and influencing their families' lives.

The most forceful model for Violet was her mother, who consistently refused help from her male relatives. That she never remarried after being widowed at age twenty-seven was a strong statement to her daughter that men were not particularly necessary. Mary Blair's self-sacrifice for her children and her indulgence of them was a potent example of true womanhood and bound Violet to her in an intense web of devotion and duty. With an erratic sister and inconsequential brother, Violet assumed the role of dutiful daughter, her mother's protector and staunchest supporter. And Mary encouraged that fealty. There is absolutely no evidence that Mary ever objected to Violet's imperious ways when she was a belle or that she disapproved in any way of her daughter's dalliance with Lippe-Weissenfeld. Their only serious disagreement came over the annual move to the country to escape the heat and humidity of Washington. Violet hated it. But because her mother desired it, she bowed to her wishes and lived at the Moorings every summer. Both women nourished that dependency and found their emotional support in each other. As the years passed and Violet's marriage failed, neither really needed anyone else, although Violet never abandoned her love for or loyalty to Albert.

As essential as her mother was to her, Violet's marriage was central to her life. It dominated her thoughts and feelings and shaped her adult life. Until the end of her life, she thought her greatest failure had been her marriage. Extremely sensitive to the conventions of society, she sought marriage, albeit on her own terms, as the natural destiny of a woman. She could have chosen to remain single, but she did not. Social convention expected women to marry, and Violet was too much the traditionalist to ignore cultural standards. The ideology of domesticity was not, however, so strong that women did not deviate from the ideal, and Violet's personal resolution of the pull between perfection and actuality was to marry Albert. With him, she thought she could embody true womanhood and keep her independence.

When her relationship with Albert did not develop as she thought it should, she created a separate life in which she found a degree of fulfillment. Beyond her social obligations in Washington society, which kept alive her days as a belle, Violet gave time to traditional benevolent organizations. Although she had supported the woman suffrage movement in the 1870s and 1880s, she did not take an active, public role. Hers was a feminism played out on a private stage. And when immigrants from southern and eastern Europe inundated the country, she was willing to reject suffrage for herself in order to deny it to new citizens.

In the closing decade of the nineteenth century, as the size of government grew and parvenus began to supplant the resident elite, Violet fought a rear-guard action to stanch the tides of change. She understood that if her class was no longer preeminent, then her own importance was diminished: the prestige of her family, her reign as a belle, and much of what she deemed significant was lost. Having failed in marriage, the core of a woman's life, Violet directed her energies to saving her country through her involvement in patriotic organizations, shoring up her social class by insisting upon the exclusiveness of the Cave Dwellers, and caring for her mother, her most enduring emotional attachment.

Sadly, Violet got what she wanted: autonomy. In the process, she lost domination of and intimacy with her partner. Strong, willful, intelligent, loyal, generous, and honest, Violet Blair Janin enriches our understanding of what it was like to be a woman in the nineteenth century.

Notes

Introduction

1. Barbara Welter was the first to explore the prescriptive literature which defined what it meant to be a "true woman" in the nineteenth century. Whether women actually lived up to the vision of perfect womanhood is not as important as the existence of the ideal in the minds of many. See Barbara Welter, "The Cult of True Womanhood: 1820–1860," *American Quarterly* 18(summer 1966): 151–74. Many have since explored the complex effect of this concept on women, among them are Nancy Cott, *The Bonds of Womanhood: "Woman's Sphere" in New England, 1780–1835* (New Haven: Yale University Press, 1977); Mary Ryan, *Womanhood in America: From Colonial Times to the Present* (New York: Franklin Watts, 1975); Nancy Woloch, *Women and the American Experience,* 2nd ed. (New York: McGraw-Hill, 1994); Anne Firor Scott, *The Southern Lady: From Pedestal to Politics, 1830–1930* (Chicago: University of Chicago Press, 1970); and Margaret Ripley Wolfe, *Daughters of Canaan: A Saga of Southern Women* (Lexington: University Press of Kentucky, 1995).

2. Kathryn Allamong Jacob, "High Society in Washington during the Gilded Age: Three Distinct Aristocracies" (Ph.D. diss., Johns Hopkins University, 1986), 305.

3. In her study of Victorian romantic love, Karen Lystra allots "considerable economic power" to Albert. Her study concentrates on their courtship and does not follow the couple throughout their marriage. Karen Lystra, *Searching the Heart: Women, Men, and Romantic Love in Nineteenth-Century America* (New York: Oxford University Press, 1989), 233.

4. Margo Culley, ed., *A Day at a Time: The Diary Literature of American Women from 1764 to the Present* (New York: The Feminist Press, 1985), 8. On the role of diaries in women's lives, see also, Jane Hunter, "Inscribing the Self in the Heart of the Family: Diaries and Girlhood in Late-Victorian America," *American Quarterly* 44(March 1992): 52, 75.

5. Violet Blair to Albert Janin, December 29, 1923, Janin Family Collection, Henry Huntington Library, San Marino, California (cited hereafter as JFC).

6. Joyce Antler, "Feminism as Life-Process: The Life and Career of Lucy Sprague Mitchell," *Feminist Studies* 1(spring 1981): 134.

7. Phyllis Rose, *Parallel Lives: Five Victorian Marriages* (New York: Vintage Books, 1983), 3–9.

8. Anthony Rotundo, "Manhood in America: Middle-Class Masculinity in the Northern United States, 1770–1910" (Ph.D. diss., Brandeis University, 1982), 11.

Chapter 1 Youth

1. Violet Blair Janin Diary (cited hereafter as VBJ Diary), February 21, 1879, Box 27, JFC.

2. Dumas Malone and Allen Johnson, eds., *Dictionary of American Biography*, 22 vols. (New York: Charles Scribner's Sons, 1933–36), 5:62–63; Rev. Henry Griswold Jesup, *Edward Jessup of West Farms, Westchester Co., New York, and His Descendents* (Cambridge: John Wilson and Son, 1887), 148–54; E. B. Smith, *Francis Preston Blair* (New York: The Free Press, 1980), 185–88; William E. Smith, *The Francis Preston Blair Family in Politics*, 2 vols. (New York: Macmillan Co., 1933), 1:208–10; Box 32, JFC.

3. See E. B. Smith, *Blair*, and W. E. Smith, *Blair Family*.

4. Violet was born on August 14, 1848; Jesup, on February 13, 1852; and Lucy James, on December 26, 1853.

5. Elizabeth Blair Lee to Samuel Phillips Lee, May 21, November 15, 1849, Blair-Lee Papers, Princeton University (cited hereafter as BLP).

6. Elizabeth Blair Lee to S. P. Lee, June 19, 1849, BLP.

7. James Blair to Mary Blair, March 31, 1850, Papers of the Blair Family, Library of Congress (cited hereafter as LC).

8. James Blair to Francis Preston Blair, April 10, 1849, Papers of the Blair Family, LC.

9. Elizabeth Blair Lee to S. P. Lee, October 3, 6, 1849, BLP.

10. James Blair to Mary Blair, March 31, 1850, Papers of the Blair Family, LC.

11. Elizabeth Blair Lee to S. P. Lee, June 8, September 8, 12, 1850, BLP.

12. Ibid., September 29, October 7, 1850; Pamela Herr, *Jessie Fremont: A Biography* (New York: Franklin Watts, 1987), 218–19.

13. Mary Blair to Elizabeth Blair Lee, May 15, August 1, 1851, November 30, [1851], BLP.

14. Ibid., August 29, 1852; Elizabeth Blair Lee to S. P. Lee, January 2, 1852, BLP; James Blair to Francis Preston Blair, November 15, 1852, Papers of the Blair Family, LC.

15. E. B. Smith, *Blair*, 187. Lucy James Blair was born on December 26, 1853.

16. VBJ Diary, November 12, 1864, JFC. Although Violet felt she was the favorite, she had been replaced in her grandfather's affections by his daughter's son, Francis Preston Blair Lee.

17. Bessie Campbell Lester to Violet Blair Janin, Christmas Eve, 1916, Box 35, JFC.

18. VBJ Diary, November 12, 1864, JFC.

19. Ibid.

20. Elizabeth Blair Lee to S. P. Lee, August 19, 21, 27, 1861, BLP.

21. Ibid., October 3, 7, 1861; May 1, 3, June 23, October 22, November 28, 1862; Mary Blair to My dear Sister, May 18, [1862], Papers of the Blair Family, LC.

22. VBJ Diary, January 9, 1865; *Washington Star*, John Clagett Proctor articles, July 25, 1945, October 25, 1942, January 5, 1936; Minna Blair to Violet Blair at Bethlehem, undated, Box 49, JFC.

23. VBJ Diary, August 28, December 3, 1865, JFC.

24. Ibid., December 28, 1864.

25. Ibid., November 12, 1864, June 8, 1865. Minna's birthday was May 28, 1850. For a solid interpretation of nineteenth-century female friendships, see Carroll Smith-Rosenberg, "The Female World of Love and Ritual: Relations between Women in Nineteenth-Century America," in Smith-Rosenberg, *Disorderly Conduct: Visions of Gender in Victorian America* (New York: Oxford University Press, 1985), 53–76.

26. Minna Blair to Violet Blair, undated, Box 49, JFC.

27. Ibid., undated, probably 1868 or 1869.

28. VBJ Diary, December 28, 1864, JFC.

29. Ibid., January 9, 1865. In 1915, Violet added this bemused notation: "Indigestion or pious books?"

30. Eliphalet Nott Potter, son of Episcopal bishop Alonzo Potter, moved from his Bethlehem position in 1869 to become associate rector at St. Paul's in Troy, New York. In 1871 he assumed the position of president of Union College, and in 1884, after refusing the bishopric of Nebraska, became president of Hobart College. See James Grant Wilson and John Fiske, eds., *Appleton's Cyclopedia of American Biography* (New York: D. Appleton and Co., 1888), 5:87.

31. VBJ Diary, April 12, 1865, JFC.

32. Elizabeth Blair Lee to S. P. Lee, February 17, 1865, BLP.

33. VBJ Diary, July 3, 1865, JFC.

34. Frank Robinson, born in 1841, joined the U.S. Volunteers in 1865, serving with the U.S.C.T. Mustered out at the end of 1867, he rejoined in 1868, retiring in 1905 as a brigadier-general. He did not marry until he was fifty years old. See *National Cyclopedia of American Biography* (New York: James T. White and Co., 1932), 22:401.

35. VBJ Diary, April 22, June 3, June 8, June 22, July 3, 1865, JFC.

36. Ibid., June 3, 1865.

37. Ibid., September 28, 1865.

38. Andrew Blair, born in the same year as Violet, 1848, was her uncle Frank's eldest son. Their aunt Elizabeth Blair Lee had already noticed the beginnings of their friendship, commenting on July 2, 1864, "[I]t is odd to see with all his boyishness how Violet's beauty attracts him. She is certainly very lovely." See Virginia J. Laas, ed., *Wartime Washington: The Civil War Letters of Elizabeth Blair Lee* (Urbana: University of Illinois Press, 1991), 398.

39. VBJ Diary, January 6, May 5, 1866, JFC.

40. Ibid., March 28, April 6, 14, 1866.

41. Ibid., May 5, 1866.

42. Ibid., May 8, June 21, 1866.

43. Ibid., June 21, 1866.

44. Ibid., August 15, 1866.

45. Ibid., March 25, 1867.

46. Ibid.

47. Ibid.

48. Minna Blair to Violet Blair, undated, Box 49, JFC; VBJ Diary, March 25, 1867, JFC.

49. VBJ Diary, March 25, 1867, JFC.

50. Ibid., August 14, 1867.

51. Ibid., March 25, 1867.

52. Charles Hurd, *Washington Cavalcade* (New York: E. P. Dutton, 1948), 117.

53. Madeleine Vinton Dahlgren, *Etiquette of Social Life in Washington,* 5th ed. (Philadelphia: J. B. Lippincott and Co., 1881), 33.

54. Randolph Keim, *Society in Washington: Its Distinguished Men and Accomplished Women—Established Customs and Notable Events* (Washington, D.C.: Harrisburg, Pa. Publishing Company, 1887), 217.

55. Hurd, *Washington Cavalcade,* 162; Barry Bulkley, *Washington Old and New* (Washington, D.C.: W. F. Roberts Co., 1913).

56. VBJ Diary, April 15, May 8, 1867, JFC.

57. Ibid., April 19, 1867.

58. Ibid., Good Friday night, 1867.

59. Ibid., April 23, 1867.

60. Ibid., April 23, May 4, 7, 11, 1867.

61. David L. Lewis, *District of Columbia: A Bicentennial History* (New York: W. W. Norton; Nashville: American Association for State and Local History, 1976), 83; Hurd, *Washington Cavalcade,* 160; Dahlgren, *Etiquette,* 14, 33.

62. VBJ Diary, February 21, 1879, JFC.

63. Ibid., May 11, 1867.

64. Frank G. Carpenter, *Carp's Washington,* ed. Frances Carpenter (New York: McGraw-Hill, 1960), 92.

65. VBJ Diary, June 21, 1867, JFC.

Chapter 2   A Belle of Washington

1. VBJ Diary, June 21, June 27, August 11, August 17, August 19, 1867, JFC.

2. Ibid., August 14, 1867.

3. Ibid., August 19, 1867.

4. Ibid., April 5, 1884.

5. Ibid., January 9, 1868.

6. Ibid., January 9, 1868.

7. Ibid., January 9, 1868.

8. Ibid., February 1, 1868.

9. Ibid., February 1, 1868.

10. Ibid., February 1, 1868.

11. Ibid., February 3, 1, 1868.

12. Ibid., February 1, 1868.

13. Ibid., March 14, 1868.

14. Kathryn Lee Seidel, *The Southern Belle in the American Novel* (Tampa: University Presses of Florida, 1985), xvi, 8, 61.

15. Anne Firor Scott, *The Southern Lady: From Pedestal to Politics, 1830–1930* (Chicago: University of Chicago Press, 1970), 23.

16. Seidel, *The Southern Belle*, 132. See also Leslie Fiedler, *Love and Death in the American Novel* (New York: Stern and Day, 1966).

17. Christie Anne Farnham, *The Education of the Southern Belle: Higher Education and Student Socialization in the Antebellum South* (New York: New York University Press, 1994), 180.

18. VBJ Diary, March 14, 1868, JFC.

19. Ibid., April 2, 1868.

20. Ibid., January 9, 1868.

21. Ibid., January 9, 1868.

22. Ibid., March 14, 1868.

23. Ibid., March 23, 1868.

24. Ibid., May 2, 1868.

25. Ibid., March 23, 28, April 2, May 2, 1868.

26. Ibid., May 25, 1868.

27. Ibid., September 22, 1868; Jesup Blair to Violet Blair, June 4, 1869, Box 3, JFC.

28. Carl Degler, *At Odds: Women and the Family in America from the Revolution to the Present* (New York: Oxford University Press, 1980), 8–9.

29. Ibid., 73–74; Mary P. Ryan, "American Society and the Cult of Domesticity, 1830–1860," (Ph.D. diss., University of California, Santa Barbara, 1971), 86, 250.

30. For a cogent summation of the relationship between mothers and daughters at midcentury, see Linda Rosenweig, *The Anchor of My Life: Middle-Class American Mothers and Daughters, 1880–1920* (New York: New York University Press, 1993), 11–14. See also Jan Lewis, "Mother's Love: The Construction of an Emotion in Nineteenth-Century America," in Andrew E. Barnes and Peter N. Stearns, eds., *Social History and Issues in Human Consciousness: Some Interdisciplinary Connections* (New York: New York University Press, 1989), 209–29.

31. E. B. Smith, *Blair*, 8.

32. VBJ Diary, June 30, 1868, JFC.

33. Ibid., June 30, 1868.

34. Ibid., July 9, 1868. For a description of the walks, grottos, flower and vegetable gardens at Silver Spring, see Gist Blair, "Annals of Silver Spring," *Records of the Columbia Historical Society* 21 (1918): 163–66.

35. VBJ Diary, February 1, May 18, July 1, 9, September 20, October 30, December 13, 1868, JFC.

36. Ibid., September 22, July 14, July 1, October 10, 1868.

37. Ibid., November 12, 13, 1868.

38. Ibid., January 24, 1869, December 13, 1868.

39. Julia Copper to Violet Blair, August 19, 1868, Box 8, JFC.

40. Newspaper cutting dated February 3, 1869, found in VBJ 1864–71 Diary, Box 27, JFC.

41. VBJ Diary, May 18, 1869, JFC.

42. Ibid., December 13, 1868, January 7, 1869.

43. For a gentle poke at Cave Dweller habits, see Marie Columbia, "Washington: Its Cave Dwellers and Its Social Secretaries," *The Delineator* (February 1905): 248–53.

44. VBJ Diary, January 17, 24, 1869, JFC.

45. Ibid., February 25, 1869.

46. Ibid., February 2, 1869.

47. Ibid., February 5, 12, 1869.

48. Ibid., January 24, 1869.

49. Ibid., February 17, 1869.

50. Ibid., February 20, 1869.

51. Ibid., February 20, 27, March 4, 1869.

52. Ibid., March 30, April 1, 1869.

53. The Sisterhood of St. John organized in 1867 and expanded its work to include the founding of the St. John's Hospital for Children in 1870. See Constance M. Green, *The Church on Lafayette Square: A History of St. John's Church, Washington, D.C., 1815–1970* (Washington: Potomac Books, 1970), 43.

54. VBJ Diary, March 8, April 30, May 8, 1869, JFC.

55. Ibid., April 30, 1869.

56. Ibid., May 8, 25, 1869.

57. Ibid., May 18, 1869.

58. Ibid., May 25, June 15, 1869.

59. Ibid., June 15, 1869.

60. Ibid., August 17, September 3, 1869.

61. Ibid., June 15, 1869.

62. Ibid., September 10, 1869.

63. Ibid., September 19, 1869.

64. Ibid., April 30, May 25, 1869.

65. Ibid., May 25, 1869.

66. Mag Zeilin Very to Violet Blair Janin, September 1 [1907], Box 55, JFC.

67. VBJ Diary, January 14, 1870, JFC.

68. Constance Green, *Washington,* 2 vols. (Princeton: Princeton University Press, 1962–63), 2:88.

69. Green, *Washington,* 1:396; Mrs. E. N. Chapin, *American Court Gossip or Life at the National Capitol* (Marshalltown, Iowa: Chapin & Hartwell Bros., 1887), 61. For a definition of elite, see George E. Marcus, "'Elite' as a Concept, Theory, and Research Tradition,"

in George E. Marcus, ed., *Elites: Ethnographic Issues* (Albuquerque: University of New Mexico Press, 1983), 7–28.

70. Green, *Washington*, 1:376; Chapin, *American Court Gossip*, 61.

71. Elden E. Billings, "Social and Economic Life in Washington in the 1890's," in *Records of the Columbia Historical Society of Washington, D.C., 1966–1968*, ed. Francis Coleman Rosenburg (Washington, D.C.: The Society, 1969), 170.

72. "The New Washington," *Century Magazine* (March 1884), reprinted in Frank Oppel and Tony Meisel, eds., *Washington, D.C., A Turn of the Century Treasury* (Secaucus, N.J.: Castle, a division of Book Sales, 1987), 131.

73. Jeanie Gould Lincoln, *Her Washington Season* (Boston: James R. Osgood and Co., 1884), 45; Jacob, "High Society in Washington," 287–89. See also, for examples of Violet's participation, VBJ Diary, December 29, 1868, January 29, 1869, JFC.

74. VBJ Diary, January 8, February 26, March 8, 12, April 1, 18, 1870, JFC.

75. James O'Kane to Violet Blair, May 12, 1870, Box 46, JFC.

76. Louis Kingsley to Violet Blair, May 2, 1870, Box 33, JFC.

77. VBJ Diary, April 25, 30, May 14, 30, September 24, 1870, JFC.

78. W. H. Emory to Violet Blair, undated, Box 11, JFC.

79. VBJ Diary, January 8, March 12, 1870, JFC.

80. Ibid., March 8, 1870.

81. Ibid., January 14, 1870.

82. Ibid., October 3, 1870.

83. Ibid., September 24, 1870.

84. Ibid., March 12, June 30, 1870.

85. Ibid., August 6, October 29, 1870.

86. Ibid., September 24, October 25, 1870.

87. Ibid., December 10, 1870.

Chapter 3 Courtship

1. VBJ Diary, January 26, 28, 30, 31, 1871, JFC.

2. Ibid., March 28, 1871.

3. Ibid., March 28, 1871.

4. Ibid., March 4, 1871.

5. Ibid., March 30, 1871.

6. Ellen Rothman, *Hands and Hearts: A History of Courtship in America* (New York: Basic Books, 1984), 200.

7. Violet Blair (or Violet Blair Janin, cited hereafter as Violet) to Albert Covington Janin (cited hereafter as Albert), January 31, [1871], Box 22, JFC; VBJ Diary, May 1, 1871, Box 27, JFC; Violet to Albert, January 26, [1872], March 23, [1872], Box 22, JFC.

8. VBJ Diary, March 28, 1871, JFC.

9. Ibid., April 15, 1871.

10. Jesup Blair to Violet, from South Boston, undated, Blair-Janin Papers, Historical Society of Washington, D.C. (hereafter cited as HS-W).

11. Academie de Paris, Universite de France to Albert C. Janin, admitting Albert to take the baccalaureate examinations, April 1862, Box 11, JFC; on his return to America, Albert to Juliet C. Janin, June 5, 1863, Box 15, JFC.

12. "Reminiscences of My School Life in Germany," Albert C. Janin, Box 18, JFC.

13. "A Sketch of Early Life of Louis Alexander Janin" and "A Biography of Louis A. Janin," both by Juliet Covington Janin, Box 20, JFC; Charles Baldwin, *Baldwin Genealogical Supplement* (Cleveland, Ohio: Leader Print Co., 1889), 1056; "Louis Janin," *National Cyclopedia of American Biography* (New York: James T. White and Co., 1922), 18:11–12; obituary of Henry Janin, Box 20, JFC. See also Clark C. Spence, *Mining Engineers and the American West: The Lace-Boot Brigade, 1849–1933* (Moscow, Idaho: University of Idaho Press, 1993, originally published 1970).

14. VBJ Diary, May 13, 1871, JFC.

15. Ibid., October 27, 1871.

16. Ibid.

17. Ibid., June 3, 1871.

18. Ibid., July 15, 1871.

19. Ibid., October 18, 1871; Minna Blair to Violet, December 25, [1871], Box 49; James O'Kane to Violet, November 7, 1871, Box 46, JFC.

20. Albert to Violet, November 6, 1871, Box 15, JFC.

21. Ibid.

22. Minna Blair to Violet, November 8, [1871], JFC. Albert gave his surname its proper French pronunciation which reminded Minna of "Jane Ann."

23. Violet to Albert, November 10, 1871, JFC.

24. Ibid., November 18, [1871].

25. Albert to Violet, November 6, 1871, JFC.

26. Violet to Albert, November 25, 1871, JFC.

27. In her study of courtship, Ellen Rothman found that couples believed that honesty was "the key to a successful courtship and a happy marriage," in *Hands and Hearts,* 108–14. Although Rothman accepts the idea of separate spheres, she thinks that Caroll Smith-Rosenberg had overemphasized the degree of separateness. Rothman asserts that by a woman's early twenties, she had been exposed to male society and was able to develop emotional attachments with them. See her note on p. 333. For Carroll Smith-Rosenberg's interpretation, see her essay "The Female World of Love and Ritual: Relations between Women in Nineteenth-Century America," in *Disorderly Conduct: Visions of Gender in Victorian America* (New York: Oxford University Press, 1985), 53–76.

28. Violet to Albert, November 18, 1871, JFC.

29. Albert to Violet, December 7, 1871, JFC.

30. Ibid., December 8, 1871.

31. Karen Lystra, *Searching the Heart: Women, Men, and Romantic Love in Nineteenth-Century America* (New York: Oxford University Press, 1989), 9–10.

32. Ibid., 166.

33. Albert to Violet, November 23, 1871, JFC.

34. Violet to Albert, November 18, 1871, September 9, 1873, November 25, December 13, 1871, Ash Wednesday, 1872, JFC.

35. Ibid., November 21, 1871, January 18, 26, February 1, 26, March 16, 1872.

36. Ibid., St. Stephens Day, [December 26], 1871.

37. Ibid., December 11, 1871.

38. Rothman, *Hands and Hearts,* 162–63.

39. James O'Kane to Violet, January 20, 1874, Box 46, JFC.

40. Albert to Violet, February 4, 1872, JFC.

41. Ibid., February 8, 1872.

42. Violet to Albert, January 2, 1872, JFC.

43. Albert to Violet, February 11, 1872, JFC.

44. Violet to Albert, February 1, 1872, JFC.

45. Albert to Violet, February 22, 1872, JFC.

46. Minna Blair to Violet, February 26, [1872], JFC.

47. Ibid., March 17, [1872].

48. Violet to Albert, March 16, 1872, JFC.

49. Lystra, *Searching the Heart,* 38, 41.

50. Violet to Albert, December 11, 1871, JFC.

51. Ibid., March 1, [1873].

52. Albert to Violet, November 27, 1871, JFC.

53. Ibid., November 23, 1871.

54. Violet to Albert, November 30, 1871, JFC.

55. Albert to Juliet C. Janin, June 17, 27, 1872, Box 15, JFC.

56. Albert to Violet, April 4, 1923, Blair-Janin Papers, HS-W.

57. Box 22, JFC.

58. Minna Blair to Violet, August 26, [1872], JFC.

59. Elizabeth Blair Lee to S. P. Lee, October 16, 1872, BLP.

60. Ibid., October 20, May 23, 1872, BLP.

61. Katherine Ramsay Hill to Violet, February 1, 1874, Box 13, JFC.

62. Violet to Albert, November 9, 1872, JFC.

63. Albert to Violet, November 13, 1872, JFC.

64. Ibid., November 15, 1872.

65. Violet to Albert, September 13, November 15, [1873], JFC.

66. Nancy Cott, *The Bonds of Womanhood: Woman's Sphere in New England, 1780–1835* (New Haven: Yale University Press, 1977), 80.

67. Ellen K. Rothman, "'Intimate Acquaintance': Courtship and the Transition to Marriage in America, 1770–1900" (Ph.D. diss., Brandeis University, 1981), 229.

68. Rothman, *Hands and Hearts,* 157.

69. Degler, *At Odds,* 161–62; Rothman, "Intimate Acquaintance," 230.

70. Lystra, *Searching the Heart,* 233–35. Lystra points out that even though Violet's case is an extreme one in her conscious recognition of power, many Victorian women did not subscribe wholly to the theory of patriarchal authority.

71. Violet to Albert, January 26, 1872, November 25, 1871, JFC.

72. Ibid., April 17, [1874].

73. Ibid., March 9, [1874]

74. Ibid., February 26, 1872.

75. Albert to Violet, March 1, 1874, JFC.

76. Albert to Juliet C. Janin, June 3, 1863, JFC; quotation in June 5, 1863, Box 15, JFC.

77. Albert to Violet, December 6, 1873, JFC; Violet to Albert, November 20, [1873], JFC.

78. Albert to Violet, March 10, 1874, JFC.

79. Violet to Albert, April 9, 1874, JFC.

80. Mary Blair to Violet, May 18, 1874, Blair-Janin Papers, HS-W.

81. Ibid., March 26, [1874].

82. Ibid., November 16, [1872].

83. Ibid., March 17, 10, [1874].

84. Albert to Violet, March 17, 1874, JFC.

85. Ibid., April 9, 1874.

86. Violet to Albert, April 9, [1874], JFC.

87. Albert to Violet, April 16, 1874, JFC.

88. Violet to Albert, April 9, 22, [1874], JFC.

89. Albert to Violet, April 26, 1874, JFC.

90. Minna Blair to Violet, Wednesday, [May 20, 1874], Box 49, JFC; regarding wedding invitations, Violet to Albert, May 8, 1874; regarding the minister, Violet to Albert, October 23, [1873]; their wedding invitation, in Box 30, JFC.

91. Lystra, *Searching the Heart,* 235.

92. Nancy M. Theriot, *Mothers and Daughters in Nineteenth-Century America: The Biosocial Construction of Femininity* (Lexington: University Press of Kentucky, 1996), 30–31.

Chapter 4   A Bride

1. Mary Blair to Violet, May 19, 1874, Blair-Janin Papers, HS-W; Violet to Mary Blair, May 15, 19, 18, 28, 21, 1874, Box 22, JFC.

2. Nancy M. Theriot, *Mothers and Daughters in Nineteenth-Century America: The Biosocial Construction of Femininity* (Lexington: University Press of Kentucky, 1996), 64.

3. VBJ Diary, June 10, 1885, JFC.

4. Ibid., December 8, 1888.

5. Ibid., May 11, 1901.

6. Linda Rosenweig, *The Anchor of My Life: Middle-Class American Mothers and Daughters, 1880–1920* (New York: New York University Press, 1993), 22–25, 82–90.

7. Albert to Violet, April 28, 1874, JFC.

8. Violet to Albert, August 15, [1874], JFC.

9. Ibid., August 26, [1874].

10. Albert to Violet, July 6, 1874, JFC. On the Reconstruction period in Louisiana, see Joe Gray Taylor, *Louisiana Reconstructed: 1863–1877* (Baton Rouge: Louisiana State University Press, 1974); William Gillette, *Retreat from Reconstruction, 1869–1879* (Baton Rouge: Louisiana State University Press, 1979); Joy Jackson, *New Orleans in the Gilded Age: Politics and Urban Progress, 1800–1896* (Baton Rouge: Louisiana State University Press, 1979); Ella Lonn, *Reconstruction in Louisiana after 1868* (New York: G. P. Putnam's Sons, 1918); and Garnie W. McGinty, *Louisiana Redeemed: The Overthrow of Carpet-bag Rule, 1876–1880* (New Orleans: Pelican Publishing Co., 1941).

11. Anthony Rotundo, "Manhood in America: The Northern Middle Class, 1770–1920" (Ph.D. diss., Brandeis University, 1982). Rotundo defines gender ideal as "a *cluster* of traits, behaviors, and values that the members of a society believe a man (or a woman) should have." Although his study deals with northern, middle-class men, Rotundo points out the pervasiveness of middle-class ideals throughout society. Albert Janin's attitudes may be an indication of the nationwide applicability of the values found by Rotundo.

12. Among the many works that have found these qualities in the nineteenth-century ideal of manhood are Anthony Rotundo, *American Manhood: Transformations in Masculinity from the Revolution to the Modern Era* (New York: Basic Books, 1993); David G. Pugh, *Sons of Liberty: The Masculine Mind in Nineteenth-Century America* (Westport, Conn.: Greenwood Press, 1983); Michael Gordon, "The Ideal Husband as Depicted in the Nineteenth-Century Marriage Manual," in Elizabeth Pleck and Joseph Pleck, eds., *The American Man* (Englewood Cliffs, N.J.: Prentice Hall, 1980), 145–57; Michael Grossbert, "Institutionalizing Masculinity: The Law as a Masculine Profession," in Mark C. Carnes and Clyde Griffen, eds., *Meanings for Manhood: Constructions of Masculinity in Victorian America* (Chicago: University of Chicago Press, 1990), 133–51; Elaine Tyler May, *Great Expectations: Marriage and Divorce in Post-Victorian America* (Chicago: University of Chicago Press, 1980); Peter G. Filene, *Him/Her/Self: Sex Roles in Modern America,* 2nd ed. (Baltimore: Johns Hopkins University Press, 1986); Anthony Rotundo, "Learning about Manhood: Gender Ideals and the Middle-Class Family in Nineteenth-Century America," in J. A. Mangan and James Walvin, eds., *Manliness and Morality: Middle-Class Masculinity in Britain and America, 1800–1940* (New York: St. Martin's Press, 1987); and John Demos, "Images of the Family, Then and Now," in Demos, *Past, Present, and Personal: The Family and the Life Course in American History* (New York: Oxford University Press, 1986), 24–40.

13. Albert to Eugene Janin, August 28, 1854, Box 15, JFC.

14. Albert to Juliet C. Janin, December 18, 1859, JFC.

15. Ibid., January 5, 1861.

16. Violet to Albert, July 9, [1874], JFC.

17. Ibid., August 4, [1874].

18. VBJ Diary, August 28, 1884, JFC.

19. Violet to Albert, August 12, [1874], JFC.

20. Ibid., August 13, [1874].

21. Ibid., June 29, [1874].

22. Lystra, *Searching the Heart,* 234.

23. Albert to Violet, July 6, 1874, JFC.

24. Violet to Albert, July 17, [1874], JFC.

25. Ibid., August 26, [1874].

26. Albert to Violet, September 1, 1874, JFC.

27. Ibid., September 4, 1874.

28. Minna Blair to Violet, Saturday, [August] 29, [1874], JFC.

29. Violet to Albert, October 17, [1874], JFC.

30. Ibid., July 9, August 19, [1874].

31. For a solid overview of the history of homeopathy in the United States, see Martin Kaufman, *Homeopathy in America: The Rise and Fall of a Medical Heresy* (Baltimore: The Johns Hopkins Press, 1971). See also Anita Clair Fellman and Michael Fellman, *Making Sense of Self: Medical Advice Literature in Late Nineteenth-Century America* (Philadelphia: University of Pennsylvania Press, 1981).

32. See "Tullio Suzzara Verdi," in *Appleton's Cyclopedia,* ed. Wilson and Fiske, 6:278.

33. Violet to Albert, November 7, [1874], JFC.

34. Jane Stephens, "Breezes of Discontent: A Historical Perspective of Anxiety Based Illnesses Among Women," *Journal of American Culture* 8 (winter 1985): 5. See also Ann Douglas Wood, "'The Fashionable Diseases': Women's Complaints and Their Treatment in Nineteenth-Century America," in *Women and Health in America: Historical Readings,* ed. Judith Walzer Leavitt, (Madison: University of Wisconsin Press, 1984), 222–38.

35. Violet to Albert, November 19, [1874], JFC. See also her letters of November 10 and 16, [1874]. For a brief synopsis of some of the common treatments used by allopaths before 1880, see Roderick E. McGrew, *Encyclopedia of Medical History* (New York: McGraw Hill, 1985), 124–25. For descriptions of homeopathic treatment of women's medical difficulties, see James Compton Burnett, *Organ Diseases of Women, Notably Enlargements and Displacements of the Uterus, and Sterility, Considered as Curable by Medicines* (London: The Homeopathic Publishing Company, 1896); Henry N. Guernsey, *The Application of the Principles and Practice of Homeopathy to Obstetrics and the Disorders Peculiar to Women and Young Children* (Philadelphia: F. E. Boericke, Hahnemann Publishing House, 1886); and Morton Monroe Eaton, *A Treatise on the Medical and Surgical Diseases of Women and Their Homeopathic Treatment* (New York: Boericke and Tafel, 1880).

36. Violet to Albert, November 21, [1874], JFC.

37. Albert to Violet, November 15, 1874, JFC.

38. Ibid., November 19, 1874.

39. Violet to Albert, November 23, [1874], JFC.

40. Violet to Mary Blair, November 24, [1874], JFC.

41. Albert to Violet, November 28, 1874, JFC.

42. Ibid., March 15, 1875.

43. Violet to Albert, March 11, [1875], JFC.

44. Ibid., August 22, [1875].

45. Violet to Albert, March 15, [1875], JFC.

46. Albert to Violet, March 18, 1875, JFC.

47. Ibid., March 20, 1875.

48. Ibid., November 24, 1875. See also her indirect reference to condoms ("[W]ould it be possible for you to find something you told me about?") in Violet to Albert, November 26, [1874], JFC.

49. For a discussion of the various techniques, appliances, chemicals, and methods of birth control, see Janet Farrell Brodie, "Family Limitation in American Culture, 1830–1900" (Ph.D. diss., University of Chicago, 1982), and Michael La Sorte, "Nineteenth Century Family Planning Practices," *Journal of Psychohistory* 4 (fall 1976): 163–83. See also, Degler, *At Odds,* 224, and John De'Emilio and Estelle Freedman, *Intimate Matters: A History of Sexuality in America* (New York: Harper and Row, 1988), 59–60; on the use of condoms, see Peter Gay, *The Bourgeois Experience: Victoria to Freud,* vol. 1, *Education of the Senses* (New York: Oxford University Press, 1984), 256–57. In the earlier decades of the nineteenth century, according to Peter Gay, the French had been the first to accept the practice of birth control: "to judge by the contemporary literature, the French practiced birth control without writing about it; the English and the Americans wrote about it without practicing it." In the last decades of the century, Americans had greatly increased their birth control practices (Gay, *Education of the Senses,* 259).

50. Violet to Albert, January 26, [1875], Box 23, JFC. Colonel Sellers was a character in Mark Twain's and Charles Dudley Warner's 1873 novel *The Gilded Age.* Beriah Sellers, a perennial optimist and gifted talker, always had great schemes and dreams which never resulted in the glorious profits he anticipated.

51. For an account of Albert's Mexican adventure, including an attack by a band of Apaches, see J. Rope Browne, "A Tour Through Arizona," *Harper's New Monthly Magazine* 30, no. 177 (February 1865): 283–93. The episode is also mentioned in Albert to Alexis Janin, February 12, 1865, JFC.

52. Louis A. Janin to Albert, March 13, 1864, Box 20, JFC.

53. Albert to Juliet Janin, March 25, 1864. For his speculations, see Albert to Juliet Janin, October 28, 1863, Box 15, JFC.

54. Albert Janin 1864 Diary, December 31, 1864, Box 62, JFC.

55. Ibid. See for example, the entries of March 26, April 13, 17, May 4, 22, October 10, December 4, 1864.

56. Louis A. Janin to Juliet C. Janin, July 26, 1866, Box 20, JFC.

57. Albert to Juliet Janin, January 2, 1867, Box 15, JFC.

58. Albert to Violet, May 14, 1894, Blair-Janin Papers, HS-W.

59. Violet to Albert, January 26, [1875], JFC.

60. Ibid., March 26, [1875].

61. Albert to Violet, March 25, 27, 1875, JFC.

62. Ibid., March 30, 1875.

63. Violet to Albert, April 3, [1875], JFC.

64. Albert to Violet, April 8, 1875, JFC.

65. Ibid., April 17, 21, 1875.

66. Ibid., May 26, 1875.

67. Violet to Albert, June 17, [1875], JFC.

68. Ibid., June 24, [1875].

69. Ibid., June 9, 17, [1875].

70. Albert to Violet, June 15, 1875, JFC.

71. Violet to Mary Blair, November 15, [1875], JFC.

72. Ibid., November 16, [1875].

73. Ibid., November 26, [1875].

74. Ibid., April 7, [1875]. Among her friends were her next door neighbors Lise Chalaron and Elise Urquhart.

75. Violet to Mary Blair, April 26, [1876], JFC. See also her letters to her mother of April 5, 7, [1876], and Mary Blair to Violet, April 11, 1876, JFC.

76. Violet to Albert, June 1, [1877], JFC.

77. Albert to Violet, April 19, 1874, JFC.

78. Ibid., January 3, 1876.

79. Violet to Albert, January 15, [1877], May 31, [1877], JFC.

80. Ibid., January 28, [1876].

81. Albert to Violet, January 9, 1876, JFC.

82. Ibid., January 23, 27, 1876.

83. Ibid., July 4, 1876.

84. Ibid., July 29, 1876.

85. Violet to Albert, January 8, June 13, 28, 1876, JFC.

86. Ibid., January 8, [1876].

87. Ibid., June 28, 1876.

88. Ibid., July 31, [1876].

89. For details on its work, see Frank W. Klingberg, *The Southern Claims Commission* (New York: Octagon Books, 1978).

90. Albert to Violet, January 27, 1876, JFC.

91. Ibid., July 12, 1877.

92. Ibid., February 1, 1877.

93. Violet to Albert, February 9, [1877], JFC. Good to his word, he did indeed repay the note promptly. Albert to Mary Blair, March 24, 1877, Box 15, JFC; "James Alden," in *Dictionary of American Biography*, ed. Malone and Johnson, 1:145–46.

94. Albert to Violet, February 8, 13, 1877, JFC.

95. Violet to Albert, February 17, [1877], JFC.

96. Albert to Violet, May 30, 1877, JFC.

97. Taylor, *Louisiana Reconstructed,* 355–61.

98. Albert to Violet, June 2, 1877, JFC.

99. Violet to Albert, June 5, 12, [1877], JFC.

100. Ibid., July 14, July 3, [1876].

101. Ibid., May 24, [1877].

102. Albert to Violet, January 18, 1878, Box 16, JFC.

103. Violet to Albert, January 22, [1878], JFC.

104. Ibid., January 25, [1878].

105. Ibid., January 26, [1878].

106. Albert to Violet, January 28, 1878, JFC; Violet to Albert, February 8, [1878], JFC.

107. Violet to Albert, February 15, [1878], JFC. Dr. Verdi had published two works dealing with female health: *Maternity, a Popular Treatise for Young Wives and Mothers* in 1869 and *Mothers and Daughters: Practical Studies for the Conservation of the Health of Girls* in 1877. See "Tullio Suzzara Verdi," in *Appleton's Cyclopedia,* ed. Wilson and Fiske, 6:278.

108. Violet to Albert, February 6, 15, [1878], JFC.

109. Albert to Violet, February 27, 1878, JFC.

110. Violet to Albert, April 10, [1878], JFC.

111. Ibid., April 22, 24, [1878].

112. Albert to Violet, April 8, 1878, JFC.

113. Ibid., April 12, 1878.

114. Violet to Albert, May 3, [1878], JFC; Albert to Violet, May 1, 1878, JFC.

115. Ibid., May 6, [1878].

116. Albert to Violet, May 8, 1878, JFC.

117. Judith Walzer Leavitt and Whitney Walton, "'Down to Death's Door': Women's Perceptions of Childbirth in America," in *Women and Health in America,* ed. Leavitt, 159. See also chapter 3, "Pressures of Reality," in Gay, *Education of the Senses,* 226–77.

118. Violet to Albert, February 6, 11, April 12, [1878], JFC.

119. Albert to Violet, April 19, 22, May 13, 1878, JFC.

120. Ibid., February 13, 1878.

121. Violet to Albert, April 24, [1878], JFC.

122. Ibid., April 2, [1878].

123. Ibid., April 24, [1878].

124. VBJ Diary, January 5, 1878, JFC.

125. Ibid., January 23, 1878.

126. Ibid., March 4, 1878.

127. Ibid., February 7, 13, May 4, 1878.

128. Violet to Albert, May 13, [1878], JFC.

129. Elizabeth Blair Lee to S. P. Lee, May 16, 1878, BLP.

130. VBJ Diary, June 29, 1878, JFC.

131. Ibid.

132. Ibid., July 20, 1878.

Chapter 5 Marital Crisis

1. Violet to Albert, June 25, [1878], JFC.

2. Albert to Violet, June 28, July 19, 1878, JFC.

3. For details on the political strength of the Lottery Company, see Bertold C. Alives, "The History of the Louisiana State Lottery Company," *Louisiana Historical Quarterly* 27 (October 1944): 964–1118, and Richard Wiggins, "The Louisiana Press and the Lottery," *Louisiana Historical Quarterly* 31 (July 1948): 716–844.

4. Violet to Albert, June 29, [1878], JFC.

5. VBJ Diary, September 24, 1878, JFC.

6. Violet to Albert, May 27, [1879], JFC.

7. Albert to Violet, May 28, 1879, from New York, and another dated May 28, 1879, from New Orleans, JFC.

8. VBJ Diary, February 21, 1879, JFC.

9. Ibid., March 6, 1879.

10. Many of the papers detailing Albert's long and complicated financial and legal arrangements over the canal are located in the Blair-Janin Papers, HS-W.

11. Albert to Violet, June 5, 1879, JFC.

12. Ibid., January 9, 1880.

13. Unsigned report to William A. Booth, president of Third National Bank of New York, [1889], Box 18, JFC.

14. Albert to Violet, May 25, 1877, JFC.

15. Albert to Clement Story, March 2, 1898, Blair-Janin Papers, HS-W.

16. VBJ Diary, July 8, 1879, JFC.

17. Major E. A. Burke of New Orleans, with "a company of businessmen," bought the *Democrat*. In 1881, Burke bought the *New Orleans Times* and combined the two as the *Times-Democrat*. See *Biographical and Historical Memoirs of Louisiana . . . ,* 2 vols. (Chicago: The Goodspeed Publishing Co., 1892), 2:164. For the political implications of the sale, see Garnie W. McGinty, *Louisiana Redeemed: The Overthrow of Carpet-bag Rule, 1876–1880* (New Orleans: Pelican Publishing Co., 1941), 189–90. For explanation of the intricacies of speculation in land scrip, see Paul W. Gates, *History of Public Land Law* (Washington, D.C.: Government Publishing Office, 1968).

18. VBJ Diary, April 15, 1880, JFC.

19. Ibid., April 15, 1880.

20. Elizabeth Blair Lee to S. P. Lee, January 17, 1879, BLP.

21. Violet to Albert, February 9, 1880, JFC.

22. Albert to Violet, March 6, 1880, JFC.

23. Violet to Albert, February 23, [1880], JFC.

24. VBJ Diary, April 15, 1880, JFC.

25. Albert to Violet, April 11, 1880, JFC.

26. Violet to Albert, April 13, 1880, JFC.

27. Juliet Janin to Albert, May 29, 1880, Box 20, JFC.

28. Albert to Louis Janin, February 18, 1881, Box 15, JFC.

29. Albert to Violet, May 1, 1880, JFC.

30. Ibid., May 10, 1880.

31. Ibid., May 26, 1880.

32. Albert to Mary Blair, June 11, 1880, JFC.

33. Albert to Violet, June 10, 1880, JFC.

34. Ibid., June 18, 1880.

35. Violet to Albert, June 13, 1880, JFC.

36. Ibid., June 14, [1880].

37. Albert to Violet, June 18, 1880, JFC.

38. John Demos, *Past, Present, and Personal: The Family and the Life Course in American History* (New York: Oxford University Press, 1986), 33. See also, Rotundo, "Manhood in America," 265.

39. VBJ Diary, August 2, 1880, JFC.

40. Violet to Albert, June 22, [1880], JFC.

41. Albert to Mary Blair, June 23, 1880, JFC.

42. Ibid., June 25, 1880.

43. Juliet Janin to Albert, November 27, 1884, Box 20, JFC.

44. Ibid., June 23, [1885?].

45. Ibid., July 14, 1880.

46. Violet to Albert, July 3, [1880], JFC.

47. Ibid., July 31, [1880].

48. VBJ Diary, August 2, 1880, JFC.

49. Albert to Violet, July 29, 1880, JFC.

50. Violet to Albert, August 7, [1880], JFC; VBJ Diary, August 9, 1880, JFC.

51. Ibid., October 26, [1880].

52. Albert to Violet, December 3, 1880, JFC.

53. Violet to Albert, December 8, [1880], JFC.

54. VBJ Diary, August 14, 1880, JFC.

55. Ibid., November 2, 1880.

56. Ibid., August 2, 1880.

57. Violet to Albert, November 15, December 16, [1880], JFC.

58. Ibid., December 3, [1880].

59. Violet to Mary Blair, December 20, 24, 25, 29, 1880, JFC.

60. Violet to Albert, December 25, 1880, JFC.

61. Ibid., January 24, [1881].

62. Albert to Violet, January 6, 1881, JFC.

63. Rothman, *Hands and Hearts,* 98.

64. Violet to Albert, January 31, [1881], JFC.

65. VBJ Diary, May 23, 1881, JFC.

66. Violet to Albert, May 7, 9, [1881], JFC.

67. Ibid., June 4, [1881].

68. Ibid., June 1, [1881].

69. VBJ Diary, July 1, 1881. For her work for Wheeler, see VBJ Diary, November 28, 1882, April 4, 1883, JFC.

70. Violet to Albert, January 8, [1881], JFC.

71. Ibid., June 3, [1881].

72. Albert to Violet, June 6, 1881, JFC.

73. For details on the French and American Claims Commission, see *Rules of the French and American Claims Commission with the Convention Establishing the Commission* (Washington, D.C.: Gibson Brothers Printers, 1880), and *Report of the Secretary of State concerning the Transactions of the French and American Claims Commission,* 48th Cong. 2d sess., House of Representatives Ex. Doc. 235, Serial Set 2305, 2302, and 2306.

74. Violet to Albert, January 15, February 19, [1881], JFC.

75. Ibid., December 8, [1880], August 5, [1881].

76. Albert to Violet, August 20, 1881, JFC.

77. *Report of the Secretary of State* (see note 73 above), 94–96.

78. VBJ Diary, February 2, 1880, JFC.

79. Violet to Albert, June 7, [1881], JFC; Albert to Violet, June 8, 1881, JFC.

80. Albert to Violet, August 27, 1881, JFC.

81. Ibid., January 24, 25, August 28, 1882.

82. Ibid., September 24, 1883.

83. Ibid., September 27, 1883.

84. Ibid., April 2, 1884.

85. Ibid., October 4, 1883.

86. VBJ Diary, January 7, 1882, JFC.

87. Albert to Violet, April 26, 1883, JFC.

88. VBJ Diary May 4, 1883, JFC.

89. Ibid., August 5, 1882.

90. Ibid., September 8, 1882.

91. *New Orleans Times-Democrat,* September 2, 16, 17, 27, 28, 30, 1882.

92. Albert to Violet, October 30, 1882, JFC. See also his letters of September 5, 9, 18, 29, 17, 1882, JFC. Others did not share his optimism. A newspaper cutting entitled "Special to the *Courier Journal* and dated New Orleans, September 6, stated: "His confidence is not shared by those familiar with the district, in which there is a Democratic majority of over 4,000" (inserted in letter, Albert to Juliet Janin, September 9, 1882, Box 15, JFC).

93. VBJ Diary, September 30, 1882, JFC.

94. Ibid., September 30, 1882.

95. Albert to Violet, November 11, 1882, JFC.

96. VBJ Diary, December 9, 1882, JFC.

97. Albert to Violet, October 4, 1883. For examples of his explanations, see letters of April 26, September 17, 24, 27, 1883, JFC.

98. VBJ Diary, January 7, 1882, JFC.

99. Ibid., December 10, 1883.

Chapter 6   Separate Lives

1. VBJ Diary, January 7, 1882, February 8, 1883, JFC. For the role of women's organizations, see Karen J. Blair, *The Clubwoman as Feminist: True Womanhood Redefined, 1868–1914* (New York: Holmes and Meier, 1980), and Anne Firor Scott, *Natural Allies: Women's Associations in American History* (Urbana and Chicago: University of Illinois Press, 1992). See also Theodora Penny Martin, *The Sound of Our Own Voices: Women's Study Clubs, 1860–1910* (Boston: Beacon Press, 1987).

2. The novel was Trenfani's *Cecco d'Ascoli.* See D. Appleton and Company to Violet Blair Janin, May 20, 1882, Box 1, JFC; VBJ Diary, May 29, 1882.

3. VBJ Diary, November 28, 1882, April 4, May 12, 1883, JFC. Concerning payment of $5.85 for translations from German and Dutch, see War Department to Violet, May 8, 1887, Blair-Janin Papers, HS-W.

4. VBJ Diary, April 10, 1883, JFC.

5. Ibid., January 10, 1883.

6. Ibid., February 8, 1883.

7. Ibid., March 7, 1885.

8. Ibid., April 10, 18, 20, 1883.

9. Henry Loomis Nelson, "Washington Society," in Frank Oppel and Tony Meisel, eds., *Washington D.C.: A Turn-of-the-Century Treasury* (Secaucus, N.J.: Castle, 1987), 87.

10. VBJ Diary, March 3, 10, 1884, JFC.

11. Albert to Violet, May 1, 1884, JFC.

12. Violet to Albert, April 14, 29, [1884], JFC.

13. Albert to Violet, May 5, 1884, JFC.

14. Ibid., May 5, 1884.

15. Violet to Albert, April 29, 1884; VBJ diary, June 17, 1883, JFC.

16. VBJ Diary, June 17, 1884, JFC.

17. Violet to Albert, July 10, 15, 1884, JFC.

18. Albert to Violet, May 21, 1884, JFC.

19. Ibid., July 15, 1884.

20. Ibid., July 18, 1884.

21. Ibid., July 22, 1884.

22. VBJ Diary, July 12, 1884, JFC.

23. Ibid., June 17, 1884.

24. Ibid., July 12, 1884.

25. "Dear Pater," December 3, 1882, in *The Letters of Mrs. Henry Adams, 1865–1883,* ed. Ward Thoron (Boston: Little Brown and Co., 1936), 404.

26. Ibid., December 10, 1882, March 25, 1883, 406, 454.

27. VBJ Diary, July 17, 1884, JFC.

28. Ibid., July 18, 1884.

29. Ibid., August 19, 1884.

30. Ibid., August 28, 1884.

31. Ibid., October 8, 1884.

32. Ibid., October 18, 1884.

33. Ibid., December 31, 1884.

34. Violet to Albert, August 18, 1884, JFC.

35. Ibid., September 24, [1884].

36. VBJ Diary, July 8, 1884, JFC.

37. Violet to Albert, October 10, [1884], JFC.

38. Albert to Violet, April 14, 1884, JFC.

39. Ibid., November 3, 1884.

40. VBJ Diary, December 31, 1884, JFC.

41. Ibid., December 18, 1884, May 14, 1885.

42. Ibid., January 30, 1884.

43. Ibid., March 10, 1884.

44. Ibid., January 22, 1885.

45. Ibid., February 26, December 26, 1885.

46. Ibid., December 1, 1884. For discussion of study clubs, see Louise L. Stevenson, *The Victorian Homefront: American Thought and Culture, 1860–1880* (New York: Twayne Publishers, 1991).

47. VBJ Diary, May 25, 1885, JFC.

48. Ibid., March 7, 1885.

49. Lippe-Weissenfeld to Dear Mrs. Blair-Janin, Saturday, Box 35, JFC.

50. Unsigned letter to "Dearest Lady-friend," Thursday, Box 35, JFC.

51. VBJ Diary, March 28, 1885, JFC.

52. Albert to Violet, March 14, 1885, JFC.

53. VBJ Diary, August 13, 1885, JFC.

54. Ibid., August 26, 1885.

55. Albert to Violet, August 14, 1885, JFC.

56. VBJ Diary, September 19, November 12, 1887.

57. Minna Blair to Gist Blair, October 23, 1887, Papers of the Blair Family, LC.

58. VBJ Diary, October 3, 1885, JFC.

59. Ibid., December 14, 1885.

60. Ibid., June 26, 1886. Yet even at the height of her flirtation with Lippe, Violet showed concern for Albert's feelings, writing him in France: "I hope you were happy the few days you spent here. I tried to do what I could to make you so. If I have not done all that I might have done, I hope you will forgive it." She began that letter "My precious old Bert." See Violet to Albert, November 3, [1885], Blair-Janin Papers, HS-W.

61. VBJ Diary, January 9, 1886, JFC.

62. Ibid., February 2, 1886.

63. Ibid., October 18, 1886, January 15, 1887.

64. Ibid., February 28,1887.

65. Ibid., March 14, 1887.

66. Ibid., October 15, 22, 29, 1887.

67. Ibid., November 7, 1887.

68. Ibid., November 12, 1887.

69. Ibid., December 31, 1887.

70. Ibid., January 24, 1887.

71. Minna Blair to Violet, June 24, [1885], Box 49, JFC. Violet took her cousin's advice, as Minna reported to her brother Gist: "Vi's friend the count has gone but she seems to fill his place with plenty of very young, & very old admirers." See Minna Blair to Gist Blair, [November 23, 1887], Papers of the Blair Family, LC.

72. VBJ Diary, January 19, 1889, JFC.

73. Albert to Violet, February 16, 1885, JFC.

74. *New York World,* March 5, 1885.

75. VBJ Diary, March 14, 1885, JFC.

76. Albert to Violet, March 14, 1885, JFC. On one occasion, Violet inadvertently offered the reason for her beauty: "I had a lovely color and my eyes sparkled. I drank off a whole glass of claret just before going there." See Violet to Albert, March 1, [1885], Blair-Janin Papers, HS-W.

77. See, for example, VBJ Diary, January 9, March 31, 1886, JFC.

78. Ibid., February 22, 1888.

79. Ibid., January 15, 1887.

80. Ibid., March 14, 1887.

81. Ibid., January 4, 1887.

82. Ibid., January 24, 1887.

83. Albert to Violet, January 17, 1888, JFC.

84. Ibid., January 28, 1888.

85. VBJ Diary, November 24, December 3, 1886, JFC.

86. Ibid., January 7, 1888.

87. Ibid., February 2, 1889.

88. Ibid., January 14, 1888.

89. Ibid., December 10, 1887, January 21, 1888, March 13, 1889.

90. Ibid., January 26, 1889, May 8, 1888. For Mrs. Cleveland's popularity, see Allan Nevins, *Grover Cleveland: A Study in Courage* (New York: Dodd, Mead, and Co., 1932), 310–15.

91. VBJ Diary, February 9, 1889, JFC.

92. Ibid., February 16, 1889.

93. Ibid., November 30, December 8, 15, 22, 1888.

94. Ibid., February 2, 1889.

95. Ibid., February 9, 1889.

96. Ibid., April 1, 1889.

97. Ibid., March 13, 27, April 1, 1889.

98. Ibid., April 9, 1889.

99. Ibid., May 13, 1889.

100. Albert to Violet, June 2, 1885, JFC.

101. VBJ Diary, May 13, 1889. Kingsbury never did quite recover from his infatuation with Violet. On January 21, 1901, he wrote to her: "I only want you to know that I think of you very often and with the tenderest thoughts in the world. You are the finest woman in all the world to me and I am so sorry I did not know you when we were both young in the Juventus Mundi." See Henry Kingsbury to Violet, Box 33, JFC.

102. VBJ Diary, June 15, 1889, JFC.

103. Ibid., March 19, 1889.

104. Ibid., April 1, 1889.

105. Ibid., April 1, 1889.

106. Ibid., May 2, 1885.

107. Ibid., May 11, 18, 1885.

108. Ibid., March 14, 1887.

109. Ibid., March 14, 1887.

110. Ibid., March 31, 1886.

111. Ibid., January 19, 1889.

112. Minna Blair to Violet, undated, Box 49, JFC.

113. VBJ Diary, January 9, 1886, JFC.

114. Ibid., February 25, 1887.

115. Ibid., March 14, 31, 1887.

116. Ibid., November 12, 1887.

117. Ibid., May 12, 1888.

118. Ibid., April 1, 1889.

119. Ibid., September 2, 1889.

120. Ibid., April 22, June 4, 1892.

121. Ibid., March 23, 1895.

Chapter 7 The Final Years

1. VBJ Diary, May 26, 1894, JFC.

2. Ibid., March 14, 1891.

3. Albert to Violet, August 16, 1890, JFC.

4. Ibid., February 16, 1891. The post office lasted until 1900, when lack of business forced the government to close it. See Albert to Violet, January 4, 1900, JFC.

5. Henry Janin to E. H. Farrar, April 22, 1892, Box 18, JFC. In the prior year, his brothers Louis and Alexis had refused to lend him more money for the canal: "We will not advance any money, and in return are willing to waive all claims." See Louis Janin to Albert, May 18, 1891. Blair-Janin Papers, HS-W.

6. Mary Blair had agreed to Albert's proposition to use more of her bonds in June 1890; instead of returning them as planned, he renewed his note in August 1890 and had never been able to repay his note or restore Mary's bonds to her. See VBJ Diary, June 21, August 23, 1890, JFC.

7. VBJ Diary, January 28, 1893, JFC.

8. Ibid., August 12, 1893.

9. Ibid., January 28, 1893.

10. Ibid., May 14, 1896.

11. Ibid., April 24, 1897, January 21, 1893.

12. Ibid., Christmas, 1896.

13. Ibid., November 12, 1887.

14. Violet to Albert, December 3, [1880], JFC; VBJ Diary, August 14, 1880, JFC.

15. VBJ Diary, July 13, 1886, JFC.

16. Ibid., July 13, 1888, March 9, April 18, 1896.

17. Ibid., November 12, 1897.

18. Ibid., May 8, July 10, 1897, January 15, 1898.

19. Ibid., February 22, December 31, 1890.

20. Ibid., February 18, 1893.

21. Ibid., December 31, 1894.

22. Ibid., January 30, 1892.

23. Ibid., May 14, 1895.

24. Ibid., February 11, 1899.

25. Ibid., May 13, 1899.

26. Ibid., May 18, 1901.

27. Ibid., January 26, November 16, 1901, January 25, 1902.

28. Mary Henry to Violet, September 4, 1892, August 25, 1896, Box 13, JFC.

29. VBJ Diary, March 11, 1893, JFC.

30. Ibid., February 15, 1896.

31. Ibid., February 10, March 25, 1890.

32. James A. Gannon Sr., "Washington at the Turn of the Century," in *Records of the Columbia Historical Society of Washington, D.C., 1963–1965,* ed. Frances Coleman Rosenberg (Washington, D.C.: The Society, 1966), 315. See also, Green, *Washington,* I, 376.

33. Jacob, "High Society in Washington," 268, 300. For a detailed analysis of Washington society at the end of the nineteenth century, see Jacob's chapter 8, "'Dying Snails': The Old Elite Withdraws Into Its Shell," in "High Society in Washington," 267–308. For a complete study of nineteenth-century Washington society, see Kathryn Allamong Jacob, *Capital Elites: High Society in Washington, D.C., after the Civil War* (Washington: Smithsonian Institution Press, 1995). See also, Emily Edson Briggs, *The Olivia Letters: Being Some History of Washington City for Forty Years as Told by the Letters of a Newspaper Correspondent* (New York and Washington: Neale Publishing, 1906), 340; Mark Twain and Charles Dudley Warner, *The Gilded Age: A Tale of Today,* 2 vols. (New York: Harper and Brothers, 1915 ed., originally published 1873), 2:14; and Marie Columbia, "The Capital City and the Smart Set," *Delineator* 55(January 1905): 81–82.

34. Jacob, "High Society in Washington," 278.

35. VBJ Diary, February 28, 1895, JFC. Charles Hurd accurately points out the contradiction in the Cave Dwellers' position: "An anomaly existed in the very fact that the old families who now looked down on politicians as a class of upstarts had shared almost entirely a political background in their origins" [*Washington Cavalcade* (New York: E. P. Dutton, 1948), 160]. Kathryn Jacob labels Violet "one of the most formidable of the Antiques" ("High Society in Washington," 275).

36. Marietta Minnigerode Andrews, *My Studio Window: Sketches of the Pageant of Washington Life* (New York: E. P. Dutton, 1928), 34.

37. Elden E. Billings, "Social and Economic Life in Washington in the 1890's," in *Records of the Columbia Historical Society,* ed. Rosenberg, 169; Randolph Keim, *Society in Washington: Its Distinguished Men and Accomplished Women—Established Customs and Notable Events* (Harrisburg: Pennsylvania Publishing Company, 1887), 217.

38. VBJ Diary, May 20, 1893, JFC.

39. Ibid., February 11, 1893.

40. Ibid., April 27, 1895.

41. Ibid., January 24, April 18, 1891, May 6, 1899.

42. See, for example, the notice in the *American Historical Register and Monthly Gazette of the Historic, Military and Patriotic Hereditary Societies of the United States of America* 2 (July 1895): 1309. Their DAR numbers indicate charter membership: Elizabeth Lee's number is 171 and Violet Janin's is 174. There were 818 charter members. See Mary S. Lockwood, Historian-General, 1890–1891, *Lineage Book of the Charter Members of the Daughters of the American Revolution* (Harrisburg, Pa.: Harrisburg Publishing Company, 1895). Violet resigned as registrar of the Mary Washington chapter in 1913; Elizabeth Lee was regent until her death in 1906.

43. VBJ Diary, May 7, 1892, JFC; *American Historical Register . . .* 2 (July 1895): 1293.

44. Wallace Evans Davies, *Patriotism on Parade: The Story of Veterans' and Hereditary Organizations in America, 1783–1900* (Cambridge: Harvard University Press, 1955), 46.

45. Frederic Cople Jaher, *The Urban Establishment: Upper Strata in Boston, New York, Charleston, Chicago, and Los Angeles* (Urbana: University of Illinois Press, 1982), 276.

Although the study does not include Washington, D. C., the general attitudes and activities Jaher found in the cities under study seem to be applicable also to the capital. There has been no sociological study of Washington in this period.

46. E. Daigby Baltzell, *The Protestant Establishment: Aristocracy and Caste in America* (New York: Random House, 1964), 112–15. Similar motivation led to the formation of Phi Beta Kappa. See G. Kurt Piehler, "Phi Beta Kappa and the Rites of Spring," *OAH Newsletter* (August 1990): 3, 18.

47. Barbara Miller Solomon, *Ancestors and Immigrants: A Changing New England Tradition* (Cambridge: Harvard University Press, 1956), 81–83; Baltzell, *The Protestant Establishment,* 111–12.

48. VBJ Diary, January 7, 1893, JFC.

49. Ibid., August 17, 1878, JFC.

50. Ibid., October 7, 1882.

51. Ibid., May 24, 1886.

52. Violet to Albert, May 7, 1894, Blair-Janin Papers, HS-W.

53. John Higham, *Strangers in the Land: Patterns of American Nativism 1860–1925,* 2d ed. (New York: Atheneum, 1965), 5–11.

54. Ibid., 95–96.

55. VBJ Diary, January 16, 1897, JFC.

56. *Report of the Daughters of the American Revolution 1890 to 1897* (Washington: Government Printing Office, 1899), 35–36.

57. Violet to Albert, April 25, 1923, JFC.

58. Davies, *Patriotism on Parade,* 82.

59. VBJ Diary, May 7, 1892, JFC.

60. Ibid., April 25, 1896.

61. Ibid., January 16, 1897.

62. Violet to Albert, March 21, 1874, JFC.

63. VBJ Diary, April 4, 1891, JFC. The next generation also garnered her approval. When P. Blair Lee, one of Blair Lee's sons, married Elizabeth Wayne, a descendant of the Revolutionary War general Anthony Wayne, Violet was pleased that she was eligible for membership in the Colonial Dames. See Violet to Albert, February 23, 1927, JFC.

64. VBJ Diary, January 27, 1883, November 1, December 18, 1884, January 22, 1885, September 27, November 24, 1888, May 31, 1889, JFC.

65. Ibid., November 24, 1886.

66. Ibid., July 20, 1889.

67. Ibid., January 1, 1884, September 21, 1886, June 30, 1888.

68. Ibid., June [July?] 18, 1888.

69. Ibid., April 25, 1891.

70. Ibid., April 22, 30, 1892.

71. See for example, VBJ Diary, September 21, 1886, October 22, 1892, April 30, 1892.

72. J. H. Pulte, *Woman's Medical Guide; containing essays on the Physical, Moral and*

Educational Development of Females and the Homeopathic Treatment of their diseases in all periods of life together with Directions for the Remedial Use of Water and Gymnastics (Cincinnati: Moore, Anderson, Wilstach and Keys, 1853), 326. For an example of one who tried to define and describe neurasthenia and differentiate it from hysteria, see Thomas D. Savill, *Clinical Lectures on Neurasthenia* (New York: William Wood and Company, 1899), 22–32, 35–39. For examples of modern historical comment on the interpretation of women's nervous disorders, see Carroll Smith Rosenberg, "The Hysterical Woman: Sex Roles and Role Conflict in Nineteenth-Century America," in *Disorderly Conduct: Visions of Gender in Victorian America,* Rosenberg, (New York: Oxford University Press, 1985), 197–216; Edward Shorter, "Paralysis: The Rise and Fall of a 'Hysterical' Sympton," *Journal of Social History* 19 (summer 1986): 549–82; Mark S. Micale, "Hysteria and Its Historiography: A Review of Past and Present Writings (II)," *History of Science* 27 (1989): 319–51; and F. G. Gosling and Joyce M. Ray, "The Right to Be Sick: American Physicians and Nervous Patients, 1885–1910," *Journal of Social History* 20 (winter 1986): 251–67. For a feminist interpretation that relates women's hysteria to their powerlessness in the nineteenth century, see Jennifer L. Pierce, "The Relation between Emotion, Work and Hysteria: A Feminist Reinterpretation of Freud's *Studies on Hysteria,*" *Women's Studies* 16 (1989): 255–70.

73. VBJ Diary, March 22, 1902, JFC.

74, Ibid., August 30, 1900.

75. Albert to Violet, June 21, 1893, JFC. His youngest brother, Alexis, added his advice to that of his brothers in urging Albert to abandon the canal venture: "pull yourself together, charge the past to experience account, and make a fresh start before it is too late." See Alexis Janin to Albert, December 16, 1895, Box 19, JFC.

76. Albert to Violet, October 2, 1895, JFC.

77. Albert to Violet, May 15, 1895, Blair-Janin Papers, HS-W; newspaper clipping of sheriff's sale of the canal, to be held on May 11, 1895, Blair-Janin Papers, HS-W.

78. Albert to Violet, December 10, 1895, March 18, 26, May 2, 1896. Blair-Janin Papers, HS-W.

79. Albert to Violet, July 3, 1896, JFC.

80. VBJ Diary, October 12, 1895, May 11, July 11, Christmas, 1896, November 20, 1897, JFC.

81. Ibid., January 16, 1897.

82. Albert to Violet, January 21, 1897, JFC.

83. Violet to Albert, May 13, 1897, JFC.

84. VBJ Diary, April 24, August 2, 1897, JFC.

85. Violet to Albert, August 2, 1897, JFC.

86. Albert to Violet, August 11, 1897, JFC.

87. Ibid., December 17, August 27, 1897. Enclosed with this letter was the following document, also dated August 27, 1897: "I hereby declare that it is my intention to abandon my residence in Louisiana and to resume my residence at Washington, in the District of Columbia, so soon as I shall succeed in disposing of my property interests in this state to reasonable advantage—possibly in a year from now, but not later than the end of the year 1899." It was signed, "Albert C. Janin." See also Albert to Register of Voters, October 17, 1899, declaring Montgomery County as his legal residence, Blair-Janin Papers, HS-W.

88. Albert to Violet, March 31, 1899, JFC.

89. Violet to Albert, May 18, 1899, JFC.

90. Albert to Violet, June 29, 1899, Blair-Janin Papers, HS-W.

91. Albert to Violet, June 18, 1900, JFC.

92. VBJ Diary, December 31, 1897, January 15, 1898, JFC.

93. Albert to Violet, April 15, 1900, JFC.

94. Henry Janin to Albert, July 11, no year, Box 20, JFC.

95. Albert to Violet, November 25, 1900, Blair-Janin Papers, HS-W.

96. Violet to Albert, November 1, 28, December 7, 1900, JFC.

97. VBJ Diary, September 24, November 5, 1904, JFC.

98. Ibid., October 3, 1905.

99. Although the financial records of Mammoth Cave are not complete, some comparative figures indicate the growth in revenue after Albert took charge. The annual report for 1903 through 1904 states that $11,505.80 was distributed to the heirs; in 1906 through 1907, that figure rose to $18,598.09. In the monthly report for August 1896, Mary Blair received $176.22; in the same month in 1903, her dividend was $126.84, and in 1905 it was $411.94. See Mammoth Cave Records, Boxes 38 and 39, JFC. See also Albert's extensive files on Mammoth Cave in the Blair-Janin Papers, HS-W.

100. When her will was filed for probate in 1933, Violet's estate was valued at $425,140. See the *Washington Post,* February 12, 1933. Included was over $100,000 derived from the sale of Mammoth Cave in December 1928. See Cecil E. Goode, *World Wonder Saved: How Mammoth Cave Became a National Park* (Mammoth Cave, Ky.: The Mammoth Cave National Park Association, 1986), 32–33.

101. VBJ Diary, two loose pages signed "V.B.J.," inserted into 1914 diary among the October entries, JFC.

102. For details on the events of Albert's illness, see VBJ Diary, October 8, 10, 1914, Box 29, JFC; and Minna Blair Richey to Julia Clark Jesup, August 2, [1914], Box 51, JFC.

103. VBJ diary, October 10, 1914; Minna Blair Richey to Violet, Sunday 13th [1914], Box 50.

104. VBJ Diary, December 26, 1914, JFC.

105. Ibid., January 2, 1915.

106. Albert to Violet, April 4, 1923, Blair-Janin Papers, HS-W.

107. Violet to Albert, July 28, 1916, JFC.

108. Ibid., [October] 15, 1916.

109. Ibid., August 20, 1920.

110. W. M. Ewing, M.D., To Whom It May Concern, March 1, 1926, Box 11, JFC.

111. Albert to Violet, July 9, 1923, JFC.

112. Violet to Albert, February 6, 1924, JFC.

113. VBJ pocket diaries, June 10, October 20, November 11, December 10, 1924, March 16, April 9, May 24, October 28, 1925, July 28, November 11, December 3, 1926, July 7, October 14, 1927, JFC.

114. See, for example, Felicia Villanueva to Mrs. Janin, February 20, March 7, 10, 22, April 1, 3, 1924, Box 56, JFC; and Chester McCarty to Mrs. Janin, December 31, 1926, Box 36, JFC.

115. Burley Dennison to Mrs. Janin, February 24, 1925, Box 19, JFC.

116. Chester McCarty to Mrs. Janin, April 11, 1927, Box 36, JFC; *Washington Post,* May 30, May 31, 1928; VBJ pocket diary, October 14, 1927, Box 29, JFC.

117. Goode, *World Wonder Saved,* 32–33.

118. Sophia Radford de Meissner, historian, "Forty Years of the National Society of the Colonial Dames of America in the District of Columbia," printed pamphlet, Records of the District of Columbia Colonial Dames, Dumbarton House, Washington, D.C.

119. David Bornet, Assistant Trust Officer of National Savings and Trust Company, to Thomas Corcoran, American Security and Trust, December 22, 1922, Archives of the Washington National Cathedral; *Cathedral Age* (Michaelmas, 1931): 62; George J. Cleaveland, "Washington Cathedral Library," *Cathedral Age* (Christmas, 1952): 14.

120. *Washington Post,* January 16, 1933; *Washington Daily News,* January 16, 1933; *Minutes of the Twenty-first Biennial Council, 1933, of the National Society of the Colonial Dames of America, Washington, D.C., May 2, 3, 4, & 5* (Richmond, Va.: Whitlet and Shepperson, 1933), 21–24.

Bibliography

Primary Sources

MANUSCRIPT COLLECTIONS

Archives of the Washington National Cathedral. Washington, D.C.
Blair-Janin Papers. Historical Society of Washington, D.C.
Blair-Lee Papers. Harvey Firestone Library. Princeton University.
Janin Family Collection. Henry Huntington Library. San Marino, California.
Papers of the Blair Family. Library of Congress.
Records of the District of Columbia Colonial Dames. Dumbarton House.
    Washington, D.C.

GOVERNMENT DOCUMENTS

Department of Interior. U.S. General Land Office. Maps of the State of Louisiana,
    1887, 1896.
*Rules of the French and American Claims Commission with the Convention Establishing
    the Commission.* Washington, D.C.: Gibson Brothers Printers, 1880.
U.S. Congress. *Report of the Secretary of State concerning the Transactions of the French
    and American Claims Commission.* 48th Cong., 2d sess., House of Representatives
    Executive Document 235.

NEWSPAPERS

New Orleans Times-Democrat, 1882.
New York Herald, 1868, 1869, 1870, 1874.
New York Times, 1874–1900.
New York World, 1883, 1885.
Washington Chronicle, 1895.
Washington Evening Star, 1867–1874.
Washington Post, 1900, 1928, 1933.
The Woman's Protest, 1912–1918.

CITY AND GOVERNMENT DIRECTORIES

Boyd's Business Directory and Guide to the Cities of Washington, Georgetown and Alexandria. Washington, D.C.: Boyd's Directory Company, 1867, 1871, 1887.

New York City Directory. New York: Doggett and Rode, 1879–1880.

Soard's New Orleans City Directory. New Orleans: L. Soards and Company, 1874.

U.S. Congressional Directory. Washington, D.C.: Government Printing Office, 1869, 1870, 1874, 1880, 1881, 1883, 1884, 1885.

PUBLISHED LETTERS, MEMOIRS, JOURNALS, AND ADVICE BOOKS

Adams, Marion Hooper. *The Letters of Mrs. Henry Adams, 1865–1883.* Edited by Ward Thoron. Boston: Little Brown, 1936.

Ames, Blanche, comp. *Chronicles from the Nineteenth Century: Family Letters of Blanche Butler Ames and Adelbert Ames.* Privately printed, 1957.

Andrews, Marietta M. *My Studio Window: Sketches of the Pageant of Washington Life.* New York: E. P. Dutton, 1928.

Benstock, Shari, ed. *The Private Self: Theory and Practice of Women's Autobiographical Writings.* Chapel Hill: University of North Carolina Press, 1988.

Blackwell, Alice Stone. *Growing Up in Boston's Gilded Age: The Journal of Alice Stone Blackwell, 1872–1874.* Edited by Marlene Deahl Merrill. New Haven: Yale University Press, 1990.

Briggs, Emily Edson. *The Olivia Letters: Being Some History of Washington City for Forty Years as Told by the Letters of a Newspaper Correspondent.* New York: Neale Publishing Company, 1906.

Bulkley, Barry. *Washington, Old and New.* Washington: Washington Printing Company, 1914.

Carpenter, Frank G. *Carp's Washington.* Edited by Frances Carpenter. New York: McGraw-Hill, 1960.

Chapin, Elizabeth M. *American Court Gossip, or Life at the Nation's Capitol.* Marshalltown, Iowa: Chapin and Hartwell Bros., 1887.

Dahlgren, Madeleine Vinton. *Etiquette of Social Life in Washington.* 5th ed. Lancaster, Pa.: Inquirer Publishing Co., 1881.

Duffey, Mrs. E. B. *What Women Should Know: A Woman's Book About Women, Containing Practical Information for Wives and Mothers.* Philadelphia: J. M. Stoddart, 1873.

Duffield, Isabel McKenna. *Washington in the 90's: California Eyes Dazzled by the Brilliant Society of the Capitol.* San Francisco: Press of Overland Monthly, 1929.

Lasser, Carol, and Marlene Merrill, eds. *Friends and Sisters: Letters between Lucy Stone and Antoinette Brown Blackwell, 1846–1893.* Urbana: University of Illinois Press, 1987.

Lee, Elizabeth Blair. *Wartime Washington: The Civil War Letters of Elizabeth Blair Lee.* Edited by Virginia Jeans Laas. Urbana: University of Illinois Press, 1991.

Lincoln, Jeanie Gould. *Her Washington Season.* Boston: James R. Osgood and Co., 1884.

Oppel, Frank, and Tony Meisel, eds. *Washington, D.C.: A Turn of the Century Treasury.* Secaucus, N.J.: Castle, 1987.

Poore, Ben Perley. *Perley's Reminiscences of Sixty Years in the National Metropolis.* 2 vols. Philadelphia: Hubbard Brothers, 1886.

Slayden, Ellen Maury. *Washington Wife: Journal of Ellen Maury Slayden from 1897–1919.* New York: Harper and Row, 1962.

Sterling, Ada, ed. *A Belle of the Fifties: Memoirs of Mrs. Clay of Alabama.* New York: Doubleday, Page and Co., 1904.

Thomas, Ella Gertrude Clanton. *The Secret Eye: The Journal of Ella Gertrude Clanton Thomas, 1848–1889.* Edited by Virginia Ingraham Burr. Chapel Hill: University of North Carolina Press, 1990.

Secondary Sources

MONOGRAPHS, BIOGRAPHIES, AND REFERENCE WORKS

Alpern, Sara, and Joyce Antler, Elisabeth Israels Perry, and Ingrid Winther Scobie, eds. *The Challenge of Feminist Biography: Writing the Lives of Modern American Women.* Urbana: University of Illinois Press, 1992.

Baldwin, Charles. *Baldwin Genealogical Supplement.* Cleveland, Ohio: Leader Print Co., 1889.

Baltzell, E. Digby. *Philadelphia Gentlemen: The Making of a National Upper Class.* New York: Fredd Press, 1958.

———. *The Protestant Establishment.* New York: Random House, 1964.

Banner, Lois W. *Women in Modern America: A Brief History.* 2nd ed. New York: Harcourt Brace Jovanovich, 1984.

Barker-Benfield, G. J. *The Horrors of the Half-Known Life: Male Attitudes toward Women and Sexuality in Nineteenth-Century America.* New York: Harper and Row, 1976.

Basch, Norma. *In the Eyes of the Law: Women, Marriage and Property in Nineteenth-Century New York.* Ithaca: Cornell University Press, 1982.

Beer, Thomas. *The Mauve Decade: American Life at the End of the Nineteenth Century.* New York: A. A. Knopf, 1926.

Berg, Barbara. *The Remembered Gate: Origins of American Feminism, the Woman and the City, 1800–1860.* New York: Oxford University Press, 1978.

Biographical and Historical Memoirs of Louisiana, embracing an authentic and comprehensive account of the chief events in the history of the state, a special sketch of every parish and a record of the lives of many of the most worthy and illustrious families and individuals. 2 vols. Chicago: The Goodspeed Publishing Company, 1892.

Blair, Karen J. *The Clubwoman as Feminist: True Womanhood Redefined, 1868–1914.* New York: Holmes and Meier Publishers, 1980.

Bleser, Carol, ed. *The Hamonds of Redcliffe*. New York: Oxford University Press, 1981.

Brandt, Allan M. *No Magic Bullet: A Social History of Venereal Disease in the United States since 1880*. New York: Oxford University Press, 1985.

Brehm, Sharon S. *Seeing Female: Social Roles and Personal Lives*. Westport, Conn.: Greenwood Press, 1988.

Burnett, James Compton. *Organ Diseases of Women, Notably Enlargements and Displacements of the Uterus, and Sterility, Considered as Curable by Medicines*. London: The Homeopathic Publishing Company, 1896.

Burt, Nathaniel. *The Perennial Philadelphians: The Anatomy of an American Aristocracy*. Boston: Little, Brown, 1963.

Calhoun, Arthur W. *A Social History of the American Family from Colonial Times to the Present*. 3 vols. Cleveland: Arthur Clarke and Co., 1918.

Callahan, Edward W., ed. *List of Officers of the Navy of the U.S. and of the Marine Corps from 1775 to 1900*. First published 1901. New York: Haskell House, 1969.

Carnes, Mark C., and Clyde Griffen, eds. *Meanings for Manhood: Constructions of Masculinity in Victorian America*. Chicago: University of Chicago Press, 1990.

Chafe, William H. *The Paradox of Change: American Women in the 20th Century*. New York: Oxford U. Press, 1991.

Coles, Robert. *Privileged Ones: The Well-Off and the Rich in America*. Boston: Little, Brown, 1977.

Conrad, Susan Phinney. *Perish the Thought: Intellectual Women in Romantic America, 1830–1860*. New York: Oxford University Press, 1976.

Coontz, Stephanie. *The Social Origins of Private Life: The History of American Families, 1600–1900*. New York: Verso, 1988.

Cott, Nancy. *The Bonds of Womanhood: Woman's Sphere in New England, 1780–1815*. New Haven: Yale University Press, 1977.

———. *The Grounding of Modern Feminism*. New Haven: Yale University Press, 1987.

Cott, Nancy, and Elizabeth Pleck, eds. *A Heritage of Her Own: Toward a New Social History of American Women*. New York: Simon and Schuster, 1979.

Culley, Margo., ed. *A Day at a Time: The Diary Literature of American Women from 1764 to the Present*. New York: Feminist Press, 1985.

Daniel, Robert. *American Women in the Twentieth Century: A Festival of Life*. New York: Harcourt Brace Jovanovich, 1987.

Davies, Wallace Evans. *Patriotism on Parade: The Story of Veterans' and Hereditary Organizations in America, 1783–1900*. Cambridge: Harvard University Press, 1955.

Degler, Carl N. *At Odds: Women and the Family in America from the Revolution to the Present*. New York: Oxford University Press, 1980.

DeLeon, Thomas Cooper. *Belles, Beaux and Brains of the Sixties*. New York: G. W. Dillingham, 1909.

D'Emilio, John, and Estelle Freeman. *Intimate Matters: A History of Sexuality in America*. New York: Harper and Row, 1988.

Demos, John. *Past, Present, and Personal: The Family and the Life Course in American History*. New York: Oxford University Press, 1986.

Demos, John, and Sarane Spence Boocock, eds. *Turning Points: Historical and Sociological Essays in the Family.* Chicago: University of Chicago Press, 1978.

Donaldson, Frances F. *The President's Square: The Cosmos Club's and Other Historic Homes on Lafayette Square.* New York: Vantage Press, 1968.

Douglas, Ann. *The Feminization of American Culture.* New York: Avon, 1978.

DuBois, Ellen. *Feminism and Suffrage: The Emergence of an Independent Women's Movement in America, 1848–1869.* Ithaca: Cornell University Press, 1978.

Eaton, Morton Monroe. *A Treatise on the Medical and Surgical Diseases of Women and Their Homeopathic Treatment.* New York: Boericke and Tafel, 1880.

Ehrenreich, Barbara, and Deidre English. *Complaints and Disorders: The Sexual Politics of Sickness.* Old Westbury, N.Y.: Feminist Press, 1974.

Epstein, Barbara. *The Politics of Domesticity: Women, Evangelism and Temperance in Nineteenth–Century America.* New York: Wesleyan University Press, 1981.

Farnham, Christie Anne. *The Education of the Southern Belle: Higher Education and Student Socialization in the Antebellum South.* New York: New York University Press, 1994.

Fellman, Anita Clair, and Michael Fellman. *Making Sense of Self: Medical Advice Literature in Late Nineteenth–Century America.* Philadelphia: University of Pennsylvania Press, 1981.

Fiedler, Leslie. *Love and Death in the American Novel.* New York: Stern and Day, 1966.

Filene, Peter G. *Him/Her/Self: Sex Roles in Modern America.* 2nd ed. Baltimore: Johns Hopkins University Press, 1966.

Flexner, Eleanor. *Century of Struggle: The Woman's Rights Movement in the United States.* Cambridge: Belknap Press of Harvard University Press, 1959.

Freud, Sigmund. *Dora—An Analysis of a Case of Hysteria.* New York: Collier Books, 1963.

Friedman, Jean E. *The Enclosed Garden: Women and Community in the Evangelical South, 1830–1900.* Chapel Hill: University of North Carolina Press, 1985.

Gates, Paul W. *History of Public Land Law.* Washington, D.C.: Government Printing Office, 1968.

Gay, Peter. *The Bourgeois Experience: Victoria to Freud.* Vol. 1, *Education of the Senses.* New York: Oxford University Press, 1984.

Geertz, Clifford. *The Interpretation of Cultures.* New York: Basic Books, 1973.

Gillette, William. *Retreat from Reconstruction, 1869–1879.* Baton Rouge: Louisiana State University Press, 1979.

Glassberg, David. *American Historical Pageantry: The Uses of Tradition in the Early Twentieth Century.* Chapel Hill: University of North Carolina Press, 1990.

Goode, Cecil E. *World Wonder Saved: How Mammoth Cave Became a National Park.* Mammoth Cave, Ky.: The Mammoth Cave National Park Association, 1986.

Goode, James. *Capital Losses: A Cultural History of Washington's Destroyed Buildings.* Washington, D.C.: Smithsonian Press, 1979.

Gordon, Linda. *Woman's Body, Woman's Right: A Social History of Birth Control in America.* New York: Penguin, 1977.

Gordon, Michael, ed. *The American Family in Social-Historical Perspective.* 3rd ed. New York: St. Martin's Press, 1983.

Green, Constance. *The Church on Lafayette Square: A History of St. John's Church, Washington, D.C., 1815–1970.* Washington, D.C.: Potomac Books, 1970.

———. *Washington: A History of the Capital, 1800–1950.* 2 vols. Princeton: Princeton University Press, 1962–63.

Green, Harvey. *The Light of the Home: An Intimate View of the Lives of Women in Victorian America.* New York: Pantheon Books, 1983.

Grossberg, Michael. *Governing the Hearth: Law and Family in Nineteenth-Century America.* Chapel Hill: University of North Carolina Press, 1985.

Grund, Francis J. *Aristocracy in America.* New York: Harper Torchbooks, 1959.

Guernsey, Henry N. *The Application of the Principles and Practice of Homeopathy to Obstetrics and the Disorders peculiar to Women and Young Children.* Philadelphia: F. E. Boericke, Hahnemann Publishing House, 1886.

Haller, John S., and Robin M. Haller. *The Physician and Female Sexuality in Nineteenth-Century America.* Urbana: University of Illinois Press, 1974.

Halttunen, Karen. *Confidence Men and Painted Women: A Study of Middle-Class Culture in America, 1830–1870.* New Haven: Yale University Press, 1982.

Hareven, Tamara, ed. *The Family and the Life Course in Historical Perspective.* New York: Academic Press, 1978.

———, ed. *Family and Kin in Urban Communities, 1700–1930.* New York: New Viewpoints, 1977.

Hayden, Dolores. *The Grand Domestic Revolution: A History of Feminist Designs for American Homes, Neighborhoods, and Cities.* Cambridge: MIT Press, 1981.

Heilbrun, Carolyn. *Writing a Woman's Life.* New York: Ballantine Books, 1988.

Heitman, Francis. *Historical Register and Dictionary of the United States Army from its Organization, Sept. 29, 1789, to March 2, 1903.* 2 vols. Washington, D.C.: Government Printing Office, 1903.

Herr, Pamela. *Jessie Benton Fremont: A Biography.* New York: Franklin Watts, 1987.

Hewitt, Nancy A. *Women's Activism and Social Change: Rochester, New York, 1822–1872.* Ithaca: Cornell University Press, 1984.

Higham, John. *Strangers in the Land: Patterns of American Nativism, 1860–1925.* 2nd ed. New York: Atheneum, 1965.

Hogeland, Ronald, ed. *Women and Womanhood in America.* Lexington, Mass.: D.C. Heath, 1973.

Howe, Daniel Walker, ed. *Victorian America.* Philadelphia: University of Pennsylvania Press, 1976.

Hurd, Charles. *Washington Cavalcade.* New York: E. P. Dutton, 1948.

Jackson, Joy. *New Orleans in the Gilded Age: Politics and Urban Progress, 1800–1896.* Baton Rouge: Louisiana State University Press, 1969.

Jacob, Kathryn Allamong. *Capital Elites: High Society in Washington, D.C., after the Civil War.* Washington: Smithsonian Institution Press, 1995.

Jaher, Frederic Cople. *The Urban Establishment: Upper Strata in Boston, New York, Charleston, Chicago, and Los Angeles.* Urbana: University of Illinois Press, 1982.

————, ed. *America in the Age of Industrialism: Essays in Social Structure and Cultural Values.* New York: Free Press, 1968.

————, ed. *The Rich, the Well Born, and the Powerful: Elites and Upper Classes in History.* Urbana: University of Illinois Press, 1973.

Jesup, Rev. Henry Griswold. *Edward Jessup of West Farms, Westchester Co., New York, and His Descendants.* Cambridge: John Wilson and Son, 1887.

Kaufman, Martin. *Homeopathy in America: The Rise and Fall of a Medical Heresy.* Baltimore: The Johns Hopkins Press, 1971.

Keiffer, Chester L. *Maligned General: A Biography of Thomas Sidney Jesup.* San Rafael, Calif.: Presidio Press, 1979.

Keim, Rudolph. *Society in Washington, Its Noted Men, Accomplished Women, Established Customs and Notable Events, 1887.* Harrisburg: Pennsylvania Publishing Co., 1887.

Klingberg, Frank W. *The Southern Claims Commission.* New York: Octagon Books, 1978.

Konolige, Kit, and Frederica Konolige. *The Power of Their Glory: America's Ruling Class, the Episcopalians.* New York: Simon and Schuster, 1978.

Kraditor, Aileen S. *The Ideas of the Woman Suffrage Movement, 1890–1920.* New York: Columbia University Press, 1965; New York: W. W. Norton, 1981.

Lasch, Christopher. *The New Radicalism in America, 1889–1963: The Intellectual as a Social Type.* New York: Knopf, 1965.

Leavitt, Judith Walzer. *Brought to Bed: Childbearing in America, 1750–1950.* New York: Oxford University Press, 1986.

————, ed. *Women and Health in America: Historical Readings.* Madison: University of Wisconsin Press, 1984.

Lemons, J. Stanley. *The Woman Citizen: Social Feminism in the 1920s.* Urbana: University of Illinois Press, 1973.

Lewis, David L. *District of Columbia: A Bicentennial History.* New York: W. W. Norton and Nashville: American Association of State and Local History, 1976.

Lonn, Ella. *Reconstruction in Louisiana after 1868.* New York: G. P. Putnam's Sons, 1918.

Lystra, Karen. *Searching the Heart: Women, Men, and Romantic Love in Nineteenth-Century America.* New York: Oxford University Press, 1989.

Mangan, J. A., and James Wolvin, eds. *Manliness and Morality: Middle-Class Masculinity in Britain and America, 1800–1940.* New York: St. Martin's Press, 1987.

Marcus, George E., ed. *Elites: Ethnographic Issues.* Albuquerque: University of New Mexico Press, 1983.

Martin, Edward Sandford. *The Unrest of Women.* New York: D. Appleton, 1913.

May, Elaine Tyler. *Great Expectations: Marriage and Divorce in Post-Victorian America.* Chicago: University of Chicago Press, 1980.

McDarrnell, Colleen. *The Christian Home in Victorian America, 1840–1900.* Bloomington: University of Indiana Press, 1986.

McGinty, Garnie W. *Louisiana Redeemed: The Overthrow of Carpet-bag Rule, 1876–1880.* New Orleans: Pelican Publishing, 1941.

McGrew, Roderick E. *Encyclopedia of Medical History.* New York: McGraw-Hill, 1985.

Melder, Keith E. *Beginnings of Sisterhood: The American Woman's Rights Movement, 1800–1850.* New York: Schocken Books, 1977.

Mintz, Steven. *A Prison of Expectations: The Family in Victorian Culture.* New York: New York University Press, 1983.

Mintz, Steven, and Susan Kellogg. *Domestic Revolutions: A Social History of American Family Life.* New York: Free Press, 1988.

Mitchell, Juliet, and Ann Ockley, eds. *What is Feminism?* New York: Pantheon Books, 1986.

Mosher, Clelia Duel. *The Mosher Survey: Sexual Attitudes of Forty-five Victorian Women.* Edited by James Mahood and Christina Wenburg. New York: Arno Press, 1980.

Motz, Marilyn Ferris. *True Sisterhood: Michigan Women and Their Kin, 1820–1920.* Albany: State University of New York Press, 1983.

Motz, Marilyn Ferris, and Pat Browne. *Making the American Home: Middle Class Women and Domestic Material Culture, 1840–1940.* Bowling Green, Ohio: Bowling Green University Press, 1988.

Nevins, Allan. *Grover Cleveland: A Study in Courage.* New York: Dodd, Mead and Company, 1932.

O'Neill, William L. *Divorce in the Progressive Era.* New Haven: Yale University Press, 1967.

———. *Everyone Was Brave: A History of Feminism in America.* Chicago: Quadrangle Books, 1971.

Page, Thomas Nelson. *The Old Dominion: Her Making and Her Manners.* New York: Charles Scribner's Sons, 1918.

———. *The Old South.* Chautauqua, N.Y.: Chautauqua Press, 1919.

Payne, Elizabeth Anne. *Reform, Labor, and Feminism: Margaret Dreier Robins and the Women's Trade Union League.* Urbana: University of Illinois Press, 1988.

Pessen, Edward. *Riches, Class and Power before the Civil War.* Lexington, Mass.: D. C. Heath, 1973.

Pleck, Elizabeth, and Joseph H. Pleck, eds. *The American Man.* Englewood Cliffs, N.J.: Prentice-Hall, 1980.

Pugh, David G. *Sons of Liberty: The Masculine Mind in Nineteenth-Century America.* Westport, Conn.: Greenwood Press, 1983.

Pulte, J. H. *Woman's Medical Guide; containing essays on the Physical, Moral and Educational Development of Females and the Homeopathic Treatment of Their diseases in all periods of life together with Directions for the Remedial Use of Water and Gymnastics.* Cincinnati: Moore, Anderson, Wilstach, and Keys, 1853.

Rose, Phyllis. *Parallel Lives: Five Victorian Marriages.* New York: Vintage Books, 1984.

———. *Writing of Women: Essays in a Renaissance.* Middletown, Conn.: Wesleyan University Press, 1985.

Rosenweig, Linda. *The Anchor of My Life: Middle-Class Mothers and Daughters, 1880–1920.* New York: New York University Press, 1993.

Rothman, David J. *The Discovery of the Asylum: Social Order and Disorder in the New Republic.* Boston: Little, Brown, 1971.

Rothman, Ellen K. *Hands and Hearts: A History of Courtship in America.* New York: Basic Books, 1984.

Rothman, Sheila M. *Woman's Proper Place: A History of Changing Ideals and Practices, 1870 to the Present.* New York: Basic Books, 1978.

Rotundo, Anthony. *American Manhood: Transformations in Masculinity from the Revolution to the Modern Era.* New York: Basic Books, 1993.

Ryan, Mary P. *Cradle of the Middle Class: The Family in Oneida County, New York, 1790–1865.* New York: Cambridge University Press, 1981.

———. *Womanhood in America from Colonial Times to the Present.* New York: New Viewpoints, 1975.

———. *Women in Public: Between Banners and Ballots, 1825–1880.* Baltimore: Johns Hopkins Press, 1990.

Savill, Thomas D. *Clinical Lectures on Neurasthenia.* New York: William Wood and Co., 1879.

Schlesinger, Arthur, and Dixon Ryan Fox, eds. *A History of American Life X.* New York: Macmillan, 1933.

Scott, Anne Firor. *Natural Allies: Women's Associations in American History.* Urbana and Chicago: University of Illinois Press, 1992.

———. *The Southern Lady: From Pedestal to Politics, 1830–1930.* Chicago: University of Chicago Press, 1970.

Scott, Anne Firor, and Andrew MacKay Scott. *One Half the People: The Fight for Woman Suffrage.* Urbana: University of Illinois Press, 1975.

Seidel, Kathryn. *The Southern Belle in the American Novel.* Tampa: University of South Florida Press, 1985.

Sklar, Kathryn Kish. *Catherine Beecher: A Study in Domesticity.* New Haven: Yale University Press, 1973.

Sloane, Florence Adel. *Maverick in Mauve: The Diary of a Romantic Age.* Garden City, N.Y.: Doubleday, 1983.

Smith, E. B. *Francis Preston Blair.* New York: Free Press, 1980.

Smith, William E. *The Francis Preston Blair Family in Politics.* 2 vols. New York: Macmillan Company, 1933.

Smith-Rosenberg, Carroll. *Disorderly Conduct: Visions of Gender in Victorian America.* New York: Oxford University Press, 1985.

Snitow, Anne, Christine Stansell, and Sharon Thompson, eds. *Powers of Desire: The Politics of Sexuality.* New York: Monthly Review Press, 1983.

Solomon, Barbara Miller. *Ancestors and Immigrants: A Changing New England.* Cambridge: Harvard University Press, 1956.

Spence, Clark C. *Mining Engineers and the American West: The Lace-Boot Brigade, 1849–1933.* Moscow, Idaho: University of Idaho Press, 1970 and 1993.

Stevenson, Louise L. *The Victorian Homefront: American Thought and Culture, 1860–1880.* New York: Twayne Publishers, 1991.

Sutherland, Daniel E. *Americans and Their Servants: Domestic Service in the United States from 1800 to 1920.* Baton Rouge: Louisiana State University Press, 1981.

Taylor, Joe Gray. *Louisiana Reconstructed: 1863–1877.* Baton Rouge: Louisiana State University Press, 1974.

Theriot, Nancy M. *Mothers and Daughters in Nineteenth-Century America: The Biosocial Construction of Femininity.* Lexington: University Press of Kentucky, 1996.

Tilly, Louis A., and Patricia Gurin, eds. *Women, Politics and Change in Twentieth-Century America.* New York: Russell Sage Foundation, 1990.

Trollope, Anthony. *The Way We Live Now.* London: Chapman and Hall, 1875.

Verbrugge, Martha H. *Able-Bodied Womanhood: Personal Health and Social Change in Nineteenth-Century Boston.* New York: Oxford University Press, 1988.

Walters, Ronald. *Primers for Prudery: Sexual Advice to Victorian America.* Englewood Cliffs, N.J.: Prentice, 1974.

Ware, Susan, ed. *Modern American Women: A Documentary History.* Chicago: Dorsey Press, 1989.

Warmoth, Henry Clay. *War, Politics, and Reconstruction: Stormy Days in Louisiana.* New York: McMillan, 1930.

Weaver, Richard M. *The Southern Tradition at Bay.* New Rochelle, N.Y.: Arlington House, 1968.

Welter, Barbara. *Dimity Convictions: The American Woman in the Nineteenth Century.* Athens: Ohio University Press, 1976.

Wendell, Barrett. *Privileged Classes.* New York: Charles Scribner's Sons, 1908.

Wertz, Richard W., and Dorthy C. Wertz. *Lying-In: A History of Childbirth in America.* New York: Free Press, 1977.

Wilson, James, and John Fiske, eds. *Appleton's Cyclopedia of American Biography.* 7 vols. New York: James T. White and Co., 1888.

Woloch, Nancy. *Women and the American Experience.* New York: Alfred A. Knopf, 1984.

ARTICLES IN BOOKS AND PERIODICALS

Alives, Bertold C. "The History of the Louisiana State Lottery Company." *Louisiana Historical Quarterly* 27 (October 1944): 964–1118.

Anderson, George M. "An Early Commuter: The Letters of James and Mary Anderson." *Maryland Historical Magazine* 75 (fall 1980): 217–32.

Antler, Joyce. "Feminism as Life-Process: The Life and Career of Lucy Sprague Mitchell." *Feminist Studies* 7 (spring 1981): 134–57.

———. "Was She a Good Mother? Some Thoughts on a New Issue for Feminist Biography." In *Women and the Structure of Society: Selected Research from the Fifth Berkshire Conference on the History of Women,* edited by Barbara J. Harris and Jo Anne K. McNamara, 53–66. Durham, N.C.: Duke University Press, 1984.

Baker, Paula. "The Domestication of Politics: Woman and American Political Society, 1780–1920." *American Historical Review* 89 (June 1984): 620–47.

Barker-Benfield, G. J. "The Spermatic Economy: A Nineteenth-Century View of Sexuality." *Feminist Studies* 1 (1972): 45–74.

Basch, Francoise. "Women's Rights and the Wrongs of Marriage in Mid-Nineteenth-Century America." *History Workshop* 22 (autumn 1986): 18–40.

Basch, Norma. "The Emerging Legal History of Women in the United States: Property, Divorce, and the Constitution." *Signs* 12 (autumn 1986): 97–117.

Billings, Elden E. "Social and Economic Life in Washington in the 1890's." In *Records of the Columbia Historical Society of Washington, D.C., 1966–1968,* edited by Frances Coleman Rosenberg, 167–81. Washington, D.C.: The Society, 1969.

Blair, Gist. "Annals of Silver Spring." *Records of the Columbia Historical Society* 21 (1918): 155–85.

Bogdan, Janet. "Care or Cure? Childbirth Practices in Nineteenth-Century America." *Feminist Studies* 4 (June 1978): 92–98.

Boylan, Anne M. "Timid Girls, Venerable Widows, and Dignified Matrons: Life Cycle Patterns among Organized Women in New York and Boston, 1797–1840." *American Quarterly* 38 (winter 1986): 779–97.

Bridges, William. "Family Patterns and Social Values in America, 1825–1875." *American Quarterly* 17 (spring 1965): 3–11.

Browne, J. Rope. "A Tour Through Arizona." *Harper's New Monthly Magazine* 30, no. 177 (February 1865): 283–93.

Cashin, Joan E. "The Structure of Antebellum Planter Families: 'The Ties That Bound Us Was Strong.'" *Journal of Southern History* 56 (February 1990): 55–70.

Chafetz, Janet Salzman, and Gary Dworken. "In the Face of Threat: Organized Antifeminism in Comparative Perspective." *Gender and Society* 1 (1987): 33–60.

Chudacoff, Howard P. "The Life Course of Women: Age and Age Consciousness, 1865–1915." *Journal of Family History* 5 (fall 1980): 274–92.

Columbia, Maria. "The Capital and the Smart Set." *Delineator* 55 (January 1905): 79–83.

———. "Washington: Its Cave Dwellers and Its Social Secretaries." *Delineator* 55 (February 1905): 248–53.

Conway, Jill. "Women Reformers and American Culture, 1870–1930." *Journal of Social History* 5 (1971–72): 164–77.

Cott, Nancy. "Feminist Theory and Feminist Movements: The Past before Us." In *What is Feminism?,* edited by Juliet Mitchell and Ann Oakley. New York: Pantheon Books, 1986.

———. "'Passionless': An Interpretation of Victorian Sexual Ideology, 1790–1850." *Signs* 4 (1978): 219–36.

———. "What's in a Name? The Limits of 'Social Feminism'; or, Expanding the Vocabulary of Women's History." *Journal of American History* 76 (December 1989): 809–29.

Decker, Hannah S. "Freud and Dora: Constraints on Medical Progress." *Journal of Social History* 14 (spring 1981): 445–64.

Degler, Carl N. "What Ought To Be and What Was: Women's Sexuality in the Nineteenth Century." *American Historical Review* 79 (December 1974): 1467–90.

DuBois, Ellen, Mari Jo Buhle, Temma Kaplan, Gerda Lerner, and Carroll Smith-Rosenberg. "Politics and Culture in Women's History: A Symposium." *Feminist Studies* 6 (spring 1980): 26–64.

Dye, Nancy Schrom. "Review Essay on the History of Childbirth." *Signs* 6 (1986): 97–108.

Dye, Nancy S., and Daniel B. Smith. "Mother Love and Infant Death, 1750–1920." *Journal of American History* 73 (September 1986): 329–53.

Freedman, Estelle. "Separation as Strategy: Institution Building and American Feminism, 1870–1930." *Feminist Studies* 5 (fall 1979): 512–29.

———. "Sexuality in Nineteenth-Century America: Behavior, Ideology, and Politics." *Reviews in American History* 10 (December 1982): 196–215.

Gannon, James A., Sr. "Washington at the Turn of the Century." In *Records of the Columbia Historical Society of Washington, D.C., 1963–1965,* edited by Frances Coleman Rosenberg, 313–19. Washington, D.C.: The Society, 1966.

Gay, Peter. "Victorian Sexuality: Old Texts and New Insights." *American Scholar* 49 (1980): 372–78.

Gibbs, Phillip A. "Self Control and Male Sexuality in the Advice Literature of Nineteenth-Century America, 1830–1860." *Journal of American Culture* 9 (summer 1986): 37–41.

Gordon, Michael. "The Ideal Husband as Depicted in Nineteenth-Century Marriage Manuals." In *The American Man,* edited by Elizabeth Pleck and Joseph Pleck, 145–57. Englewood Cliffs, N.J.: Prentice Hall, 1980.

———. "From an Unfortunate Necessity to a Cult of Mutual Orgasm: Sex in American Marital Education Literature, 1830–1940." In *Studies in the Sociology of Sex,* edited by James Henslin, 53–71. New York: Appleton, 1971.

Gosling, F. G., and Joyce M. Ray. "The Right to Be Sick: American Physicians and Nervous Patients, 1885–1910." *Journal of Social History* 20 (winter 1986): 251–67.

Grossbert, Michael. "Institutionalizing Masculinity: The Law as a Masculine Profession." In *Meanings for Manhood: Constructions of Masculinity in Victorian America,* edited by Mark C. Carnes and Clyde Gridden, 133–51. Chicago: University of Chicago Press, 1990.

Haller, John. "From Maidenhood to Menopause: Sex Education for Women in Victorian America." *Journal of Popular Culture* 6 (summer 1972): 46–70.

Hamilton, Virginia Van der Veer, ed. "'So Much in Love . . .': The Courtship of a Bluegrass Belle—Rosalie Stewart's Diary, December 1890–July 1891." *Register of the Kentucky Historical Society* 88 (winter 1990): 24–44.

Hareven, Tamara K. "The History of the Family and the Complexity of Social Change." *American Historical Review* 96 (February 1991): 95–124.

———. "Modernization and Family History: Perspectives on Social Change." *Signs* 2 (1976): 190–206.

Harsin, Jill. "Syphilis, Wives, and Physicians: Medical Ethics and the Family in Late Nineteenth-Century France." *French Historical Studies* 16 (spring 1989): 72–95.

Herman, Sondra R. "Loving Courtship or the Marriage Market? The Ideal and Its Critics, 1871–1911." In 3rd ed. of *Our American Sisters: Women in American Life and Thought,* edited by Jean E. Friedman and William Shade, 329–47. Lexington, Mass.: D. C. Heath, 1982.

Hewitt, Nancy A. "Beyond the Search for Sisterhood: American Women's History in the 1980s." *Social History* 10 (October 1985): 299–321.

Hogeland, Ronald W. "The Female Appendage: Feminism Life-Styles in America, 1820–1860." *Civil War History* 17 (1971): 101–14.

Holt, Shan. "The Anatomy of a Marriage: Letters of Emma Spaulding Bryant, 1873." *Signs: Journal of Women in Culture and Society* 17 (autumn 1991): 187–204.

Horn, Margo. "'Sisters Worthy of Respect': Family Dynamics and Women's Roles in the Blackwell Family." *Journal of Family History* 8 (winter 1983): 369–82.

Hunter, Jane. "Inscribing the Self in the Heart of the Family: Diaries and Girlhood in Late-Victorian America." *American Quarterly* 44 (March 1992): 51–81.

Kasson, John F. "Civility and Rudeness: Urban Etiquette and the Bourgeois Social Order in Nineteenth-Century America." In Vol. 9 of *Prospects: The Annual of American Cultural Studies,* edited by Jack Salzman, 143–67. New York: Cambridge University Press, 1984.

Kelley, Mary. "The Sentimentalists: Promise and Betrayal in the Home." *Signs* 4 (spring 1979): 434–46.

Kenney, Alice P. "'Evidence of Regard': Three Generations of American Love Letters." *Bulletin of the New York Public Library* 76 (1972): 92–119.

Kerber, Linda. "Separate Spheres, Female Worlds, Woman's Place: The Rhetoric of Women's History." *Journal of American History* 75 (1988): 9–39.

Lasch, Christopher, and William R. Taylor. "Two 'Kindred Spirits': Sorority and Family in New England, 1839–1846." *New England Quarterly* 36 (1963): 23–41.

LaSorte, Michael A. "Nineteenth-Century Family Planning Practices." *Journal of Psychohistory* 4 (fall 1976): 163–83.

Lasser, Carol. "'Let Us Be Sisters Forever': The Sororal Model of Nineteenth-Century Female Friendship." *Signs* 14 (autumn 1988): 158–81.

Leavitt, Judith W. "Under the Shadow of Maternity: American Women's Responses to Death and Debility Fears in Nineteenth-Century Childbirth." *Feminist Studies* 12 (spring 1986): 129–54.

Leavitt, Judith W., and Whitney Walton. "'Down to Death's Door': Women's Perceptions of Childbirth in America." In *Women's Health in America: Historical Readings,* edited by Judith Leavitt, 155–65. Madison: University of Wisconsin Press, 1984.

Lerner, Gerda. "Priorities and Challenges in Women's History Research." *Perspectives: Newsletter of the American Historical Association* 26 (April 1988): 17–20.

Lewis, Jan. "Mother's Love: The Construction of an Emotion in Nineteenth-Century America." In *Social History and Issues in Human Consciousness: Some Interdisciplinary Connections,* edited by Andrew E. Barnes and Peter N. Stearns, 209–29. New York: New York University Press, 1989.

Marcus, George E. "'Elite' as a Concept, Theory, and Research Tradition," In *Elites: Ethnographic Issues,* edited by G. E. Marcus, 7–27. Albuquerque: University of New Mexico Press, 1983.

May, Elaine T. "The Pressure to Provide: Class, Consumerism, and Divorce in Urban America, 1880–1920." *Journal of Social History* 12 (winter 1978): 180–93.

McGovern, James R. "The American Woman's Pre–World War I Freedom in Manners and Morals." *Journal of American History* 55 (September 1968): 315–33.

Melder, Keith. "Ladies Bountiful: Organized Women's Benevolence in the Nineteenth Century." *New York History* 48 (1967): 231–54.

Micale, Mark. "Hysteria and Its Historiography: A Review of Past and Present Writings (II)." *History of Science* 27 (December 1989): 319–52.

Morantz, Regina. "Making Women Modern: Middle-Class Women and Health Reform in Nineteenth-Century America." *Journal of Social History* 10 (1976–77): 490–507.

———. "The Perils of Feminist History." *Journal of Interdisciplinary History* 4 (spring 1974): 649–60.

Morantz, Regina, and Sue Zschoche. "Professionalism, Feminism, and Gender Roles: A Comparative Study of Nineteenth-Century Medical Therapeutics." *Journal of American History* 67 (December 1980): 568–88.

Nelson, Henry Loomis. "Washington Society." In *Washington, D.C.: A Turn of the Century Treasury,* edited by Frank Oppel and Tony Meisel, 84–93. Secaucus, N.J.: Castle, 1987.

"Obituary of Henry Janin," *Monthly Bulletin, American Institute of Mining Engineers* 53 (May 1911): xxviii–xxxvi.

Pessen, Edward. "The Egalitarian Myth and the American Social Reality: Wealth, Mobility, and Equality in the 'Era of the Common Man.'" *American Historical Review* 76 (1971): 989–1034.

Piehler, G. Kurt. "Phi Beta Kappa and the Rites of Spring." *OAH Newsletter* 18 (August 1990): 3, 18.

Pierce, Jennifer L. "The Relationship between Emotion, Work, and Hysteria: A Feminist Reinterpretation of Freud's *Studies in Hysteria.*" *Women's Studies* 16 (March/April 1989): 255–70.

Reynolds, David S. "The Feminization Controversy: Sexual Stereotypes and the Paradoxes of Piety in Nineteenth-Century America." *New England Quarterly* 53 (1980): 96–105.

Riley, Glenda G. "The Subtle Subversion: Changes in the Traditionalist Image of the American Woman." *Historian* 32 (February 1970): 210–27.

Rosenberg, Charles. "Sexuality, Class, and Role in Nineteenth-Century America." *American Quarterly* 25 (1973): 131–53.

Rosenzweig, Linda. "'The Anchor of My Life': Middle-Class American Mothers and College-Educated Daughters, 1880–1920." *Journal of Social History* 25 (fall 1991): 5–25.

Ryan, Mary P. "The Explosion of Family History." *Reviews in American History* 10 (December 1982): 181–95.

Savage, Gail. "'The Wilful Communication of a Loathsome Disease': Marital Conflict and Venereal Disease in Victorian England." *Victorian Studies* 34 (autumn 1990): 35–54.

Scholten, Catherine. "'On the Importance of the Obstetrick Art': Changing Customs of Childbirth in America." *William and Mary Quarterly* 34 (1977): 426–45.

Scott, Anne. "Women, Religion, and Social Change in the South, 1830–1930." In *Religion and the Solid South,* edited by Samuel S. Hill, 92–121. Nashville: Abingdon Press, 1972.

Seidel, Kathryn. "The Southern Belle as an Antebellum Ideal." *Southern Quarterly* 15 (July 1977): 387–401.

Seidman, S. "The Power of Desire and the Danger of Pleasure: Victorian Sexuality Reconsidered." *Journal of Social History* 24 (autumn 1990): 47–68.

———. "Sexual Attitudes of Victorian and Post-Victorian Women: Another Look at the Mosher Survey." *Journal of American Studies* 23 (April 1989): 68–72.

Shade, William G. "'A Mental Passion': Female Sexuality in Victorian America." *International Journal of Women's Studies (Canada)* 1 (1978): 13–29.

Shorter, Edward. "Paralysis: The Rise and Fall of a 'Hysterical' Symptom." *Journal of Social History* 19 (summer 1986): 549–82.

Sicherman, Barbara. "Review Essay: American History" *Signs* 1 (winter 1975): 461–85.

Smith, Daniel Scott. "Family Limitation, Sexual Control, and Domestic Feminism in Victorian America." *Feminist Studies* 1 (1973): 40–57.

Smith-Rosenberg, Carroll. "Beauty, the Beast, and the Militant Woman: A Case Study of Sex Roles and Social Stress in Jacksonian America." *American Quarterly* 23 (October 1971): 562–84.

———. "The Female World of Love and Ritual: Relations between Women in Nineteenth-Century America." *Signs* 1 (1975): 1–30.

———. "The Hysterical Woman: Sex Role and Role Conflict in Nineteenth-Century America." *Social Research* 39 (1972): 652–78.

———. "Puberty to Menopause: The Cycle of Femininity in Nineteenth-Century America." *Feminist Studies* 1 (1973): 58–72.

———. "Sex as Symbol in Victorian Purity: An Ethnohistorical Analysis of Jacksonian America." In *Turning Points: Historical and Sociological Essays on the Family,* edited by John Demos and Sarane Spence Boocock. Chicago: University of Chicago Press, 1978.

Smith-Rosenberg, Carroll, and Charles Rosenberg. "The Female Animal: Medical and Biological Views of Women in Nineteenth-Century America." *Journal of American History* 59 (1973): 331–56.

Stearns, Carol Z., and Peter N. Stearns. "Victorian Sexuality: Can Historians Do It Better?" *Journal of Social History* 18 (1984–85): 626–33.

Stephens, Jane. "Breezes of Discontent: A Historical Perspective of Anxiety Based Illnesses among Women." *Journal of American Culture* 8 (winter 1985): 3–9.

Stevenson, Louise L. "Women Anti-Suffragists in the 1915 Massachusetts Campaign." *New England Quarterly* 52 (1979): 80–93.

Stowe, Steven M. "The Not-So-Cloistered Academy: Elite Women's Education and Family Feeling in the Old South." In *The Web of Southern Social Relations: Women, Family, and Education,* edited by Talter J. Fraser, F. Frank Saunders Jr., and Jon Le Wahelyn. Athens: University of Georgia Press, 1985.

———. "The *Thing* Not Its Vision: A Woman's Courtship and Her Sphere in the 'Southern Planter Class.'" *Feminist Studies* 9 (spring 1983): 113–30.

Waite, Lucy. "The Mechanical Treatment of Uterine Displacements." In Vol. 4 of *The Medical Visitor,* edited by T. S. Hayne, 339–40. Chicago: John Morris Company, 1888.

Walsh, John F. "Wiggery's Onward March." *Reviews in American History* 19 (September 1991): 353–58.

Welter, Barbara. "Coming of Age in America: The American Girl in the Nineteenth Century." In *Dimity Convictions: The American Woman in the Nineteenth Century,* 3–20. Athens: Ohio University Press, 1976.

———. "The Cult of True Womanhood: 1820–1860." *American Quarterly* 18 (summer 1966): 151–74.

Wesselhoeft, Conrad. "Some Observations on Neurasthenia and Its Treatment." In *Transactions of the World's Congress of Homeopathic Physicians and Surgeons, Chicago, Illinois, May 29 to June 3, 1893.* Philadelphia: Sherman and Company, 1894.

Wiggins, Richard. "The Louisiana Press and the Lottery." *Louisiana Historical Quarterly* 31 (July 1948): 716–844.

Wood, Ann. "'The Fashionable Disease': Women's Complaints and Their Treatment in Nineteenth-Century America." *Journal of Interdisciplinary History* (1973): 25–52.

DISSERTATIONS

Brodie, Janet Farrell. "Family Limitation in American Culture, 1830–1900." Ph.D. diss., University of Chicago, 1982.

Camhi, Jane Jerome. "Women against Women: American Antisuffragism, 1880–1920." Ph.D. diss., Tufts University, 1973.

Giele, Janet Zollinger. "Social Change in the Feminine Role: A Comparison of Woman's Suffrage and Woman's Temperance, 1870–1920." Ph.D. diss., Radcliffe College, 1961.

Jablonsky, Thomas J. "Duty, Nature, and Stability: The Female Anti-Suffragists in the United States, 1894–1920." Ph.D. diss., University of California, Los Angeles, 1978.

Jacob, Kathryn Allamong. "High Society in Washington during the Gilded Age: 'Three Distinct Aristocracies.'" Ph.D. diss., Johns Hopkins University, 1986.

LaGanke, Lucile. "The National Society of the Daughters of the American Revolution—Its History, Politics, and Influence, 1890–1949." Ph.D. diss., Western Reserve University, 1951.

Lyons, Anne W. "Myth and Agony: The Southern Woman as Belle." Ph.D. diss., Bowling Green State University, 1974.

Rothman, Ellen K. "'Intimate Acquaintance': Courtship and the Transition to Marriage in America, 1770–1900." Ph.D. diss., Brandeis University, 1981.

Rotundo, E. Anthony. "Manhood in America: Middle-Class Masculinity in the Northern United States, 1770–1910." Ph.D. diss., Brandeis University, 1982.

Ryan, Mary P. "American Society and the Cult of Domesticity, 1830–1860." Ph.D. diss., University of California, Santa Barbara, 1971.